HANDBOOK OF
GREAT
AIRCRAFT
OF WWII

HANDBOOK OF
GREAT
AIRCRAFT
OF WWII

Dr Alfred Price and Mike Spick

HERMES
HOUSE

This edition is published by Hermes House, an imprint of Anness Publishing Ltd, 108 Great Russell Street, London WC1B 3NA; info@anness.com

www.hermeshouse.com; www.annesspublishing.com; twitter: @Anness_Books

Anness Publishing has a new picture agency outlet for images for publishing, promotions or advertising. Please visit our website www.practicalpictures.com for more information.

A CIP catalogue record for this book is available from the British Library.

Publisher: Joanna Lorenz
Senior Editor: Felicity Forster
Production Controller: Pirong Wang

PUBLISHER'S NOTE
Although the information in this book is believed to be accurate and true at the time of going to press, neither the authors nor the publisher can accept any legal responsibility or liability for any errors or omissions that may have been made.

CONTENTS

Introduction 7

The Supermarine Spitfire 9

Prologue 10
Cutaway Diagram 12
A Fighter is Born 14
Spitfire in Action 20
Spitfire Spyplanes 32
The Spitfire Spreads its Wings 38
Regaining Control of the Skies 44
Enter the Griffon 50
More Spitfire Spyplanes 54
Spitfire Fighter-Bomber 58
Post-War Spitfires 62
Appendix 70

The Avro Lancaster 73

Prologue 74
Cutaway Diagram 76
The Manchester 78
The Lancaster Described 82
Into Service 92
Main Force 102
Bombers vs. Fighters 114
Special Squadrons 124
Appendix 134

The Messerschmitt 109 137

Prologue 138
Cutaway Diagram 140
Early Career 142
Tested in Battle 150
Enter the 'Friedrich' 160
'Gustav' and 'Kurfurst' 166

The North American P-51 Mustang 177

Prologue 178
Cutaway Diagram 182
Birth of a Fighter 184
Allison Mustangs in Service 194
The Rolls-Royce Engine 204

The Boeing B-17 Flying Fortress 213

Prologue 214
Cutaway Diagram 218
Origins 220
Into Battle 228
War in Europe 236
The Final Round 250

INTRODUCTION

In writing this book we have aimed at producing a general interest account of the five truly outstanding combat aircraft of World War II. It has been no easy matter to decide which types to include, and which to omit. In the end, after much thought, we selected the Supermarine Spitfire, the Avro Lancaster, the Messerschmitt 109, the North American P-51 Mustang and the Boeing B-17 Flying Fortress.

After describing their design and development, we devote much space to relating the combat career of each type. To present as vivid a picture as possible of how they performed their assigned combat tasks, we have included numerous first-person accounts from pilots who flew these planes in action.

When describing the German Messerschmitt 109 fighter, several published accounts have used the abbreviation Bf 109 for this aircraft. Bf stood for Bayerische Flugzeugwerke, Bavarian Aircraft Factory, and those intent on being pedantic insist on using this form. However, official Luftwaffe documents use both the 'Bf' and the 'Me' forms of abbreviation for this aircraft. So both are correct. In this account we have used the simpler and more direct form 'Me'.

Mike Spick and Alfred Price

THE SUPERMARINE SPITFIRE

PROLOGUE

A dozen Spitfires of No. 411 (Canadian) Squadron, flying in three separate four-plane sections, traced lazy patterns in the sky high above the important Luftwaffe airfield. Leading Yellow Section was Flight Lieutenant Dick Audet, a 22-year old of French extraction flying his 53rd operational sortie. During the previous months he had carried out numerous bombing and strafing attacks on ground targets, but he had yet to encounter enemy aircraft in the air.

The Spitfires' mission was to engage German aircraft taking off from the airfield or on the landing approach to it. Suddenly Audet caught sight of a dozen hostile fighters in loose formation far below. He gave a clipped radio call to inform his commander of the enemy presence and to say that he was about to engage. Then Audet led his Section into a steep diving turn, moving his force as rapidly as possible into a firing position behind the German planes. It was to be a classic fighter 'bounce', with no quarter asked or given. In his combat report Audet later wrote:

"The enemy were four Messerschmitt 109s and eight Focke Wulf 190s, flying line astern. I attacked an Me 109, the last aircraft in the formation. At 200 yards I opened fire and saw strikes all over the fuselage and wing roots. The 109 burst into flames and trailed black smoke.

"I now went around in a defensive circle until I spotted an FW 190. I attacked from 250 yards down to 100 yards and from 30 degrees from line astern.

Below: Flight Lieutenant Dick Audet scored five victories during his first encounter with enemy aircraft, on 29 December 1944.
Right: Spitfire Mark IXs of Audet's unit, No. 411 Squadron, warming their engines at their base at Heesch in Holland, before a mission.

I saw strikes all over the cockpit and to the rear of the fuselage. It burst into flames. I saw the pilot slumped in his cockpit.

"Ahead was a 109 going down in a slight dive. It pulled up sharply into a climb, and the cockpit canopy flew off. I gave a short burst at about 300 yards and the aircraft whipped down in a dive. The pilot attempted to bail out, but his chute ripped to shreds. I saw the 109 hit the ground and smash into flaming pieces.

"I next spotted an FW 190 being pursued by a Spitfire pursued in turn by an FW 190. I called this pilot – one of my Yellow Section – to break, and attacked the 109 from the rear. We went down in a steep dive. I opened fire at 250 yards and it burst into flames. I saw it go into the ground and burn.

"Several minutes later, while attempting to re-form my section, I spotted an FW 190 at about 2000 feet. I dived on him and he turned into me from the right. He then flipped around in a left-hand turn, and attempted a head-on attack. I slowed down to wait for him to fly into range. At about 200 yards I gave a short burst. I could not see any strikes but he flicked violently and continued to do so until he crashed."

Within 10 minutes Dick Audet had shot down five enemy aircraft, to gain for himself the coveted status of fighter ace. Other pilots in the squadron witnessed the feat, and it would later be confirmed by analysis of his combat camera film. During the action, other pilots in Audet's squadron destroyed three more enemy fighters.

Although the Spitfire had been in service for six years, the versions in service at the end of 1944 were still formidable fighting machines. Yet, paradoxically, the fighter was designed for a purpose quite different from that flown by Dick Audet on that December afternoon. The Spitfire was designed solely as an air defence interceptor, to engage and destroy enemy bombers attempting to attack targets in the British Isles. The Spitfire fulfilled that task brilliantly, and was equally effective in hunting down enemy fighters over their own territory. In those and a dozen other roles, the sleek-lined little fighter illustrated its versatility.

SUPERMARINE SPITFIRE VB

1   Aerial stub attachment
2   Rudder upper hinge
3   Fabric-covered rudder
4   Rudder tab
5   Sternpost
6   Rudder tab hinge
7   Rear navigation light
8   Starboard elevator tab
9   Starboard elevator structure
10 Elevator balance
11 Tailplane front spar
12 IFF aerial
13 Castoring non-retractable
    tailwheel
14 Tailwheel strut
15 Fuselage double frame
16 Elevator control lever
17 Tailplane spar/fuselage
    attachment
18 Fin rear spar (fuselage
    frame extension)
19 Fin front spar (fuselage
    frame extension)
20 Port elevator tab hinge
21 Port elevator
22 IFF aerial
23 Port tailplane
24 Rudder control lever
25 Cross shaft
26 Tailwheel oleo access place
27 Tailwheel oleo shock-absorber
28 Fuselage angled frame
29 Battery compartment
30 Lower longeron
31 Elevator control cables
32 Fuselage construction
33 Rudder control cables
34 Radio compartment
35 Radio support tray

36 Flare chute
37 Oxygen bottle
38 Auxiliary long-range fuel tank
    (29 gallon/132 litre)
39 Dorsal formation light
40 Aerial lead-in
41 HF aerial
42 Aerial mast
43 Cockpit aft glazing
44 Voltage regulator
45 Canopy track
46 Structural bulkhead

47 Headrest
48 Plexiglass canopy
49 Rear-view mirror
50 Entry flap (port)
51 Air bottles (alternative rear
    fuselage stowage)
52 Sutton harness
53 Pilot's seat (moulded Bakelite)
54 Datum longeron
55 Seat support frame
56 Wingroot fillet
57 Seat adjustment lever

58 Rudder pedal frame
59 Elevator control
    connecting tube
60 Control column spade grip
61 Trim wheel
62 Reflector gunsight
63 External windscreen armour
64 Instrument panel
65 Main fuselage fuel tank
    (48 gallon/218 litre)
66 Fuel tank/longeron
    attachment fittings

67 Rudder pedals
68 Rudder bar
69 King post
70 Fuselage lower fuel tank
   (37 gallon/168 litre)
71 Firewall/bulkhead
72 Engine bearer attachment
73 Steel tube bearers
74 Magneto
75 'Fishtail'/exhaust manifold
76 Gun heating 'intensifier'
77 Hydraulic tank

78 Fuel filler cap
79 Air compressor intake
80 Air compressor
81 Rolls-Royce Merlin 45 engine
82 Coolant piping
83 Port cannon wing fairing
84 Flaps
85 Aileron control cables
86 Aileron push tube
87 Bellcrank
88 Aileron hinge
89 Port aileron

90 Machine-gun access panels
91 Port wingtip
92 Port navigation light
93 Leading-edge skinning
94 Machine-gun ports (protected)
95 20mm cannon muzzle
96 Three-blade constant-speed
   propeller
97 Spinner
98 Propeller hub
99 Coolant tank
100 Cowling fastening

101 Engine anti-vibration
    mounting pad
102 Engine accessories
103 Engine bearers
104 Main engine support member
105 Coolant pipe
106 Exposed oil tank
107 Port mainwheel
108 Mainwheel fairing
109 Carburettor air intake
110 Stub/spar attachment
111 Mainwheel leg pivot point
112 Main spar
113 Leading-edge ribs (diagonals
    deleted for clarity)
114 Mainwheel leg shock-absorber
115 Mainwheel fairing
116 Starboard mainwheel
117 Angled axle
118 Cannon barrel support fairing
119 Spar cut-out
120 Mainwheel well
121 Gun heating pipe
122 Flap structure
123 Cannon wing fairing
124 Cannon magazine drum
    (120 rounds)
125 Machine-gun support brackets
126 Gun access panels
127 .303in machine-gun barrels
128 Machine-gun ports
129 Ammunition boxes (350rpg)
130 Starboard aileron construction
131 Wing ribs
132 Single-tube outer spar section
133 Wingtip structure
134 Starboard navigation light

A FIGHTER IS BORN

The story of the Spitfire began almost exactly ten years before Dick Audet's famous action, in December 1934. Then, at the Supermarine Aviation Company's works at Southampton, Reginald Mitchell and his team finalized the layout of their new high-speed fighter for the RAF.

Mitchell had already established his name as a highly successful designer of racing floatplanes for the Schneider Trophy competition. One of his designs – the Supermarine S.5 – had won that international contest in 1927. The S.6 won it two years later in 1929. After another two-year gap the Supermarine S.6B won the trophy outright for Britain in 1931, and later went on to raise the World Air Speed record to 407mph (655km/hr).

These had been magnificent achievements but, in the nature of things, the market for high-speed racing seaplanes was extremely limited. The Supermarine company's main 'bread and butter' products were its big Southampton and Scapa flying boats which now equipped seven RAF maritime patrol squadrons.

In 1934, the fastest fighter type in the Royal Air Force was the Hawker Fury, which had a maximum speed of 207mph at 14,000ft (333km/hr at 4,270m). At that time Air Vice Marshal Hugh Dowding held the post of Air Member for Supply and Research, and was responsible for issuing to manufacturers the specifications for new aircraft required for the Royal Air Force. Dowding was an exceptionally farsighted innovator, what we would now call a 'technocrat'. He saw the vital need for a new fighter to bridge the huge gap in

performance between the Schneider Trophy racers and the biplanes that were then in service.

The early 1930s saw rapid advances in aviation technology. The Schneider Trophy racing seaplanes had demonstrated the performance advantages of using highly supercharged engines, streamlined all-metal airframes and the monoplane wing layout. These features were also being incorporated into the latest land planes, together with wing flaps to reduce the landing speeds, and retractable undercarriages.

■ MITCHELL'S FIRST FIGHTER ■

In February 1934, Reginald Mitchell's first fighter design appeared, the Supermarine Type 224. The aircraft took part in the competition to select a new fighter type for the Royal Air Force. Although it

Opposite: Production of wings at Woolston, early in 1939.

THE SCHNEIDER TROPHY AND THE SPITFIRE

The Supermarine S.6B, Reginald Mitchell's final racing floatplane design, gained the Schneider Trophy outright for Great Britain in 1931. Later that year, it raised the world absolute speed record to 407mph (655km/hr).

One frequently repeated myth about the Spitfire is that it was 'developed from' the Supermarine S.6B. This is simply not true. Certainly Mitchell learned a lot about high-speed flight from his work on the floatplanes, but that is quite different from saying that the Spitfire was 'developed from' them. In fact, the two aircraft were quite different designs, intended for quite different roles. There was not a single component of any significance in the Spitfire that resembled its counterpart in the racing seaplane.

Type Single-seat racing floatplane
Power plant One Rolls-Royce 'R' engine developing 2,350hp
Dimensions Span 30ft 0in (9.14m); length 28ft 10in (8.79m)
Weight Maximum loaded weight 6,086lb (2760kg)
Performance Maximum speed 407mph at 245ft (655km/hr at 75m), a world record

Right: The Supermarine S.6B racing floatplane won the coveted Schneider Trophy outright for Great Britain in 1931. Later that year, it captured the world absolute speed record at 407mph (655km/hr).

SUPERMARINE TYPE 224

REGINAL MITCHELL'S FIRST FIGHTER DESIGN

This single-seat interceptor fighter used a novel type of evaporative cooling for the engine, employing a steam condenser built into the leading edge of each wing. The system gave continual trouble and would probably have precluded the fighter being ordered for the RAF even if its performance had been more impressive.

Above: The Supermarine Type 224, Reginald Mitchell's unsuccessful first attempt at designing a fighter aircraft.

Type Single-seat interceptor fighter
Armament Four Vickers .303in (7.7mm) machine-guns synchronized to fire through the propeller arc
Power plant One Rolls-Royce Goshawk developing 680hp
Dimensions Span 45ft 10in (13.97m); length 29ft 5¼in (8.97m)

Weight Maximum loaded weight 4,743lb (2,151kg)
Performance Maximum speed 228mph at 15,000ft (367km/hr at 4,575m); time to climb to 15,000ft, 9½ minutes

Right: The Hawker Fury, the fastest fighter type in the RAF in 1934, had a maximum speed of 207mph (333km/hr).

was a monoplane design of all-metal construction, the fighter had a fixed undercarriage and a rather clumsy appearance. The Type 224 proved a flop. Its maximum speed was only 228mph (367km/hr) and it took 9½ minutes to reach 15,000ft (4,575m). The unusual system of evaporative cooling for the engine, using a steam condenser mounted along the leading edge of each wing, gave continual trouble. The winner of the competition, the Gloster entrant later named the Gladiator, had a maximum speed of 242mph (390km/hr) and it climbed to 15,000ft in 6½ minutes. One thing was clear: a good biplane design would outperform an over-conservative monoplane design.

Having learned that painful lesson, Reginald Mitchell persuaded the company to allow him to design a smaller, lighter and more streamlined fighter. This time he would use the new 1,000 horsepower V-12 engine, later named the Merlin, which was then under test at the Rolls-Royce company in Derby. When Air Vice Marshal Dowding saw details of the proposed new fighter, he gave it his full support and issued an official Royal Air Force specification so that the government would meet most of the cost of building a prototype.

The new fighter made its maiden flight on 5 March 1936, with Chief Test Pilot 'Mutt' Summers at the controls. This was an altogether more effective machine than its predecessor, and it aroused immediate interest. Not long afterwards, the Air Ministry allocated a name to the new fighter – 'Spitfire'. Had the decision been left to its designer, the aircraft would certainly have been named differently. When Mitchell learned of the official choice of name, he was heard to comment:

FASTEST FIGHTER

"It is claimed – and the claim seems indisputable – that the Spitfire is the fastest military aeroplane in the world. It is surprisingly small and light for a machine of its calibre (the structural weight is said to have been brought down to a level never before attained in the single-seat fighter class), and its speed and manoeuvrability are something to marvel at.

Tight turns were made at high speed after dives, and the control at low speeds was amply demonstrated. The demonstration was cramped by low clouds, but after the main flying display the machine was taken up again and gave one of the smoothest displays of high-speed aerobatics ever seen in this country."

FLIGHT MAGAZINE, 3 JULY 1936

Above: The prototype Supermarine F. 37/34, serial number K 5054, pictured at Eastleigh shortly before its maiden flight. The metal parts of the aircraft were unpainted, the aircraft carried no armament and the undercarriage was locked in the down position.

"It's the sort of bloody-silly name they would give it!"

During flight tests, the new fighter attained a maximum speed of 349mph at 16,800ft (562km/hr at 5,122m), and in the climb it reached 30,000ft (9,145m) in 17 minutes. Not only was it the fastest fighter in existence, but it was also one of the most heavily armed, for it was designed to carry eight Browning .303in (7.7mm) machine-guns in the wings.

■ LARGE ORDER ■

The Spitfire became available at exactly the right time for the Royal Air Force. In Germany the recently re-formed Luftwaffe was building up its strength rapidly. Its new monoplane fighter type, the Messerschmitt 109, was on the point of entering large-scale production. To meet the mounting threat, in June 1936 the British Government signed a contract for 310 Spitfires.

The Spitfire made its first public appearance on 18 June 1936, during a press day held at Eastleigh to show aircraft made by the Supermarine and Vickers companies. Other aircraft taking part included a Walrus amphibian (another of Mitchell's designs) and the prototype Wellington bomber. With press photographers eagerly snapping away, Jeffrey Quill started the

Spitfire's engine and taxied to one end of the grass runway. Then he pushed open the throttle to begin his take-off run and the lightly loaded aircraft rapidly gained speed. Before getting airborne the pilot made a brief scan of his instruments, and noticed the needle of the oil pressure gauge suddenly drop to zero. That left him in an unenviable position. He had no room to stop before reaching the airfield boundary, and on the other side of it lay the sprawling buildings of the Southern Railway Company's locomotive works. Fearing that the engine might seize up at any moment, the pilot eased the aircraft into the air and reduced power to the minimum necessary

to hold it there. Then he took it round in a shallow turn, aiming to get it back to the airfield as soon as possible. The engine maintained its healthy roar, but as Quill lined up for the landing, he saw he was a little too low. He eased open the throttle for one last burst of power, the engine responded, and he made a safe landing. Examination of the engine revealed that an oil pipe

PROTOTYPE SPITFIRE

Type Single-seat interceptor fighter
Armament Eight .303in (7.7mm) Browning machine-guns with 350 rounds per gun
Power plant One Rolls-Royce Merlin Type C liquid cooled V-12 engine with single-speed supercharger developing 990hp
Dimensions Span 40ft (12.1m); length 29ft 11in (9.17m)
Weight Maximum loaded 5,395lb (2,446kg)
Performance Maximum speed 349mph at 16,800ft (562km/hr at 5,122m); service ceiling 35,400ft (10,790m)

Above: **Close to disaster! Jeffrey Quill taking off in the prototype Spitfire during the press day at Eastleigh on 18 June 1936. A few seconds before this photograph was taken, when it was too late to abort the take-off, an oil pipe had come adrift. In the** background is the sprawling Southern Railway works over which the aircraft had to pass before it returned to the airfield. By skilful flying, Quill took the fighter in a wide circuit and landed before the engine seized. Had the prototype been lost that day, it is possible that the RAF might have cancelled its order, in which case the Spitfire would not have gone into production. *Below left:* **The Supermarine works at Woolston on the outskirts of Southampton, close beside the River Itchen.**

had come adrift, allowing the lubrication system to run dry. The engine was changed and sent to Rolls-Royce for examination, but it had suffered remarkably little damage from this treatment.

Had the prototype been lost during its first air display, the consequences to the nation hardly bear thinking about. Only the one Spitfire existed, and it had not completed its initial performance trials with the Royal Air Force. If it had crashed, the Royal Air Force would probably have cancelled the contract and ordered other types of fighter instead. That would have had a disastrous effect on the capability of Fighter Command during the Battle of Britain, four years later.

Thanks to Jeffrey Quill's skilful flying, however, there had been no crash. Five days later the Spitfire resumed flying with a new engine. On 27 June, Flight Lieutenant Hugh Edwardes-Jones demonstrated the aircraft before a large crowd at the Royal Air Force Pageant at Hendon. Two days later, 'Mutt' Summers flew it at the Society of British Aircraft Constructors' air display at Hatfield. The demonstrations aroused enormous public interest in the fighter, and drew lyrical descriptions in the press.

■ ON DISPLAY ■

The prototype completed its initial service trials at Martlesham Heath in July 1936, and returned to Eastleigh for modification. The fighter received a newer version of the Merlin, giving slightly greater power, and eight machine-guns were fitted in the wings.

Not all aspects of the Spitfire's flight trials went off smoothly. One of the most serious problems was that the fighter's guns did not work reliably at high altitude. During the initial firing trials in March 1937, all eight guns fired perfectly at 4,000ft (1,220m). It was a different story a few days later, when an RAF pilot climbed the Spitfire to 32,000ft (9,755m) over the North Sea for the first high-altitude firing. It nearly ended in tragedy. One gun fired 171 rounds before it failed, another fired 8 rounds, one fired 4 rounds, and the remaining five guns failed to fire at all. That was bad enough, but when the Spitfire touched down at Martlesham Heath after the test, the shock of the landing released the previously frozen-up breech blocks. Three of the weapons loosed off a round in the general direction of Felixstowe, fortunately without hitting anyone.

> ## ". . . the Spitfires will be useless as fighting aircraft . . ."

During the next 18 months, Supermarine engineers tried various schemes to solve the problem of gun freezing, using hot air ducted from the aircraft's glycol radiator. Yet the guns were still not functioning reliably in July 1938 when the first production Spitfires were delivered to the Royal Air Force. This led the Chief of the Air Staff, Marshal of the Royal Air Force Sir Cyril Newall, to comment during a secret meeting of the Air Council: "If the guns will

"MY GOD, IT'S MADE OF TIN!"

Whenever the prototype Spitfire landed away from its base, it was the subject of great interest. At that time, most airframes comprised a wood or light metal framework with a covering of linen fabric. The streamlined all-metal monoplane Spitfire with its enclosed cockpit and retractable undercarriage made every other aircraft in the Royal Air Force look positively prehistoric!

During a test flight in December 1936, Jeffrey Quill ran short of fuel, and he landed the Spitfire at the fighter airfield at Tangmere near Chichester. As he taxied in, a crowd of curious RAF ground crewmen gathered to meet it. Then, Quill recalled: "I taxied to a standstill and shut down, and could hear a tapping sound rather like raindrops hitting the aircraft. But it was a clear day. I checked I had shut everything down, but the tapping sound continued. Then as I climbed out I saw the reason. Several mechanics were standing around the rear fuselage, tapping it with their knuckles disbelievingly. 'My God,' one of them exclaimed, 'It's made of tin!'"

not fire at heights at which the Spitfires are likely to encounter enemy bombers, the Spitfires will be useless as fighting aircraft . . ."

It took until October 1938 to resolve the problem. Then, on the 14th, a service pilot took the prototype to high altitude and fired off the entire contents of the ammunition boxes without a single stoppage. The gun-heating modification was then incorporated in all Spitfires on the production line.

During the test programme, the prototype Spitfire survived two serious accidents. During the first, in March 1937, it made an emergency wheels-up landing following an engine failure; and almost exactly a year later it suffered an undercarriage collapse on landing, following a fatigue fracture of one of the main wheel legs. On both occasions, the aircraft resumed flying after repairs. By the end of 1938, production Spitfires

were emerging from the assembly hangar at Eastleigh at an encouraging rate, and the test programme of the prototype was complete. In those days there were no sentimental ideas about preserving historic aircraft, and the first Spitfire went to Farnborough for use as a 'hack' aircraft. On 4 September 1939, the day after Britain entered the Second World War, the aircraft suffered serious damage in a fatal landing accident. The venerable aircraft could have been repaired, but since there was no further use for it, the machine was scrapped.

The prototype Spitfire had cost the public purse a mere £15,776. Rarely has the money of British taxpayers been better spent.

Below: The prototype Spitfire wearing drab military camouflage, in 1938. The muzzles of the two outer machine-guns can be seen protruding from the wing.

SPITFIRE IN ACTION

Having gained the initial order for 310 Spitfires, the Supermarine I Company found that fulfilling the contract was more difficult than expected. Previously the company had built small batches of flying boats for the Royal Air Force, and its work force numbered only about 500. The new all-metal fighter required specialized manufacturing techniques, and at a time when the aircraft industry was expanding, it was difficult to recruit workers with the necessary skills. As a result, there were delays in getting the fighter into production.

In August 1938, 29 months after the maiden flight of the prototype, No. 19 Squadron at Duxford received the first Spitfires. It took until December for the unit to get its full complement of aircraft, then other squadrons began to re-equip with the type. By this time Hugh Dowding had been promoted to Air Chief Marshal and held the post of Commander-in-Chief RAF Fighter Command. By a quirk of history, the man who had done so much to bring the Spitfire into being was now to direct these fighters into action.

When Great Britain declared war on Germany in September 1939, Royal Air Force Fighter Command possessed 187 Spitfires in front-line units. Nos. 19, 41, 54, 65, 66, 72, 74, 602, 603 and 611 Squadrons were fully equipped with Spitfires and No. 609 Squadron was in the process of converting to the type.

Spitfires first saw action on 6 September 1939, during the so-called 'Battle of Barking Creek'. Because of a technical fault at the radar station at Canewdon in Essex, aircraft flying west of the station appeared on the screen as if their position was east of the radar (i.e. in the direction from which a German raiding force heading for London would make

Main left: The cockpit of an early production Spitfire I.
Inset left: Spitfires of No. 19 Squadron practising formation flying, early in 1939.

SPITFIRE I

Type Single-seat interceptor fighter
Armament Eight Browning .303in (7.7mm) machine-guns with 350 rounds per gun
Power plant One Rolls-Royce Merlin II liquid cooled V-12 engine with single-speed supercharger developing 1,030 horsepower
Dimensions Span 36ft 10in (10.98m); length 29ft 11in (9.11m)
Weight Maximum loaded weight 5,819lb (2,639kg)
Performance Maximum speed 362mph at 18,500ft (583km/hr at 5,640m); service ceiling 31,900ft (9,725m)

Top: Spitfires and Hurricanes from several squadrons lined up at Digby in Lincolnshire. The aircaft had assembled there prior to a massed flypast over cities in the Midlands, to mark Empire Air Day on 20 May 1939. (No. 72 Squadron Archive)
Above and overleaf: The 600th production Spitfire during its testing in April 1940. During the Battle of Britain, this aircraft served with No. 64 Squadron.

Spitfires first saw action on 6 September 1939, during the so-called 'Battle of Barking Creek'

its approach). The operators at Canewdon reported 20 unidentified aircraft heading towards London from the east, and to meet the threat, several fighter squadrons were scrambled. Within

For the next hour, complete and utter chaos reigned over the Thames estuary

minutes the 'incoming formations' being tracked on the radar, all of them now designated as 'hostile', increased to 12. Despite the poor weather, it looked as if the Luftwaffe was about to launch its expected onslaught on the capital. The defences came to full alert

A GERMAN PILOT'S OPINION OF THE SPITFIRE

Below: Spitfires in captivity. By the beginning of the Battle of Britain, the Germans had captured four Spitfires in flying or repairable condition.
Bottom: A captured Spitfire painted in bogus British markings and used in propaganda photographs.

"I was able to fly a captured Spitfire at Jever. My first impression was that it had a beautiful engine. It purred. The engine of the Messerschmitt 109 was very loud. Also the Spitfire was easier to fly, and to land, than the Me 109. The 109 was unforgiving of any inattention. I felt familiar with the Spitfire from the very start.

That was my first and lasting impression. But with my experience with the 109, I personally would not

have traded it for a Spitfire. I had the impression, though I did not fly the Spitfire long enough to prove it, that the 109 was the faster, especially in the dive. Also, I think the pilot's view was better from the 109. In the Spitfire one flew further back, a bit more over the wing."

OBERLEUTNANT HANS SCHLOLLER-HALDY,
MESSERSCHMITT 109 PILOT,
FIGHTER GESCHWADER 54

and soon afterwards an anti-aircraft gun battery opened fire at 'twin-engined bombers' passing overhead. Shortly after that, the leader of a Spitfire squadron broadcast a 'Tally Ho!' call, to indicate that he had enemy planes in sight and was about to engage. For the next hour, complete and utter chaos reigned over the Thames Estuary. Squadrons of fighters cruised between the banks of cloud, seeking enemy planes but finding only friendly ones. There were several brief fire fights, each one broken off when it became evident that the 'opponents' were 'friendlies'. In the end, shortage of

Right: Spitfires of No. 41 Squadron photographed during the Battle of Britain.

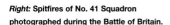

Above: Spitfires of Nos. 222 and 603 Squadrons at Hornchurch at the time of the Battle of Britain. Note the steam roller in the background, to roll flat the filled-in bomb craters on the airfield.
Right: The Messerschmitt 109E was the most formidable opponent facing RAF Fighter Command during the Battle of Britain.

fuel forced the Spitfires and Hurricanes to return to their airfields, and then the situation resolved itself. In fact, there had never been any German aircraft in the area. The fiasco cost the RAF three aircraft destroyed; two Hurricanes shot down by Spitfires of No. 74 Squadron and a Blenheim shot down by anti-aircraft fire. One RAF pilot was killed.

Following the action, Fighter Command launched a thoroughgoing official inquiry to determine what had gone wrong and prevent a recurrence. One lesson, which has to be re-learned for each war, was the folly of opening

"During the Battle of Britain one had to take every opportunity to train new pilots. Young pilots would arrive on the squadron with only six or seven hours' flying time on the Spitfire. One or two practice sorties could make all the difference to their ability to survive in combat. When we were at 30 minutes available, I might ring operations and ask permission to take one of the new pilots into the air for 'follow my leader' practice. If one could take them up, one could point out their failings and tell them: 'You won't survive ten minutes in battle if you fly like that!' The object was to tell them why and lead them round, not to frighten them."

SQUADRON LEADER DONALD MACDONELL, COMMANDER OF NO. 64 SQUADRON

Left: Spitfire X4110 had a service life of only 15 minutes. On the morning of 18 August 1940 this brand new aircraft arrived at No. 602 Squadron at Westhampnett as a replacement. Before there was time to paint on the squadron markings, Flight Lieutenant Dunlop Urie took it into action, and in an encounter with Me 109s the fighter suffered severe damage. Despite splinter wounds to both feet, Urie landed the machine at base. The Spitfire's back was broken and it never flew again.

Spitfires and Hurricanes flew large numbers of sorties to cover the evacuation of Dunkirk

fire on aircraft that had not been positively identified as 'hostile'. Another was the danger of looking at the reports from one radar in isolation (other stations along the coast had reported seeing no aircraft approaching from the east, but the absence of plots had been ignored). A further lesson was the need to fit IFF (identification friend or foe) radar equipment in all RAF fighters, and the programme to build and install this equipment received top priority.

Spitfires encountered genuinely hostile aircraft for the first time on 16 October 1939, when aircraft of Nos. 602 and 603 Squadrons rose to intercept nine Junkers 88s running in to make a dive-bombing attack on Royal Navy warships in the Firth of Forth. Flight Lieutenant Pat Gifford of No. 603 Squadron shot down one of the bombers and Flight Lieutenants

Pinkerton and McKellar of No. 602 Squadron destroyed another. A third Ju 88 suffered damage.

The Spitfire first encountered German aircraft en masse on 21 May 1940, when the rapid advance of the German army into Belgium and France brought the war to within reach of Royal Air Force fighters operating from airfields in Kent. During the weeks that followed, Spitfires and Hurricanes flew large numbers of sorties to cover the evacuation of Allied troops from Dunkirk.

■ BATTLE OF BRITAIN ■

At the beginning of July 1940, RAF Fighter Command possessed 50 squadrons of modern single-seat fighters – 31 with Hurricanes and 19 with Spitfires. The Battle of Britain opened with Luftwaffe attacks on convoys of shipping passing through the English

Above: Pilot Officer Robert Doe of No. 234 Squadron was credited with 11 enemy aircraft destroyed and two shared destroyed. He then moved to a Hurricane squadron and shot down three more. Doe suffered serious injuries during a crash landing in January 1941, and these prevented him flying for several months.

Above right: Dunlop Urie, his feet bandaged, waiting to be taken to hospital.

Right: Squadron Leader Donald MacDonell commanded No. 64 Squadron during the Battle, and was credited with nine enemy aircraft destroyed and one shared destroyed. He was shot down in March 1941, and spent the rest of the war in captivity.

WAITING AT READINESS

During the Battle of Britain, RAF fighter squadrons waiting to go into action were held on the ground at what was known as Readiness 5 Minutes. The fighters sat in their earth-and-brick revetments around the perimeter of the airfield, and from time to time the ground crews would run the engines to warm the oil and ensure the planes could take off immediately. Squadron Leader Don MacDonell, commander of No. 64 Squadron during the Battle, explained what it was like having to wait on the ground until the next German attack was detected.

"When we were at Readiness the pilots would be relaxing at the dispersal area – reading, chatting, playing cards. Each Flight had a separate crew room, so no pilot was too far from his Spitfire. I would be out of my office, wearing flying kit and Mae West, with the Flight I was to lead on that day. Each pilot's parachute was laid out on the seat of his aircraft, with the straps laid over the armour plating at the back of the cockpit.

Every time the telephone rang there would be a ghastly silence. The orderly would answer it and often one would hear something like: 'Yes, Sir... yes, Sir... Yes, Sir... Sergeant Smith wanted on the phone.' And everyone would breathe again."

Channel. The purpose of the attacks was to disrupt the coastal traffic and also to force the Royal Air Force into action. As time passed, the fighting over the Channel became progressively more ferocious, and the Luftwaffe began sending free hunting patrols over southern England.

These actions were but a prelude to the main campaign by the Luftwaffe, which began on 13 August, aimed at destroying Fighter Command as an effective force. That day, German aircraft launched multi-pronged attacks on the Royal Navy bases at Portland and Southampton, and on the airfields at Detling and Eastchurch.

> ### *There were repeated attacks on Fighter Command airfields in the south of England*

During the next three and a half weeks there were repeated attacks on Fighter Command airfields in the south of England. The Luftwaffe failed in its aim of knocking out Fighter Command, however. Every major airfield in the No. 11 Group area took hard knocks.

Above left: **Flying Officer Leonard Haines of No. 19 Squadron was credited with eight enemy 'kills' and four shared destroyed. He died in a flying accident in April 1941.**

Above: **Squadron Leader Derek Boitel-Gill commanding No. 152 Squadron was credited with eight aircraft destroyed. He died in a flying accident in September 1941.**

"SCRAMBLE!"

In Fighter Command the code-word 'Scramble' meant 'get airborne as rapidly as possible'. When pilots received the order, they ran as if their lives depended on it – because they did. Each 30-second delay in getting airborne meant 1,000ft (305m) less altitude they had when they met the enemy. And everyone knew that a Spitfire caught in the climb was easy meat for a Messerschmitt attacking in a dive. Squadron Leader Donald MacDonell explained the procedure for getting airborne:

"The orderly answering the telephone would shout "Scramble!" at the top of his voice and each pilot would dash for his aircraft. By the time one got there a mechanic would already have started the engine; the other would be holding the parachute up and help me strap it on. Once that was done I would clamber into the cockpit. He would pass my seat straps over my shoulders and help me fasten them. When I gave the thumbs-up he would slam shut the side door and I would pull tight the various straps. Next I would pull on my helmet, plug in the R/T lead and check that the engine was running properly. If all was well I would wave to the groundcrew to pull away the chocks, open the throttle, and move forward out of my blast pen and across the grass to the take-off position. Once there I would line up, open the throttle wide open and begin my take-off run with the rest of my pilots following as fast as they could. The whole thing, from the scramble order to the last aircraft leaving the ground, took about a minute and a half.

"As soon as Spitfires were all off the ground and climbing, I would inform operations. The Sector Controller would come back and tell me where he wanted me to go and at what altitude. While the squadron was forming up I would climb in a wide spiral at low boost, until everyone was in place. Then I would open up to a high throttle setting to get to altitude as fast as possible."

SPITFIRE FIGHTER DEPLOYMENT, SEPTEMBER 1940

Spitfire units on the afternoon of 14 September, before the decisive action of the Battle of Britain on the next day. The first figure indicates aircraft serviceable; figure in brackets shows aircraft unserviceable.

NO. 10 GROUP, HQ BOX, WILTSHIRE
Middle Wallop Sector
No. 152 Squadron 17 (2) Warmwell
No. 609 Squadron 15 (3) Middle Wallop
St Eval Sector
No. 234 Squadron 16 (1) St Eval
Group Total   48 (6)

NO. 11 GROUP, HQ UXBRIDGE, MIDDLESEX
Biggin Hill Sector
No. 72 Squadron 10 (7) Biggin Hill
No. 92 Squadron 16 (1) Biggin Hill
No. 66 Squadron 14 (2) Gravesend

Hornchurch Sector
No. 603 Squadron 14 (5) Hornchurch
No. 41 Squadron 12 (6) Rochford
No. 222 Squadron 11 (3) Rochford
Tangmere Sector
No. 602 Squadron 15 (4) Westhampnett
Group Total   92 (28)

NO. 12 GROUP, HQ WATNALL, NOTTINGHAMSHIRE
Duxford Sector
No. 19 Squadron 14 (0) Fowlmere
Coltishall Sector
No. 74 Squadron 14 (8) Coltishall
Wittering Sector
No. 266 Squadron 14 (5) Wittering
Digby Sector
No. 611 Squadron 17 (1) Digby
Kirton-in-Lindsey Sector
No. 616 Squadron 14 (4) Kirton-in-Lindsey
No. 64 Squadron 7 (3) Leconfield
              6 (3) Ringway
Group Total   86 (24)

NO. 13 GROUP, HQ NEWCASTLE, NORTHUMBERLAND
Catterick Sector
No. 54 Squadron 15 (2) Catterick
Usworth Sector
No. 610 Squadron 14 (5) Acklington
Turnhouse Sector
No. 65 Squadron 15 (5) Turnhouse
Group Total   44 (12)

Spitfires at Operational Training Units
              26 (24)

Spitfire production during week prior to 14 September 38

Replacement Spitfires held at Maintenance Units, 14 September 1940
Ready for immediate issue to units   47
Ready for issue within four days   10

Below left: Sergeant Basil Whall flew with No. 602 Squadron and was credited with seven enemy aircraft destroyed and two shared destroyed. In October 1940, he suffered fatal injuries when he tried to land his damaged aircraft after a combat sortie. *Below right:* Lieutenant Arthur 'Admiral' Blake, a Fleet Air Arm pilot loaned to RAF Fighter Command, flew with No. 19 Squadron. Credited with four enemy aircraft destroyed and one shared destroyed, he was shot down and killed in October 1940.

Above: The wrecked shell of the Supermarine factory at Woolston, pictured after the devastating German air attack on 26 September 1940.

However, there was an efficient damage-repair organization, and in the event only one airfield, that at Manston in Kent, was put out of action for more than a few hours. Only in rare instances were the raiders able to catch RAF fighters on the ground. By the time the German bombers arrived to deliver their attack on an airfield, the Spitfires and Hurricanes based there were usually airborne and well clear. Fighters able to fly but not fight took off on 'survival scrambles' with orders to keep clear of the area until the threat had passed. Aircraft unable to fly were wheeled into the protective revetments, or dispersed around the airfield where they were difficult to hit. As a result of these measures, the front-line fighter units lost fewer than 20 fighters destroyed on the ground, despite the almost daily attacks on airfields throughout a 25-day period.

On 7 September, the Luftwaffe shifted its attack to London, concentrating its main effort against the sprawling dock area to the east of the city. During the following week, there were three further attacks on the capital. Then on 15 September, Battle of Britain Day, the Luftwaffe mounted two separate raids on London.

"IT DEMONSTRATED THE DETERMINATION AND BRAVERY WITH WHICH THE TOMMIES WERE FIGHTING OVER THEIR OWN COUNTRY"

Early on the afternoon of 15 September 1940, as the Heinkel 111s of Bomber Geschwader 26 were passing Maidstone on their way home, the formation suddenly came under attack from Spitfires. Leutnant Roderich Cescotti, one of the German pilots, recalled:

"A few Tommies succeeded in penetrating our fighter escort. I saw a Spitfire dive steeply through our escort, level out and close rapidly on our formation. It opened fire, from ahead and to the right, and its tracers streaked towards us. At that moment a Bf 109, which we had not seen before, appeared behind the Spitfire and we saw its rounds striking the Spitfire's tail. But the Tommy continued his attack, coming straight for us, and his rounds slashed into our aircraft. We could not return the fire for fear of hitting the Messerschmitt. I put my left arm across my face to protect it from the plexiglass splinters flying around the cockpit, holding the controls with my right hand. With only the thin plexiglass between us, we were eye-to-eye with the enemy's eight machine-guns. At the last moment the Spitfire pulled up and passed very close over the top of us. Then it rolled on its back, as though out of control, and

went down steeply trailing black smoke. Waggling its wings, the Messerschmitt swept past us and curved in for another attack. The action lasted only a few seconds, but it demonstrated the determination and bravery with which the Tommies were fighting over their own country."

Cescotti's Heinkel had taken several hits, but he was able to hold position in formation. He made a normal landing at his base at Wevelghem in Belgium.

Almost certainly the courageous Spitfire pilot was Flying Officer Peter Pease of No. 603 Squadron, who was shot down at the time, the place, and in the manner described by Cescotti. When the blazing fighter smashed into the ground a few miles south-east of Maidstone, Pease was still in the cockpit.

The son of Sir Richard Pease, Arthur Peter Pease, studied at Eton and Cambridge University before joining the Royal Air Force at the beginning of the war. In July 1940, he was posted to No. 603 Squadron based at Dyce airfield near Aberdeen, and later that month he shared in the destruction of a Heinkel 111. Early in August the Squadron moved to

Hornchurch, north-east of London, to take part in the defence of southern England. On 3 September, Pease was credited with shooting down a Messerschmitt 109, and four days later his Spitfire suffered battle damage and he made a crash landing at Hornchurch. Just over a week later, on 15 September, Peter Pease died in action.

Above: Flying Officer Peter Pease of No. 603 Squadron, whose courageous attack is described by Roderich Cescotti.

"I FELT JOLLY GLAD TO BE DOWN ON THE GROUND WITHOUT HAVING CAUGHT FIRE"

"We were just going in to attack when somebody yelled 'Messerschmitts' over the R.T. and the whole squadron split up. Actually it was a false alarm. Anyway, being on my own I debated what to do. The bombers were my object, so I snooped in under the 110s and attacked the bombers (about 40–50 Heinkel 111s) from the starboard beam.

"I got in a burst of about three seconds when – Crash! and the whole world seemed to be tumbling in on me. I pushed the stick forward hard, went into a vertical dive and held it until I was below cloud. I had a look round. The chief trouble was that petrol was gushing into the cockpit at the rate of gallons all over my feet, and there was a sort of lake of petrol in the bottom of the cockpit. My knee and leg were tingling all over as if I had pushed them into a bed of nettles. There was a bullet hole in my windscreen where a bullet had come in and entered the dashboard, knocking away the starter button. Another bullet, I think an explosive one, had knocked away one of my petrol taps in front of the joystick, spattering my leg with little splinters and sending a chunk of something through the backside of my petrol tank near the bottom. I had obviously run into some pretty good crossfire from the Heinkels. I made for home at top speed to get there before all my petrol ran out. I was about 15 miles from the aerodrome and it was a heart-rending business with all that petrol gushing over my legs and the constant danger of fire. About five miles from the 'drome smoke began to come from under my dashboard. I thought the whole thing might blow up at any minute, so I switched off my engine. The smoke stopped. I glided towards the 'drome and tried putting my wheels down. One came down and the other remained stuck up. I tried to get the one that was down up again. It was stuck down. There was nothing for it but to make a one-wheel landing. I switched on my engine again to make the aerodrome. It took me some way and then began to smoke again, so I hastily switched off. I was now near enough and made a normal approach and held off. I made a good landing, touching down lightly. The unsupported wing slowly began to drop. I was able to hold it up for some time and then down came the wingtip on the ground. I began to slew round and counteracted as much as possible with the brake on the wheel which was down. I ended up going sideways on one wheel, a tail wheel and a wingtip. Luckily, the good tyre held out and the only damage to the aeroplane, apart from that done by the bullets, was a wingtip that is easily replaceable.

"I hopped out and went off to the M.O. to get a lot of metal splinters picked out of my leg and wrist. I felt jolly glad to be down on the ground without having caught fire."

PILOT OFFICER ERIC MARRS OF NO. 152 SQUADRON, DESCRIBING HIS ACTION ON 30 SEPTEMBER 1940

Left: **A pilot of No. 313 (Czech) Squadron running to his Spitfire during a scramble take-off.**

No. 11 Group of Fighter Command, which bore the brunt of the defence of the capital, possessed 310 serviceable single-seat fighters. Of that total, 218 were Hurricanes and 92 were Spitfires. To meet the two attacks on London, the RAF fighter controllers used the same defensive tactics against each. About one-third of the available squadrons, Hurricanes and Spitfires, engaged the raiding forces as they made their way across Kent to the capital. The purpose of these attacks was twofold: first, to destroy as many German bombers as possible; and secondly, to force the escorting Me 109s to fly at full throttle to ward off the British fighters and so deplete their limited supply of fuel. Meanwhile, the main body of defending fighters assembled over the east and south-east outskirts of London. It was there that the two great clashes occurred, and most of the aircraft were shot down.

■ BATTLE OF BRITAIN DAY ■

The first attack took place shortly before noon. The raiding force comprised 21 Messerschmitt 109 fighter-bombers and 27 Dornier 17 bombers, with an escort of about 180 Me 109s. The fighter-bombers were to attack rail targets throughout the London area, while the Dorniers were to hit the concentration of rail lines and junctions at Battersea. Two hours later, there was a much heavier attack on a series of targets in the London dock area, involving 114 Dornier 17s and Heinkel 111s escorted by some 450 Me 109s and a few Me 110s.

Above: WAAF mechanics helping the pilot strap into a Spitfire Mark II of No. 411 (Canadian) Squadron, at Digby in Lincolnshire in 1941.
Right: A few Mark II Spitfires were modified for the Air Sea Rescue role, and carried two cylindrical drums in parachutes in the rear fuselage. These contained an inflatable rubber dinghy and ration packs to drop to survivors.

During the late afternoon of the 15th, the Luftwaffe also launched smaller attacks on targets on the south coast. Twenty-six Heinkels bombed the Royal Navy base at Portland, and a small force of Messerschmitt 109 and 110 fighter-bombers tried unsuccessfully to hit the Supermarine plant at Southampton.

That day, 55 German aircraft were destroyed, most of them falling to fighter attack. The RAF lost eight Spitfires and 21 Hurricanes. The Spitfire force suffered a loss rate of 4.2 per hundred sorties, while the Hurricane force suffered a loss rate of 6.4 per hundred sorties. In action, the Spitfire's superior performance meant it had a 50 per cent better chance of survival compared with the Hurricane.

The German losses on 15 September fell far short of the 185 aircraft the

defenders claimed as destroyed. Yet the action is rightly deemed to mark the climax of the Battle. Two days later, Adolf Hitler ordered an indefinite postponement of Operation Sealion, the planned invasion of Britain. The ships and barges concentrated at ports along the Channel coast returned to their normal tasks, and it was clear that the threat of invasion had passed.

■ MARK II ■

Towards the end of the Battle of Britain, the Spitfire Mark II entered service. Similar in most respects to the Mark I, the new variant was powered by the Merlin 12 engine, giving an additional 110 horsepower. With the installation of armour protection and additional items of equipment, however,

the Mark II weighed 350lb (159kg) more than the early production Mark I. Because of this, the additional engine power merely restored the fighter's performance to its earlier level. The Spitfire emerged from the Battle of Britain with a proven record of success in the limited role of home-defence fighter. Yet this very success would inhibit its ability to achieve more in that role. Having suffered heavy losses during the Battle, the Luftwaffe gave up the idea of trying to mount large-scale daylight attacks on targets in Britain. If the Spitfire was to continue to play a major part in the war, it would have to do so in roles other than that of home-defence fighter. As we shall observe next, it had already started to do so.

MAINTAINING SPITFIRE PRODUCTION

On 26 September 1940, a raiding force of 59 Heinkel 111s mounted a devastating attack on the two main Supermarine factories at Woolston and Itchen. The bombers wrecked most of the factory buildings at both sites, striking a body blow at Spitfire production.

On the day following the attack, Lord Beaverbrook, Winston Churchill's tireless Minister of Aircraft Production, visited Southampton to inspect the damage. On his decision, the two wrecked factories were abandoned. Production of Spitfires was to be dispersed into several smaller units in towns and cities. Fortuitously, most of the machine tools and production jigs at Woolston and Itchen had survived the attack. Also, the final assembly hangers at Eastleigh airfield had not been touched. Supermarine executives toured Southampton, Winchester, Salisbury, Trowbridge, Reading and Newbury and the surrounding areas, looking at every large open building. Motor repair garages, laundries and bus stations were the obvious choices. Accompanying each Supermarine executive was a policeman who carried a letter of introduction from the Chief Constable of the area, requesting cooperation but giving no reason for the visit. Where a building was considered suitable for use in the dispersed production scheme, the not-always-delighted owner received official papers requisitioning the building. As each new site was acquired, the Spitfire production jigs and tools were brought in and set up.

By the end of October, 35 separate premises had been taken over for the programme and production had begun at 16 of them. Also by this time, the large-scale production had started at the huge purpose-built Nuffield organization factory at Castle Bromwich near Birmingham.

Never again would Spitfire production be as vulnerable to air attack as it had been in September 1940.

Above right and below: Following the attack on the Supermarine factories, Spitfire production was dispersed into several small units in the surrounding towns and cities. These photographs show Spitfire wing leading edges being manufactured at the requisitioned garage of Anna Valley Motors Ltd at Salisbury.

Below right: A remarkable photograph taken from a Messerschmitt 110 reconnaissance aircraft over Snodland, Kent, showing Spitfires of No. 64 Squadron climbing into position to intercept the aircraft. The Messerschmitt suffered severe damage in the ensuing engagement, and the radio operator was killed.

In time of war, it is difficult to exaggerate the importance of aerial reconnaissance. To plan effective air attacks, staff officers require the best possible information on each target. They need to know where bombs should be aimed to cause maximum damage. They also need to know the layout of the defences around each target, so they can route the bombers to avoid the worst of them. Without such information, attacking forces will inflict less damage and suffer heavier losses than would otherwise be the case. The best source of such information is aerial photography.

Today, the idea of using an unarmed reconnaissance aircraft to make a high speed dash through enemy territory to photograph targets is well accepted. It was not always so. Before the Second World War, most air forces employed modified bombers to fly long-range reconnaissance missions. Lacking the performance to avoid the defences, these machines had to carry guns and gunners to fight their way through to targets.

Shortly before the outbreak of war, Flying Officer Maurice 'Shorty' Long-bottom, an enterprising young RAF officer, suggested a better means of securing reconnaissance photographs. In a memorandum, he set down his views on the future of strategic aerial recon-naissance. Longbottom suggested that reconnaissance should be done "in such a manner as to avoid the enemy fighters and AA defences as completely as pos-sible". The best way of doing that, he thought, was by "the use of a single small machine, relying solely on its speed, climb and ceiling to avoid detection. . ."

Longbottom believed the ideal aircraft would be a Spitfire with the guns, ammunition, radio and other unneces-sary equipment removed. With addi-tional fuel tanks and cameras installed in their place, he argued that such an aircraft would have the range to reach distant targets. It would, moreover, have the speed and altitude performance to penetrate the enemy defences at will.

The Air Ministry greeted Longbottom's memorandum with polite interest, but initially the paper was pigeon-holed. The RAF was desperately short of modern

Left: Compare the 1939 inset photograph with the main one, of Bullihgen, taken in April 1944 from a Spitfire at the same altitude, with a camera fitted with a 36in (91.4cm) lens. Considerably more ground detail is visible. Comparison of these photos shows the great advances made in aerial cameras during the war years.

Top: Spitfire PR IC used for high-altitude photographic missions. This aircraft carried its vertically mounted cameras in a blister under the starboard wing, seen in the open position for the removal of the film magazines. *Middle:* Spitfire PR IF. This aircraft carried its vertically mounted cameras in the rear fuselage, and was fitted with blister fuel tanks under the wings to give it increased range.

Above: Spitfire PR IG used for low-altitude 'dicing' missions, to photograph targets beneath cloud. These aircraft wore a very pale shade of pink (the colour was the same as the bottom of cloud on overcast days). The window for the oblique camera is at the top left of the fuselage roundel.

RECONNAISSANCE VARIANTS

PR IA Original PR variant, one 5in (12.7cm) lens camera mounted in each wing. No additional fuel.

PR IB One 8in (20.3cm) lens camera in each wing. Additional fuel: 29 gallon (132 litre) tank in the rear fuselage.

PR IC As PR IB, but with the two 8in (20.3cm) lens cameras mounted in tandem in a blister fairing under the starboard wing. Additional fuel: 29 gallon (132 litre) tank in the rear fuselage; 30 gallon (136.5 litre) blister tank under the port wing.

PR ID First major redesign of the Spitfire for the reconnaissance role. Carried two 8in (20.3cm) or two 20in (50.8cm) lens cameras in the rear fuselage. Additional fuel: large fuel tank built integrally with the leading edge of the wing, capacity 114 gallons (518 litres); 29 gallon (132 litre) tank in the rear fuselage. This variant replaced the Marks IA, IB, IC and IF in front-line service during 1941. When fitted with the Merlin 45 engine it became the PR 5D, then it was redesignated as the PR Mark 4.

PR IE Designed for the low-altitude reconnaissance role; only one example produced. Oblique camera under each wing, pointing at right angles to the line

of flight. Additional fuel: 29 gallon (132 litre) tank in rear fuselage.

PR IF Carried two 8in (20.3cm) or two 20in (50.8cm) lens cameras in the rear fuselage. Additional fuel: 30 gallon (136.5 litre) blister tank under each wing; 29 gallon (132 litre) tank in the rear fuselage.

PR IG Designed for low-altitude reconnaissance role. One oblique camera mounted in the rear fuselage could point either to port or to starboard. In addition,

Above: **A reconnaissance Spitfire at high altitude. When over enemy territory, pilots went to great pains to avoid leaving condensation trails, since these betrayed their position and made them vulnerable to fighter interception.**

there was one 14in (35.6cm) and one 5in (12.7cm) lens camera mounted vertically in the rear fuselage. Additional fuel: 29 gallon (132 litre) tank in the rear fuselage.

Left and opposite right: **Exterior and interior of the huge Spitfire production facility at Castle Bromwich, Birmingham. Morris Motors Ltd built the factory, under contract to the British Government. The plant produced some 12,000 Spitfires – more than half of the total. At its peak, it turned out 320 Spitfires per month.**

Left: **Dramatic low-altitude photograph of the German cruiser *Hipper* in dry dock, at the heavily defended port of Brest.**

fighters, and needed every available Spitfire for the defence of Great Britain, Air Chief Marshal Dowding was unwilling to release these precious air-craft for other roles, no matter how per-suasive the arguments might appear.

It took only six weeks of war to change people's minds. The main RAF

SPYPLANE PILOT

"During the early [photographic reconnaissance] missions there was no such thing as cockpit heating in our Spitfires. For the high altitude missions we wore thick suits with electrical heating. Trussed up in our Mae West and parachute, one could scarcely move in the narrow cockpit of the Spitfire. When flying over enemy territory one had to be searching the sky the whole time for enemy fighters. On more than one occasion I started violent evasive action to shake off a suspected enemy fighter, only to discover that it was a small speck of dirt on the inside of my perspex canopy!

"A big worry over enemy territory was that one might start leaving a condensation trail without knowing it, thus pointing out one's position to the enemy. To avoid that we had small mirrors fitted in the blisters on each side of the canopy, so that one could see the trail as soon as it started to form. When that happened one could either climb or descend until the trail ceased. If possible, we liked to climb above the trail's layer because then fighters trying to intercept us had first to climb through the trail's layer themselves and could be seen in good time."

PILOT OFFICER GORDON GREEN, SPITFIRE PILOT, PHOTOGRAPHIC RECONNAISSANCE UNIT

reconnaissance aircraft then in use, the low performance Blenheim, was quite inadequate for the task. Only rarely could they photograph targets any distance inside enemy territory, and they suffered heavy losses whenever they tried.

■ SECRET NEW UNIT ■

Following strong representations from the Air Ministry, Air Chief Marshal Dowding reluctantly agreed to release a couple of Spitfires for the reconnaissance role. The aircraft went to a highly secret new unit based at Heston north of London, headed by Wing Commander Sidney Cotton. Appropriately, one of the officers who helped him set up the unit was 'Shorty' Longbottom himself.

Cotton's first step was to modify the Spitfires for the new role and commence operations over enemy territory, to prove the validity of Longbottom's proposals. Each aircraft was fitted with a pair of cameras, mounted in each wing in the space previously occupied by the guns and ammunition boxes. Metal plates sealed off the empty gun ports, and groundcrewmen applied plaster of Paris to fill the joints in the skinning. Then each aircraft received a coat of polish to give it a smooth, high-gloss, finish. With these changes, the maximum speed of the reconnaissance Spitfires was about 12mph (about 20km/hr) faster than the fighter version.

In November 1939, the Spitfire reconnaissance unit under the cover-designation 'No. 2 Camouflage Unit' moved to Seclin near Lille in France to begin operational trials. On the 18th, Longbottom, now a Flight Lieutenant, took off to photograph the German city of Aachen and the nearby fortifications. Flying at 33,000ft (10,000m), a very high altitude in those days, he found navigation more difficult than expected. When his films were developed, they showed a strip of Belgian territory to the south of Aachen. Longbottom learned the lesson well, and when he returned to the area four days later, he made a successful photographic run over the German border defences.

During the weeks that followed, the two Spitfires photographed several targets in western Germany, including the Ruhr industrial area. Significantly, and in distinct contrast to the Blenheims, the Spitfires flew their missions without loss or even serious interference from the German defences.

Photographs taken from 33,000ft (10,000m) with 5in (12.7cm) focal-length cameras produced very small-scale pictures, however. The interpreters could pick out roads, railways, villages and major fortifications. But even with prints enlarged as much as the grain of the film allowed, it was not possible to see troop positions or individual vehicles. If the Spitfire's capabilities were to be fully exploited, longer-lens cameras would be needed. Work began to develop these. Apart from that proviso, the flights proved the essential soundness of Longbottom's proposals. As a result, Air Chief Marshal Dowding agreed to release a dozen more Spitfires for the reconnaissance role.

In January 1940, an improved photographic reconnaissance Spitfire was ready for operations, the PR IB (for details of this and other reconnaissance variants, see opposite; the earlier variant became known as the PR IA). In February, Longbottom demonstrated

Left: Seamstresses applying the fabric covering to Spitfire rudders, in one of the component production halls at Castle Bromwich. The Spitfire's rudder weighed only 18lb (8kg), but was strong enough to withstand the side forces engendered when manoeuvring at high speed.

the usefulness of the PR IB's additional range capability when he photographed the important German naval bases at Wilhelmshaven and Emden.

Soon afterwards, Cotton's unit was renamed the Photographic Development Unit, the new title revealing its true role for the first time. Early in 1940, the operations in France were reorganized and a further unit, No. 212 Squadron, formed at Seclin to conduct the Spitfire reconnaissance missions from there.

Below: A showpiece of the British aircraft industry, the Castle Bromwich plant had a constant stream of important visitors. Here, Winston Churchill is seen chatting with Alex Henshaw, Chief Test Pilot at the factory. Between the summer of 1940 and 1946, Henshaw personally tested no fewer than 2,360 Spitfires, about one in ten of those built.

■ LONG-RANGE VISION ■

In March 1940, a so-called 'long-range' reconnaissance version of the Spitfire appeared, the PR IC, with a further fuel tank to increase its reach. On 7 April, Longbottom took this aircraft to Kiel, the first RAF aircraft to photograph the important naval base since the outbreak of war.

Little over a month later, on 10 May 1940, German forces launched their powerful Blitzkrieg attack on France, Holland and Belgium. During the hectic weeks that followed, No. 212 Squadron photographed each stage of the relentless advance of the German Panzer columns. The squadron then withdrew to England, where its aircraft and personnel were incorporated in the PDU at Heston.

Thus far, the reconnaissance Spitfires had flown their missions at medium or high altitude, and photographed their targets from directly above. Most of the RAF's aerial photography would continue to be done that way, but there was another technique that allowed close-up shots or photography of targets below cloud. A few Spitfires were fitted with the so-called oblique camera installation, with a camera pointing

at right angles to the line of flight and a few degrees below the horizontal. On 7 July 1940, Flying Officer Alistair Taylor proved the value of the new installation. Despite a 700ft (213m) cloud base and heavy rain, which would have precluded vertical photography, he took good photographs of shipping inside Boulogne harbour as he flew past the outer mole. From then on, low-altitude photography, nicknamed 'dicing' because of the risks involved, became an important additional role for the reconnaissance Spitfires.

Also in July 1940, the Photographic Development Unit underwent yet another name change. It became the Photographic Reconnaissance Unit (PRU), and at the same time Wing Commander Geoffrey Tuttle replaced Sidney Cotton as its commander. The changes of name and commander made no difference to the way the unit operated, however.

> ### *Longbottom took the PR IC to Kiel, the first RAF aircraft to photograph the important naval base*

At the end of July, a further Spitfire reconnaissance variant appeared, the 'super-long-range' PR IF. This variant had a radius of action about 100 miles (160km) greater than the Type IC. Operating from airfields in East Anglia, it could photograph targets as far afield as Berlin.

Throughout the summer of 1940, reconnaissance Spitfires kept a daily watch on the German preparations for the invasion of Britain. Each day they sallied forth to photograph each of the ports along the Channel coast, observing the growing assemblies of barges and shipping at each. Then on 20 September,

"IT WAS ALL RATHER LIKE A FOX HUNT..."

"During the early [photographic reconnaissance] missions to cover Brest [in 1941] we lost about five pilots fairly quickly. After the first couple had failed to return the Flight Commander, Flight Lieutenant Keith Arnold, asked Benson [the headquarters of the reconnaissance units] to send some reserve pilots. They duly arrived. Both took off for Brest that evening and neither came back. That was a very sobering incident.

"The important thing with any photographic mission was to take the photos if one could, and get them back to base. As the 'boss' of PRU, Wing Commander Geoffrey Tuttle, often used to say, 'I want you to get home safely not just because I like your faces, but because if you don't the whole sortie will be a waste of time!' So it was no use trying to play hide and seek with the Luftwaffe. If one had lost surprise during the approach to a heavily defended target, the best thing was to abandon the mission. One could go back another time when things might be better. Looking back at my time with the PRU, I get a lot of satisfaction from the knowledge that although I played my part in the war, I never had to fire a shot in anger. In one sense we in the reconnaissance business had things easy. All the time it was impressed on us: bring back the photographs or, if you can't, bring back the aeroplane. An infantryman taking part in the Battle of Alamein could not suddenly decide 'This is ridiculous, I'm going home!' He just had to go on. But if we thought we had lost the element of surprise we were not only permitted to turn back, we were expected to do so. On the other hand there were times when I knew real fear. When one was 15 minutes out from Brest on a low altitude sortie, one's heart was beating away and as the target got nearer one's mouth got completely dry. Anyone who was not frightened at the thought of going in to photograph one of the most heavily defended targets in Europe, was not human.

"Whenever it was possible to photograph a target, flak could engage us: if we could see to photograph they could see to open up at us. But throughout my time as a reconnaissance pilot my luck held. I never once saw an enemy fighter, nor was my aircraft ever hit by flak. Indeed only once during the time we were flying those missions over Brest did one of our aircraft come back with any damage, and that was only minor. It was all rather like a fox hunt – either the fox got away unscathed or else it was caught and killed. There was rarely anything in between."

PILOT OFFICER GORDON GREEN, SPITFIRE PILOT, PHOTOGRAPHIC RECONNAISSANCE UNIT

---

three days after Adolf Hitler's order to postpone the invasion, a reconnaissance Spitfire returned bearing the first hard evidence of the change in German plans. Its photographs of Cherbourg harbour showed that five destroyers and a torpedo boat had left the port since the previous reconnaissance. In the weeks that followed, almost every successive reconnaissance flight revealed fewer ships and barges in each port as the vessels resumed their normal tasks. The threat to Great Britain had passed.

■ TO STETTIN ■

The 'long-range' and 'extra-long-range' versions of the Spitfire opened new vistas for photographic reconnaissance and the targets it could cover. Yet in terms of range, the modified fighter could do even better. Supermarine redesigned the wing to take a huge additional fuel tank that took up almost the entire leading edge back to the main spar. In October 1940, the first Spitfires modified in this way, the PR ID, became available for operations.

When carrying its full load of fuel, the PR ID was difficult to handle, as Flight Lieutenant Neil Wheeler explained. "You could not fly it straight and level for the first half hour or hour after take-off. Until you had emptied the rear tank, the aircraft hunted the whole time. The centre of gravity was so far back that you couldn't control it. It was the sort of thing that would never have got in during peacetime, but war is another matter." Once part of the fuel load had been consumed, however, the Type D handled well, and its extra range gave it a dramatic extension of reconnaissance cover. On 29 October 1940, one of these aircraft photographed the port of Stettin on the Baltic (now Sczecin in Poland) and returned after 5 hours and 20 minutes airborne. Other remarkable missions followed in rapid succession: to Marseilles and Toulon in the extreme south of France, and to Trondheim in Norway.

The final reconnaissance variant of the Spitfire I was the Type G, optimized for the low-altitude photographic role with an oblique camera mounted in the rear fuselage. This version retained the fighter's standard armament of eight .303in (7.7mm) machine-guns to enable it to defend itself against enemy fighters.

By the beginning of 1941, the reconnaissance Spitfires possessed the range to photograph targets almost anywhere in western Europe. At this point in the Spitfire story, however, this account must return to the new challenges facing the fighter version, because, following developments in the war situation in northern Europe and the Mediterranean theatre, the aircraft was about to face a further severe test.

Above: Test pilots striding out to fly brand new Spitfires off the production line at Castle Bromwich. Alex Henshaw is second from the right.

THE SPITFIRE SPREADS ITS WINGS

n the spring of 1941, a new production version of the Spitfire appeared, the Mark V. This was fitted with the Merlin 45 engine which gave increases of, respectively, 440 and 330 horsepower over the versions fitted to the Marks I and II. The main production version of the Spitfire V carried an armament of two 20mm cannon and four .303in (7.7mm) machine-guns.

SPITFIRE V

Type Single-seat general-purpose fighter
Armament Four Hispano 20mm cannon with 120 rounds per gun, or two Hispano 2mm cannon with 120 rounds per gun and four Browning .303in (7.7mm) machine-guns with 350 rounds per gun, or eight .303in (7.7mm) Browning machine-guns with 350 rounds per gun; maximum bomb load two 250lb (113kg) bombs
Power plant One Rolls-Royce Merlin 45 liquid cooled V-12 engine developing 1,470hp
Dimensions Span 36ft 10in (10.98m), 32ft 6in (9.9m, clipped wings); length 29ft 11in (9.11m)
Weight Maximum loaded weight 6,070lb (2,752kg)
Performance Maximum speed 371mph at 20,000ft (597km/hr at 6,100m); service ceiling 38,000ft (11,585m)

Left and inset: Spitfire VC fitted with four 20mm cannon, being loaded on the aircraft carrier USS *Wasp* docked at Glasgow in April 1942. The wingtips had been removed and placed in the open cockpit, so that the aircraft could be brought by road from the nearby Abbotsinch airfield.
Above right: A remarkable modification to a Spitfire carried out in Germany, when the Daimler-Benz company at Stuttgart fitted a DB 605 engine into a captured Mark V and carried out flight tests with the combination.
Right: Spitfire in trouble – a still from a combat film taken by the Luftwaffe fighter ace Major Gerhard Schoepfel of Fighter Geschwader 26, showing cannon shells bursting on the fuselage.

Also during 1941, Fighter Command moved from the defensive to the offensive, mounting large-scale sweeps over occupied Europe. Simultaneously Spitfire production rose to a point where it exceeded losses, allowing an expansion in the number of units operating the fighter. During the Battle of Britain, 19 squadrons had operated Spitfires. By September 1941, there were 27. And by the end of 1941, Fighter Command had 46 squadrons equipped with Spitfires.

The Mark V had a performance significantly better than the earlier variants of the Spitfire, yet it was not good enough. In the summer of 1941, the Luftwaffe introduced a new and even more effective fighter into service: the Focke Wulf 190.

When this new German fighter first appeared in action over northern France, its performance came as a severe shock to Fighter Command. The Focke Wulf was 25–30mph (40–48km/hr) faster than the Spitfire V at most altitudes, and it could out-climb, out-dive and out-roll the British fighter. The Spitfire V's only advantage over its new opponent was that it could turn tighter.

Fortunately for the Royal Air Force, however, at this time the Luftwaffe was heavily committed to supporting the campaign in Russia. As a result, the size of the fighter force retained in the west, and in particular that part of it operating FW 190s, would remain relatively small.

■ SPITFIRES TO MALTA ■

The next major challenge to face the Spitfire came early in 1942, and this time the venue was far to the south. Malta was the cornerstone of Britain's strategy in the central Mediterranean. Torpedo-bombers operating from the island took

Left: In September 1942, the US manned 'Eagle' Squadrons of the RAF were officially transferred to the US Army Air Force with their aircraft. This aircraft went with No. 121 Squadron to become part of the 335th Fighter Squadron of the 4th Fighter Group.

a steady toll of ships carrying supplies and reinforcements to sustain the Axis ground forces in North Africa. Yet the beleaguered island lay within 100 miles (160km) of Axis airfields in Sicily, and it suffered frequent and destructive air attacks. Malta's continued survival depended on the efficiency of her air defences, but the Hurricanes based on the island were outclassed by the Messerschmitt 109Fs opposing them.

Only the Spitfire V could engage the Me 109F on equal terms, but getting these aircraft to the island would be no easy task. The distance from Gibraltar to Malta was far beyond the Spitfire's

Right: US Army Air Force mechanics carrying out an engine change on a Spitfire.

Below: Armourers of No. 72 Squadron cleaning the barrel and removing the ammunition drum from the Hispano 20mm cannon.

> *When the new German fighter first appeared it came as a severe shock to Fighter Command*

normal ferry range. Moreover, the strength of the Axis naval and air forces besieging the island precluded any large-scale delivery of fighters by sea. The Hurricanes already on Malta had been transported half way by aircraft carrier, which launched them to fly the rest of the way to the island. The Spitfires would have to use the same method, but even that would not be easy; from fly-off point to Malta was a distance of approximately 660 miles (1,062km).

To enable the Spitfire to reach Malta from a launch point, engineers at Supermarine designed a 90 gallon (409 litre) drop tank. The first delivery of Spitfires took place on 7 March 1942, when under Operation Spotter 15 of them took off from HMS *Eagle*. Before the end of the month, the carrier made two further delivery runs, bringing to 31 the number of Spitfires flown to the island.

Above: The flight deck of *Wasp* pictured late on the afternoon of 19 April, as the carrier prepared to fly off her brood of Spitfires soon after first light the following morning. Ranged in front and to the left of them are the carrier's own Wildcat fighters, which would take off first to cover the operation.
Left: The Focke Wulf 190 fighter was a formidable opponent for the Spitfire Mark V.

SPITFIRE V VERSUS FOCKE WULF 190A

In July 1942, a Spitfire V was flown in a comparative trial against a captured Focke Wulf 190 fighter. During the past 10 months, RAF pilots had learned the hard way that they faced a formidable foe, but these trials revealed just how formidable that foe was. Excerpts from the official RAF report on the trials are given below.

Comparative speeds: The FW 190 was compared with a Spitfire VB from an operational squadron for speed and all-round manoeuvrability at heights up to 25,000ft (7,620m). The FW 190 is superior in speed at all heights, and the approximate differences are as follows:

At 2,000ft (610m) the FW 190 is 25–30mph (40–48km/hr) faster than the Spitfire 5B.

At 3,000ft (915m) the FW 190 is 30–35mph (48–56km/hr) faster than the Spitfire 5B.

At 5,000ft (1,525m) the FW 190 is 25mph (40km/hr) faster than the Spitfire VB.

At 9,000ft (2,744m) the FW 190 is 25–30mph (40–48km/hr) faster than the Spitfire 5B.

At 15,000ft (4573m) the FW 190 is 20mph (32km/hr) faster than the Spitfire 5B.

At 18,000ft (5,488m) the FW 190 is 20mph (32km/hr) faster than the Spitfire VB.

At 21,000 (6,400m) the FW 190 is 20–25mph (32–40km/hr) faster than the Spitfire VB.

Climb: The climb of the FW 190 is superior to that of the Spitfire VB at all heights. The best speeds for climbing are approximately the same, but the angle of the FW 190 is considerably steeper. Under maximum continuous climbing conditions, the climb of the FW 190 is about 450ft/min (137m/min) better up to 25,000ft (7,620m).

Dive: Comparative dives between the two aircraft have shown that the FW 190 can leave the Spitfire with ease, particularly during the initial stages.

Manoeuvrability: The manoeuvrability of the FW 190 is better than that of the Spitfire VB except in turning circles, when the Spitfire can quite easily out-turn it. The FW 190 has better acceleration under all conditions of flight and this must obviously be most useful during combat.

When the FW 190 was in a turn and was attacked by the Spitfire, the superior rate of roll enabled it to flick into a diving turn in the opposition direction. The pilot of the Spitfire found great difficulty in following this manoeuvre and even when prepared for it, was seldom able to allow the correct deflection. A dive from this manoeuvre enabled the FW 190 to draw away from the Spitfire which was then forced to break off the attack.

The above trials have shown that the Spitfire VB must cruise at high speed when in an area where enemy fighters can be expected. It will then, in addition to lessening the chances of being successfully 'bounced', have a better chance of catching the FW 190, particularly if it has the advantage of surprise.

Left: *Left:* Following the launch of the Spitfires on deck, those in the hangar were brought up by lift and followed them into the air. This required slick timing, as this photograph shows. A Spitfire is about to begin its take-off; the aircraft ahead of it can be seen climbing away, just above the starboard wing. Meanwhile, the lift is already on the way to the hangar to pick up the next aircraft.

■ AMERICAN HELP ■

The Spitfires arrived in the nick of time. The Luftwaffe had stepped up its onslaught on the island and the defending fighter units were heavily outnumbered. With the air situation over Malta deteriorating rapidly, on 1 April Winston Churchill sent a personal telegram to President Roosevelt asking for help:

"Air attack on Malta is very heavy. There are now in Sicily about 400 German and 200 Italian fighters. Malta can only now muster 20 to 30 serviceable fighters. We keep feeding Malta with Spitfires in packets of 16 loosed from EAGLE carrier from about 600 miles west of Malta.

"This has worked a good many times quite well but EAGLE is now laid up for a month by defects in her steering gear . . . Therefore there will be a whole month without any Spitfire reinforcements. Would you be willing to allow your carrier WASP to do one of these trips provided details are satisfactorily agreed between the Navy Staffs? With her broad lifts, capacity and length, we estimate that WASP could take 50 or more Spitfires . . ."

Within three days of receiving the telegram, the US President agreed to the request. Six days after that, *Wasp* docked at Port Glasgow to load 47 Spitfires for the island. The mission was code-named Operation Calendar.

On 13 April, the American carrier set sail, and five days later she and her escorts passed through the Strait of Gibraltar. At first light on the 20th, off the coast of Algeria, the carrier began launching the Spitfires. Forty-six of the 47 fighters that took off reached Malta safely. Such was the ferocity of the air fighting, however, during the next few days most of the precious Spitfires had been destroyed in the air or on the

Above middle: Scene on the flight deck of USS *Wasp* on the morning of 9 May 1942, as the carrier prepares to launch her aircraft for the largest resupply of aircraft to Malta. In the background, also preparing to launch her Spitfires, is HMS *Eagle*.

Above: A soldier, a sailor and an airman carrying out refuelling and rearming of a Spitfire of No. 603 Squadron at Takali, Malta, in the spring of 1942. The blast pen was constructed from empty petrol tins filled with sand.

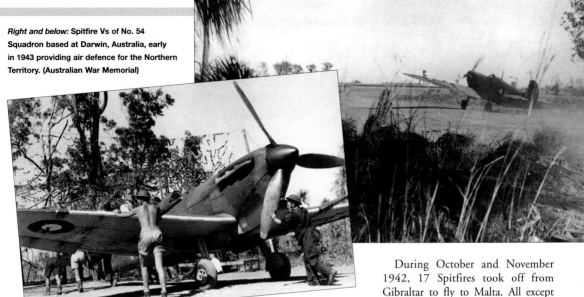

Right and below: Spitfire Vs of No. 54 Squadron based at Darwin, Australia, early in 1943 providing air defence for the Northern Territory. (Australian War Memorial)

ground. Again Malta was in crisis, and again Mr Churchill asked the US President to help. And again the latter acceded. The next resupply operation was to be the largest of them all, Operation Bowery. The American carrier returned to Glasgow on 29 April and took on a further 47 Spitfires. By then HMS *Eagle* at Gibraltar had completed her repairs, and she took on a further 17 fighters.

■ MALTA SAVED ■

As *Wasp* entered the Mediterranean a second time, *Eagle* set sail from Gibraltar to join her. The two carriers and their escorts headed east together, and shortly after dawn on 9 May they launched their Spitfires. Sixty of the 64 fighters that set out reached Malta. It was sufficient to change the course of the battle. The island's air defences were now strong enough to resist Axis air attacks, and could be topped up with 'penny packets' of Spitfires delivered by the smaller Royal Navy carriers. Never again would the island be in such peril as it had been during the first week in May 1942.

By the autumn of 1942, the RAF possessed a more cost-effective method of delivering Spitfires from Malta

from Gibraltar. Supermarine engineers had modified the Mark V to fly the distance non-stop, by fitting a 170 gallon (772 litre) drop tank under the fuselage and a 29 gallon (132 litre) auxiliary tank in the rear fuselage. With a total fuel load of 284 gallons (1,290 litres), the modified Spitfire could fly the 1,100-mile (1,770km) distance in a single hop. That was as far as from London to St Petersburg in Russia, a remarkable feat for an aircraft designed originally as a short-range interceptor.

During October and November 1942, 17 Spitfires took off from Gibraltar to fly to Malta. All except one of them made it.

Had more Spitfires been required, they too would have flown to the island, but events in the North Africa theatre of operations had removed the need. The Allied victory at El Alamein, and the subsequent expulsion of Axis forces from Libya, lifted the siege of Malta.

Meanwhile, as we shall observe in the next chapter, engineers at Rolls-Royce had solved Fighter Command's most pressing problem. With a new variant of the Merlin engine the Spitfire would be able to engage the much-feared Focke Wulf 190 on equal terms.

BY SPITFIRE TO MALTA

Pilot Officer Michael Le Bas of No. 601 Squadron described his take-off in a Spitfire from the deck of USS *Wasp*. His heavily loaded aircraft carried a 90 gallon (409 litre) drop tank under the fuselage. Ahead lay a flight of 660 miles (1,062km), about as far as from London to Prague.

"The deck officer began rotating his checkered flag and I pushed forward the throttle to emergency override to get the last ounce of power out of my Merlin. The Spitfire picked up speed rapidly in its headlong charge down the deck, but not rapidly enough. The ship's bows got closer and closer and still I had insufficient airspeed and suddenly – I was off the end. With only 60 feet to play with before I hit the water, I retracted the undercarriage and eased forward on the stick to build up speed. Down and down went the Spitfire until, about 15 feet above the waves, it reached flying speed and I was able to level out. After what seemed an age but was in fact only a few seconds, my speed built up and I was able to climb away. Nobody had told me about that at the briefing! It had been a hairy introduction to flying off an aircraft carrier. Things had happened so quickly that there was no time to think. Perhaps it was just as well."

REGAINING CONTROL OF THE SKIES

After the initial encounters with Focke Wulf 190s, Fighter Command made strong demands for an improved fighter with the performance to meet the new challenge. There could be no question of designing, building and bringing into service a completely new aircraft; on the most optimistic time scale, that would have taken at least four years. Fighter Command could not wait that long.

In fact, Rolls-Royce already had the answer to the problem in a new version of the Merlin. Previous versions of the engine used a single-stage supercharger.

The new engine employed a two-stage supercharger, in which the output from the first blower fed into the second to compress the charge of air further before it entered the carburettor. The two-stage supercharger gave a spectacular improvement in high-altitude performance. At 30,000ft (9,145m) the Merlin 45 engine with a single-stage supercharger developed about 720 horsepower. At the same altitude the same basic engine fitted with a two-stage supercharger developed about 1,020 horsepower, an increase of more than 40 per cent. The extra plumbing added only about 200lb (90kg) to the weight of the engine and increased its length by 9in (23cm). At the end of September 1941, three weeks after the debut of the Focke Wulf FW 190, an experimental Spitfire fitted with the Merlin incorporating the two-stage supercharger began flight testing.

> ## There could be no question of designing, building and bringing into service a completely new aircraft

Opposite: A Spitfire VII, the high-altitude interceptor version of the famous fighter. Note the distinctive long-span wing with pointed tips, a recognition feature of this particular variant.

SPITFIRE MARK IX

Type Single-seat general-purpose fighter and fighter-bomber
Armament Two Hispano 20mm cannon with 120 rounds per gun, four Browning .303in (7.7mm) machine-guns with 350 rounds per gun; or two Hispano 20mm cannon with 120 rounds per gun and two Browning .5in (12.7mm) machine-guns with 250 rounds per gun; maximum bomb load one 50lb (226kg) bomb and two 250lb (113kg)

Power plant One Rolls-Royce Merlin 61, 63 or 70 liquid cooled V-12 engine with two-stage supercharger; Merlin 65 developed 1,565hp
Dimensions Span 40ft 2in (12.85m, pointed wingtips), 36ft 10in (10.98m, normal wingtips) or 32ft 6in (9.9m, clipped wings); length 30ft 0in (9.14m)

Weight Maximum loaded weight 7,500lb (3,400kg)
Performance Maximum speed 40mph at 25,000ft (657km/hr at 7,622m); service ceiling 43,000ft (13,110m)

Below: Spitfire IX of No. 402 (Canadian) Squadron.

TURNING POINT IN AN AIR WAR

On the afternoon of 30 July 1942, Flight Lieutenant Donald Kingaby of No. 64 Squadron scored his 16th aerial victory. Afterwards he reported:

"I sighted approximately 12 FW 190s 2,000ft [610m] below us at 12,000ft [3,658m] just off Boulogne proceeding towards French coast. We dived down on them and I attacked a FW 190 from astern and below giving a very short burst, about half a second, from 300yd. I was forced to break away as I was crowded out by other Spits. I broke down and right and caught another FW as he commenced to dive away. At 14,000ft [4,268m] approx. I gave a burst of cannon and M/G, 400yd range hitting E/A along fuselage. Pieces fell off and E/A continued in straight dive nearly vertical. I followed E/A down to 5,000ft [1,525m] over Boulogne and saw him hit the deck just outside the town of Boulogne and explode and burn up. Returned to base at 0ft."

The combat report was little different from many others in the summer of 1942, yet this air combat marked a significant turning point in the air war over Europe. It was the first time the Spitfire Mark IX had encountered the Focke Wulf 190 in action. The latest variant of the British fighter showed that it could take on its once-feared opponent on equal terms. For the Luftwaffe, that action marked the beginning of the end of the easy-going superiority its fighters had enjoyed for most of the previous year. It would never regain that position.

Initially there were difficulties in getting the supercharger to work properly, but by the end of the year these had been resolved. The Merlin 61 Spitfire showed itself to be considerably faster than any previous version, with a maximum speed of 414mph at 27,200ft (667km/hr at 8,300m). Its rate of climb was also considerably better than that of the Spitfire V, and its service ceiling was over 41,000ft (12,500m).

■ THREE NEW VARIANTS ■

Fighter Command and Supermarine both knew a good thing when they saw it, and the new Merlin engine quickly spawned three more variants of the Spitfire. The Spitfire VII was a high-altitude interceptor version, with a pressurized cabin and a longer wingspan giving increased area. Its airframe was redesigned and strengthened to compensate for the increases in engine power and weight the fighter had incurred previously. The second of the new variants, the Spitfire VIII, was similar to the Mark VII but lacked the pressurized cabin of that type.

These two versions required a large amount of redesign, however, as well as retooling of the production lines. The changes would take time, and neither version would be available in quantity until the spring of 1943.

In the meantime, Fighter Command needed a fighter to counter the FW 190, and it needed it quickly. The solution arrived in the form of the Spitfire IX, which was essentially a Mark V with the minimum of modification necessary to take the Merlin 61 engine. Measured against peacetime stressing factors, the airframe of the Mark V was not really strong enough to accept the additional engine power and the increases in all-up weight. In wartime, however, the RAF was prepared to accept this deficiency in the name of operational expediency. No fighter pilot was going to reject the Spitfire IX in favour of the Mark V for that reason alone!

Left and above: A damaged aircraft repaired and returned to service was as valuable as a new aircraft built, and the RAF salvage teams and repair organization played a valuable role. This Spitfire of No. 403 (Canadian) Squadron had crash-landed in a suspected minefield in Normandy. After a sweep of the area to ensure that it was safe to approach the aircraft, the fighter was dismantled and loaded on to a 'Queen Mary' transporter.

The first production Spitfire IXs arrived at No. 64 Squadron at Hornchurch during June 1942, and the unit resumed operations with the new variant at the end of July. The new Spitfire quickly demonstrated that it was the equal of the Focke Wulf 190 in combat. Proof of this came a few weeks later, when a German pilot inadvertently landed his FW 190 at Pembrey in South Wales. The RAF carried out detailed flight tests with the captured aircraft to determine its exact performance, and then had it fly

SPITFIRE IX VERSUS FOCKE WULF 190A

In July 1942, a Spitfire IX was flown in a comparative trial against a captured Focke Wulf 190. Considering they were quite different aircraft, the similarities in performances were remarkable. Excerpts from the official trials report are given below.

Comparative speeds: The FW 190 was compared with a fully operational Spitfire IX for speed and manoeuvrability at heights up to 25,000ft (7,620m). The Spitfire IX at most heights is slightly superior in speed to the FW 190, and the approximate differences in speeds at various heights are as follows:

At 2,000ft (610m) the FW 190 is 7–8mph (11–13km/hr) faster than the Spitfire IX.

At 5,000ft (1,524m) the FW 190 and the Spitfire IX are approximately the same.

At 8,000ft (2,44m) the Spitfire IX is 8mph (13km/hr) faster than the FW 190.

At 15,000ft (4,573m) the Spitfire IX is 5mph (8km/hr) faster than the FW 190.

At 18,000ft (5,488m) the FW 190 is 3mph (5km/hr) faster than the Spitfire IX.

At 21,000ft (6,400m) the FW 190 and the Spitfire IX are approximately the same.

At 25,000ft (7,622m) the Spitfire IX is 5–7mph 98–11km/hr) faster than the FW 190.

Climb: During comparative climbs at various heights up to 23,000ft (7,012m), with both aircraft flying under maximum continuous climbing conditions, little difference was found between the two aircraft, although on the whole the Spitfire IX was slightly better. Above 22,000ft (6,707m) the climb of the FW 190 is falling off rapidly, whereas the climb of the Spitfire IX is increasing.

Dive: The FW 190 is faster than the Spitfire IX in a dive, particularly during the initial stage. This superiority is not as marked as with the Spitfire VB.

Manoeuvrability: The FW 190 is more manoeuvrable than the Spitfire IX except in turning circles, when it is out-turned without difficulty. The superior rate of roll of the FW 190 enabled it to avoid the Spitfire IX if attacked when in a turn, by flicking over into a diving turn in the opposition direction. As with the Spitfire VB, the Spitfire IX had great difficulty in following this manoeuvre.

The Spitfire IX's worst heights for fighting the FW 190 were between 18,000 and 22,000ft (5,486m and 6,707m) and below 3,000ft (914m). At these heights, the FW 190 is a little faster.

The initial acceleration of the FW 190 is better than the Spitfire IX under all conditions of flight, except in level flight at such altitudes where the Spitfire has a speed advantage. Then, provided the Spitfire is cruising at high speed, there is little to choose between the acceleration of the two aircraft.

The general impression gained by the pilots taking part in the trials is that the Spitfire IX compares favourably with the FW 190. Provided the Spitfire has the initiative, it undoubtedly has a good chance of shooting down the FW 190.

Left: The Spitfire VIII entered service some time after the Mark IX. This example belonged to No. 457 (Australian) Squadron, and was one of the 410 purchased by that air force for operations in the South Pacific area.

MARK VII

Type Single-seat high-altitude interceptor fighter with pressurized cabin
Armament Two Hispano 20mm cannon with 120 rounds per gun, four Browning .303in (7.7mm) machine-guns with 350 rounds per gun; aircraft assigned to ultra high-altitude interception duties sometimes carried only the four .303in machine-guns
Power plant One Rolls-Royce Merlin 61, 64 or 71 liquid cooled V-12 engine with two-stage supercharger; Merlin 61 developed 1,565hp
Dimensions Span 40ft 2in (12.85m, pointed wingtips) or 36ft 10in (10.98m normal wingtips); length 30ft 0in (9.15m)
Weight Maximum loaded weight 8,000lb (3,628kg)
Performance (Rolls-Royce Merlin 71 engine) maximum speed 424mph at 29,500ft (682km/hr at 8,994m); service ceiling 45,100ft (13,750m)

mock combats with each of the main Allied fighters. The comparison with the Spitfire IX (see preceding page) revealed that the two fighters were uncannily similar in performance.

■ MARK IX IN SERVICE ■

Initially, the Mark IX units represented only a small proportion of the Spitfire force, but even so the new variant had an immediate impact on the air situation. In combat, it was impossible to distinguish it from the Mark V, and FW 190 pilots could

never be certain which Spitfire variant they faced. As a result, the German fighters became markedly less aggressive and RAF fighter losses fell appreciably.

The first major action involving Spitfire IXs was on 19 August 1942, during the amphibious raid on Dieppe on the French coast. Four squadrons flew the new variant that day, and in the course of intensive air operations they mounted 14 squadron-sized missions comprising about 150 sorties. These resulted in claims of six enemy aircraft destroyed and two probably destroyed, for the loss of seven fighters. By the spring of 1943, the Spitfire IX equipped most of the RAF's single-seat fighter squadrons based in Great Britain. Perhaps surprisingly, the re-engineered variants of

the Spitfire intended to replace the Mark IX saw rather less use. The feared high-altitude attacks on Great Britain failed to materialize, and the order for Mark VIIs was greatly reduced. Production ended early in 1944, after about 140 had been built.

Below: Spitfire Mark VIIIs of No. 417 (Canadian) Squadron based at Canne, Italy, in 1944. These aircraft were fitted with pointed wingtips for high-altitude operations, as employed on the Mark II.

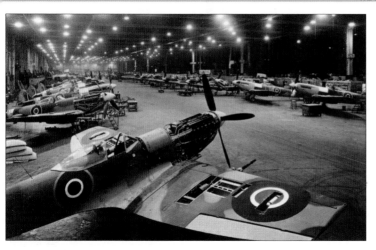

Left: The Spitfire Mark XVI was similar to the Mark IX, but was powered by the version of the Merlin engine built under licence by the American Packard Company. Late production Spitfire IXs and XVIs featured cut-down fuselages and bubble canopies, as seen on these Mark XVIs undergoing final assembly at Castle Bromwich in the spring of 1945.
Below left: Floatplane conversion of the Spitfire. A small number of aircraft were modified in this way, but none saw action.

BUBBLE CANOPY

In most cases where Spitfires were shot down by enemy fighters, the victim never saw his assailant in time to take effective evasive action. Most such attacks were mounted from the fighter's blind zone, below and behind. Any modification that reduced the likelihood of a surprise attack would increase the fighter's chances of survival in combat.

The answer was to cut back the rear fuselage behind the cockpit, and fit the fighter with a bubble canopy. A Spitfire modified in this way flew for the first time in the summer of 1943. The manufacturer's trials showed that the change brought no significant deterioration in the aircraft's handling characteristics. Experienced service pilots were hugely impressed with the improvement in view from the bubble canopy. Their report stated:

"This is an enormous improvement over the standard Spitfire rear view. The pilot can see quite easily round to his fin and past it, almost to the further edge of the tailplane, i.e. if he looks over his left shoulder he can practically see to the starboard tip of the tail. By banking the aircraft slightly during weaving action, the downward view to the rear is opened up well."

Production Spitfire Mark IXs, XIVs and XVIs fitted with bubble canopies began reaching the operational squadrons early in 1945 and they immediately became popular with pilots.

By the time the Mark VII became available in quantity, in the spring of 1943, the FW 190 menace over north-west Europe had been contained. The entire 1,658-aircraft production run of this variant went overseas to units operating in the Middle East, the Far East and Australia.

The 'stop-gap' version of the Merlin 61 Spitfire, the Mark IX, continued in production a lot longer than anyone had expected. Between them, the Super-marine and Castle Bromwich plants turned out nearly 6,000 of them.

The Spitfire XVI airframe was almost identical to that of the Mark IX, but it was powered by a version of the Merlin built by the American Packard Company. Late production Spitfire IXs and XVIs featured cut-down fuselages and bubble canopies – features which gave the pilot greatly improved vision behind and below the fighter.

The introduction of the Merlin 60 series improved the performance of the Spitfire to the point where it could fight the FW 190 on equal terms. Yet engineers at Rolls-Royce were not content to rest on their laurels. As we shall observe in the next chapter, they had something even better on offer.

In 1939, Rolls-Royce had begun development of a larger engine than the Merlin, later named the Griffon. With a cubic capacity of 65 gallons (36.75 litres), the new engine was one-third larger than its predecessor. The initial production version, with a single-stage supercharger, developed 1,735 horsepower. By clever positioning of components, the designers kept the length of the Griffon to within 3in (7.5cm), and the weight to within 600lb (272kg) of the equivalent figures for the Merlin. Moreover, the new engine's frontal area was little greater than that of its predecessor.

The Spitfire was an obvious application for the new engine, and in November 1941 an experimental Griffon prototype, the Mark IV, began flight testing. The aircraft had a maximum speed of 372mph at 5,700ft (600km/hr at 1,740m), which increased to 397mph at 18,000ft (640km/hr at 5,500m).

> *To counter the threat, the RAF issued a requirement for a low-altitude interceptor*

At about this time, the Luftwaffe commenced tip-and-run attacks on towns on the south and east coasts of England. Small forces of fighter-bombers ran in at low altitude to avoid radar detection, giving the defenders little time to react. To counter the threat, the RAF issued a requirement for a low-altitude interceptor. The Griffon Spitfire offered the best performance at low altitude, and this became the

Left: Mark XIV Spitfire of No. 402 (Canadian) Squadron. This version was the most effective variant to operate in the air superiority role during the Second World War.

SPITFIRE XII

Type Single-seat fighter optimized for operations at low and medium altitudes
Armament Two Hispano 20mm cannon with 120 rounds per gun, four Browning .303in (7.7mm) machine-guns with 350 rounds per gun
Power plant One Rolls-Royce Griffon 4 liquid cooled V-12 engine with single-stage supercharger developing 1,735 horsepower
Dimensions Span 32ft 7in (9.93m); length 30ft 9in (9.37m)

Weight Maximum loaded weight 7,400lb (3,356kg)
Performance Maximum speed 389mph at 12,500ft (626km/hr at 3,810m); service ceiling 37,350ft (11,387m)

Below: The first Griffon-powered Spitfire, pictured after the aircraft had been modified to become the prototype Mark XII low-altitude fighter.

SPITFIRE XIV

Type Single-seat fighter and fighter-reconnaissance aircraft
Armament Two Hispano 20mm cannon with 120 rounds per gun, four Browning .303in (7.7mm) machine-guns with 350 rounds per gun; or two Hispano 20mm cannon with 120 rounds per gun and two Browning .5in (12.7mm) machine-guns with 250 rounds per gun; fighter reconnaissance version carried an oblique-mounted camera in the rear fuselage

Power plant One Rolls-Royce Griffon 65 liquid cooled V-12 engine with two-stage supercharger developing 2,035hp
Dimensions Span 36ft 1in (10.98m normal wingtips) or 32ft 7in (9.93m, clipped wings); length 32ft 8in (9.96m)
Weight Maximum loaded weight 10,065lb (4,565kg)
Performance Maximum speed 439mph at 24,500ft (707km/hr); service ceiling 43,000ft (13,110m)

prototype for the Mark XII fighter. Supermarine received a production order to build 100 examples.

Like the Mark IX, the early production Mark XIIs used Mark V airframes with the minimum of modification necessary to take the new engine. Production Mark XIIs all had clipped wings, to give greater speed at low alti-tude and greater rate of roll at all altitudes. Compared with the Mark IX, the Mark XII was 14mph (22km/hr) faster at sea level and 8mph faster at 10,000ft (13km/hr at 3,050m). But above 20,000ft (6,100m), performance fell away rapidly, and the Mark XII became progressively slower than the Mark IX.

In the spring of 1943, Nos. 41 and 91 Squadrons re-equipped with Mark XIIs and commenced operations from Hawkinge airfield near Folkestone. The units flew standing patrols against enemy fighter-bombers attacking coastal targets, and on 25 May No. 91 Squadron scrambled six fighters to engage FW 190 fighter-bombers attacking Folkestone. In the ensuing combat the Spitfires claimed the destruction of six raiders, without loss to themselves.

This action proved to be a rare success for the Mark XII, however. Although it was faster than the opposing fighter types at low and medium altitudes, this was of little value during offensive sweeps over France. German fighter pilots preferred to remain at altitude, coming down only to deliver high-speed diving attacks before making zoom climbs back to altitude. Rarely would they let themselves be drawn into turning fights with Spitfires below 20,000ft (6,096m).

An obvious next step for the Spitfire was to fit it with a Griffon with a two-stage supercharger. The new engine, the Griffon 65, appeared in the spring of 1943, and developed an impressive 1,540 horsepower for take-off and 2,035hp at 7,000ft (2,134m). Six Spitfire VIIIs were modified to take the new engine, and became prototypes for the Mark XIV.

Flight tests with pre-production Mark XIVs revealed it to be an extremely effective fighter, giving a huge improvement in performance over the Mark IX. During comparative trials against a captured FW 190 and a Messerschmitt 109G, the Spitfire XIV showed itself superior to the German fighters in almost every respect.

The new variant went into production in the autumn of 1943, and by the following spring Nos. 91, 322 and 610 Squadrons had received Mark XIVs. All three units were fully operational in June when the V.1 flying bomb attacks on London commenced.

■ SPITFIRE V FLYING BOMB ■

Although the V.1s flew a straight and predictable path, usually they were not easy targets. The majority flew at speeds around 350mph (563km/hr), although the fastest reached 420mph (675km/hr) and the slowest came in at around 230mph (370km/hr). There were similar variations in altitude. Most flying bombs crossed the coast at between 3,000 and 4,000ft (915 and 1,220m), but the highest came in at around 8,000ft (2,440m) and the lowest flew at treetop height – which frequently led to their early demise!

Protecting the capital were four separate layers of defences. The first layer, extending from mid-Channel to about 10 miles (16km) short of the south coast, was the Outer Fighter Patrol Area where Spitfires and other fighters could engage the flying bombs. Next came the Gun Belt, with more than 2,500 AA guns of all calibres positioned along the strip of coast between Beachy Head and Dover; this was off-limits to fighters, allowing gunners freedom to shoot at anything that came within range. From 10 miles (16km) inland to 10 miles (16km) short of London was the Inner Fighter Patrol Area, where more fighters engaged the V.1s. The final layer, also off-limits to fighters, was the barrage

> *Although the V.1s flew a straight and predictable path, usually they were not easy targets*

balloon zone. This began 10 miles (16km) short of the London built-up area and ended at its outskirts, and above it there hovered more than 1,000 of the ungainly gasbags.

All available squadrons with Mark XIVs redeployed to airfields in Kent to defend the capital. Of the V.1s shot down by fighters, the great majority fell out of control and exploded on striking the ground. A few detonated in mid-air, but there was little risk of serious damage to the fighter unless it was within 150yd (137m) of the explosion. Fighters often suffered minor damage, however, if they struck flying pieces from the missile, or if they flew through the cloud of burning petrol from the fuel tank. Another method of bringing down a V.1 was to fly alongside it, place the fighter's wing under that of the flying bomb and then bank steeply to flip the missile out of control.

■ AIR SUPERIORITY FIGHTER ■

At the end of August 1944, Allied ground forces advancing along the north coast

---

SPITFIRE XIV COMPARED WITH FOCKE WULF 190A

Early in 1944, the Air Fighting Development Unit at Duxford flew a Spitfire XIV in a comparative trial against a captured Focke Wulf 190A. Excerpts from the official trials report are given below:

Maximum speeds: From 0–5,000ft (0–1,525m) and 15,000–0,000ft (4,573–6,100m) the Spitfire XIV is only 20mph (32km/hr) faster; at all other heights it is up to 60mph (97km/hr) faster.

Maximum climb: The Spitfire XIV has a considerably greater rate of climb than the FW 190 A at all altitudes.

Dive: After the initial part of the dive, during which the FW 190 gains slightly, the Spitfire XIV has a slight advantage.

Turning circle: The Spitfire XIV can easily turn inside the FW 190. Though in the case of a right-hand turn, this difference is not quite so pronounced.

Rate of roll: The FW 190 is very much better.

Conclusions: In defence, the Spitfire XIV should use its remarkable maximum climb and turning circle against any enemy aircraft. In the attack it can afford to 'mix it' but should beware of the quick roll and dive. If this manoeuvre is used by an FW 190 and the Spitfire XIV follows, it will probably not be able to close the range until the FW 190 has pulled out of its dive.

SPITFIRE XIV COMPARED WITH Me 109G

Early in 1944, the Air Fighting Development Unit at Duxford flew a Spitfire XIV in a comparative trial against a captured Messerschmitt 109G, the latest sub-type of the famous German fighter. Excerpts from the official trials report are given below:

Maximum speed: The Spitfire XIV is 40mph (64km/hr) faster at all heights except near 16,000ft (4,878m), where it is only 10mph (16km/hr) faster.

Maximum climb: The same result – at 16,000ft (4,877m) the two aircraft are identical, otherwise the Spitfire XIV out-climbs the Me 109G. The zoom climb is practically identical when the climb is made without opening the throttle. Climbing at full throttle, the Spitfire XIV draws away from the Me 109G quite easily.

Dive: During the initial part of the dive, the Me 109G pulls away slightly, but when a speed of 380mph (611km/hr) is reached, the Spitfire XIV begins to gain on the Me 109G.

Turning circle: The Spitfire XIV easily out-turns the Me 109G in either direction.

Rate of roll: The Spitfire XIV rolls much more quickly.

Conclusion: The Spitfire XIV is superior to the Me 109G in every respect.

Below: During mock combats, the Me 109G was no match for the Spitfire XIV.

of France overran the last of the V.1 launching sites in the Pas de Calais. The 8,617th and last flying bomb launched from that area crossed the south coast of England on the morning of 1 September.

Following the capture of the V.1 sites, the Spitfire XIV squadrons redeployed to airfields in Belgium, to resume operations against conventional enemy aircraft. Four further squadrons joined them soon afterwards, Nos. 41, 130, 350 and 403 Squadrons. For the remainder of the war, the Mark XIV was the main air superiority fighter operated by the Royal Air Force in the skies over northern Europe.

The Mark XXI was intended as the 'definitive' fighter variant of the Spitfire, and had the war continued into 1946, it was set to become the RAF's main air superiority type. Powered by the Griffon 65 engine, it featured a completely redesigned wing with a much-strengthened internal structure. It carried the four 20mm cannon armament as standard. These changes added significant weight to aircraft, however, and early production machines had unpleasant handling characteristics. It took a few months to iron out these bugs, and as a result the variant entered service only during the final few weeks of the war.

The delay in bringing the Mark XXI into action had no effect on the air war in Europe, for the Allied Air Forces defeated the Luftwaffe with the fighter types in service. Before we finish with the Second World War, however, it is necessary to review developments of the Spitfire for roles other than air combat. In the next chapter we shall observe the work done to improve the effectiveness of reconnaissance variants.

MORE SPITFIRE SPYPLANES

As the war progressed, the Royal Air Force faced increasing demands to provide reconnaissance photographs of targets deep inside occupied territory in Europe. Yet, by the summer of 1942, the improving German air defences inflicted mounting losses on the reconnaissance Spitfires. The obvious answer was to produce a higher performance reconnaissance aircraft powered by the Merlin 61 engine. The new variant, the Spitfire PR XI, combined the stregthened airframe of the Mark VIII fighter with the integral wing fuel tank and rear fuselage camera installation of the PR Marks ID and VD.

Left: Spitfire PR XI in invasion marking. Note the ports in the rear fuselage for the two vertical cameras.

Until the PR XI became available, fifteen Mark IX fighters underwent modification for the reconnaissance role. Designated PR IXs, these aircraft had the armament removed and a pair of vertical cameras installed in the rear fuselage. The version had no extra internal fuel tankage, and during operations it usually flew with a 90 gallon (409 litre) drop tank under the fuselage. No. 541 Squadron at Benson received the first PR Mark IXs in November 1942. Although the limited tankage confined the PR IX to operations over western Europe, it restored the ability to photograph defended targets without incurring serious losses.

In December 1942 the first Spitfire PR XIs began coming off the production line. The new variant could operate at altitude above 42,000ft (12,800m), some 10,000ft (3,000m) higher than previous reconnaissance version.

SPITFIRE MK XI

Type Single-seat long range reconnaissance aircraft.
War Load Two vertically mounted reconnaissance cameras, could also carry one oblique mounted camera. No armament.
Power Plant One Rolls-Royce Merlin 63 liquid cooled V-12 engine with two-stage super-charge developing 1,650hp.
Dimensions Span 36ft 10in (10.98m); length 31ft 1in (9.47m).
Weight Maximum loaded weight 8,519lb (3,863kg)
Performance Maximum Speed 417mph at 24,000ft (671km/hr at 7317m); service ceiling 44,000ft (13,415m).

Below and overleaf: Spitfire XIs of the 10th photo Group, US Army Air Force. The unit operated this variant on photographic reconnaissance mission over occupied Europe.

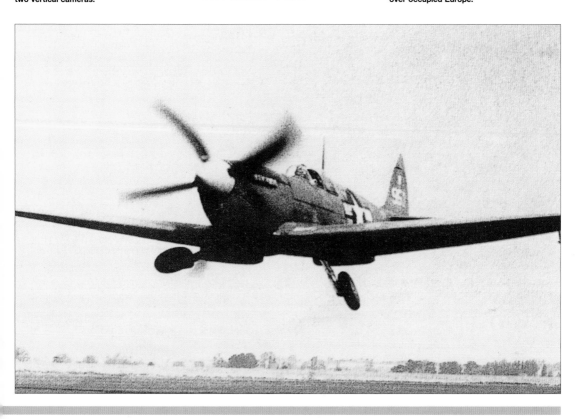

SPITFIRE XIX

Type Single-seat long-range reconnaissance aircraft.

War Load Two vertically mounted reconnaissance cameras, could also carry one oblique mounted camera. No armament.

Power Plant One Rolls-Royce Griffon 66 liquid cooled V-12 engine with two-stage super-charger developing 2,035hp.

Dimensions Span 36ft 10in (10.98m normal wing tips); length 32ft 8in (9.96m).

Weight Maximum loaded weight 10,450lb (4,739kg).

Performance Maximum speed 445mph at 26,000ft (716km/hr at 7,927m); operational ceiling in excess of 49,000ft (14,940m).

Above: PR XI of US 10th Photo Group.

Below: German pilots clamber over a captured PR XI.

The Mark XI replaced all other unarmed versions of the Spitfire in front-line reconnaissance units, and 471 examples were built. For more than a year after the variant entered service, it was almost immune to fighter interception while flying at high altitude.

In the autumn of 1943 the US 8th Air Force in Great Britain received a dozen Mark XIs. These formed the 14th Photo Squadron, 10th Photographic Group, based at Mount Farm near Oxford. The unit's role was to take pre-strike and post-strike photographs of targets attacked by the US heavy bombers. Major Walt Weitner, commander of the 14th, described his impressions of flying this version on operations:

'With all the extra clothing, the parachute, dinghy, life jacket and oxygen mask, the narrow cockpit of a Spitfire was no place for the claustrophobic! With a full load of fuel, the Spit would "lean" disconcertingly during turns when one taxied. Once the gear was up and you pulled up the nose, boy would she climb!"

The Mark XI cruised at altitudes around 39,000ft (12,000m), ascending above that altitude if enemy fighters tried to intercept it. Weitner found the Spitfire easy to handle at very high altitude:

'For high altitude work the Spit was unequalled. One had always to have hold of the stick, but it needed little pressure. In the reconnaissance business you were continually banking to search the sky all around for enemy fighter and to check the navigation.'

■ NEW VARIANTS ■

The system of allocating Spitfire numbers was anything but methodical, and the PR Mark X entered service more than a year later than the PR XI. The Mark X was similar to the Mark XI, but it was fitted with a pressurized cabin. Only sixteen examples were built, however, and the variant entered service with Nos 541 and 542 Squadrons in May 1944. The commander of the latter unit, Squadron Leader Alfred Ball, remembered the PR X with no great affection:

'I flew the PR X a few times on operations. They were not popular because of the poor visibility out of the very thick perspex canopy. Outside everything looked a slightly discoloured yellow, the perspex was not as clear as on an ordinary Spitfire. The extra weight of the pressure cabin led the Mark X to feel much heavier than the Mark XI. We preferred the unpressurized Mark XI to the Mark X.'

> **'Once the gear was up and you pulled up the nose, boy would she climb!'**

The Mark XI's near-immunity from fighter interception lasted until the spring of 1944. Then the Luftwaffe deployed its first jet fighter types, the rocket-propelled Me 163 and the turbojet powered Me 262. High flying Allied reconnaissance aircraft, unarmed and alone, offered perfect targets on which the German jet pilots could make practice interceptions.

A fighter-reconnaissance version of the Spitfire XIV entered service in small numbers, fitted with an oblique camera in the rear fuselage.

■ THE MARK XIX ■

With the increasing threat of interception from German jet fighters, there was requirement for a Griffon-powered long-range unarmed reconnaissance variant. This became the PR Mark XIX, with integral wing fuel tanks as fitted to the PR XI and its predecessors.

The new variant entered service in May 1944 and gave a huge advance in performance over the PR XI. Later production Mark XIXs had pressurized cabins, built to an improved design. Comfortably ensconced in their pressurized cabins, pilots often took this variant above 49,000ft (above 15,000m).

Altogether 225 examples of the PR XIX were built, before production of this version · ended in the spring of 1946.

Photographic reconnaissance was one role that the Spitfire's designer had not envisaged. Anoher was that of fighter-bomber.

Below: **The Mark XIX was the final reconnaissance version of the Spitfire, and remained in front-line service in the role until 1954. This example carries a 170-gallon (773-litre) ferry tank under the fuselage.**

Winston Churchill once commented that "Air power is the most difficult of all forms of military force to measure, or even to express in precise terms." One can apply those same words to air superiority. Certainly, once the enemy air force is driven from the skies, the side with air superiority possesses a great advantage. However, to exploit this advantage, types of aircraft other than the pure fighter must be brought into play. Bombers, transports and reconnaissance aircraft can then capitalize on the situation and mount effective operations to support the land battle. To assist with this, part of the fighter force will relinquish air-to-air operations and join in the attack on ground targets.

By the time of the Normandy invasion, in June 1944, the Luftwaffe had been weakened to such a point that it was rarely able to operate over northern France. Having thus secured air superiority, many Spitfire units switched to the fighter-bomber role. These aircraft became the bane of the existence of German ground troops, as they bombed and strafed anything that moved in the rear areas. Such attacks made movement on the ground extremely hazardous during the daylight hours.

■ TARGET ROMMEL ■

An action by Spitfire fighter-bombers that had far-reaching consequences for the land battle occurred on 17 July 1944. That day, Field Marshal Erwin Rommel, commander of German ground forces in Normandy, needed to travel urgently to a sector of the front where an Allied breakthrough seemed imminent. A flight of Mustangs on low-level reconnaissance observed the staff car speeding along a road near Lisieux, and reported their find. Spitfires of No. 602 Squadron, flying an armed reconnaissance over the area, were immediately ordered to investigate the sighting.

Squadron Leader Chris Le Roux, the formation leader, spotted the car and carried out a low-altitude strafing attack with cannon and machine-guns. He scored several hits and, its driver dead at the wheel, the car ran off the road and crashed into a tree.

Opposite: A pair of Spitfire IX fighter-bombers of No. 601 Squadron about to take off from Fano, Italy, to attack a target in enemy territory. The nearer aircraft carries a 500lb (226kg) bomb under the fuselage, and the aircraft in the background carries a 250lb (113kg) bomb. *Below and overleaf:* Mark IXs fitted with two 250lb (113kg) bombs under the wings.

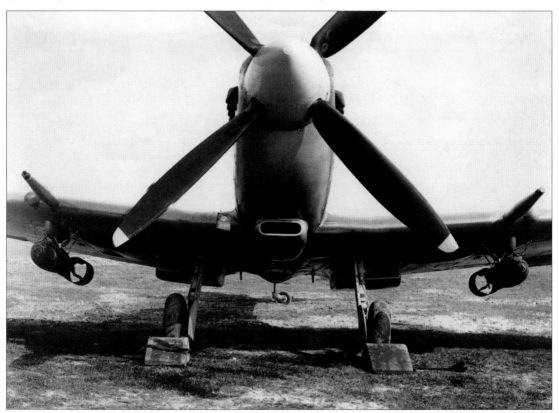

"THE EFFECT OF AIR SUPERIORITY"

". . . we always knew when we were flying over the front line either when starting out on a reconnaissance mission or when returning: the contrast was astonishing, for in German occupied territory not a thing moved; perhaps a solitary vehicle would be observed, but as soon as the driver or look-out saw an aeroplane the vehicle stopped. Over our own territory masses of tents and convoys were to be seen; and that was the effect that air superiority, or the complete lack of it, had on land forces and their everyday existence."

GROUP CAPTAIN G. MILLINGTON,
COMMANDER NO. 285 (RECONNAISSANCE)
WING IN ITALY, 1944, IN HIS BOOK
THE UNSEEN EYE

Rommel suffered a fractured skull and severe concussion, and had to be replaced at a critical stage in the land battle.

■ BOMB LOADS CARRIED ■

The bomb loads carried by Spitfires flying ground attack missions depended on the nature of the target and its distance from base. The greater the distance the aircraft had to fly, the smaller the bomb load it could carry. Normally the Spitfires carried two 250lb (113kg) bombs under the wings or a 500-pounder (226kg) under the fuselage. However, if the target was relatively close to base, the aircraft might carry the 500-pounder as well as two 250-pounders. Once the bombs had been dropped, the fighter could switch to the ground-attack role, its powerful armament making it an effective ground-strafing aircraft. When operating in the fighter-bomber role, Spitfires usually flew in sections of four or six, depending on the type of target and the weight of attack required.

Once the bombs had dropped, the fighter's powerful gun armament made it an effective ground-strafing aircraft

Flying Officer David Green flew Spitfires with No. 73 Squadron over Italy and Yugoslavia during the final months of the war. He describes the normal tactics for a dive-bombing attack in a Spitfire:

"Carrying two 250lb bombs, the Spitfire made a very fine dive-bomber. It could attack accurately and didn't need a fighter escort because as soon as the bombs had been released it was a fighter. The briefing beforehand had to be good enough for us to be able to fly right up to the target even if we had never been there before, identify it and bomb it. Because

AIR SUPPORT FOR THE ARMY, MORNING OF 10 NOVEMBER 1944

Squadron	Aircraft	Time up	Remarks
No. 7 SAAF	6 Spitfire	09.45	Bombed medium gun position
No. 1 SAAF	6 Spitfire	10.00	Bombed field guns near Forli
No. 601	6 Spitfire	10.15	Bombed field guns near Forli; light AA fire; one aircraft failed to pull out of dive possibly due to flak hit, pilot killed
No. 2 SAAF	6 Spitfire	10.20	Two aircraft returned early; rest bombed gun position and carried out strafing attacks; heavy AA from target, no losses
No. 92	6 Spitfire	10.25	Bombed gun positions S. Faenza
No. 92	6 Spitfire	10.30	Bombed and strafed gun and mortar positions near Faenza
No. 4 SAAF	6 Spitfire	10.40	Dive-bombed gun positions
No. 2 SAAF	6 Spitfire	11.05	Bombed 3 gun positions, target well strafed; light AA from target
No. 4 SAAF	6 Spitfire	11.35	Bombed gun positions

the flak was often accurate we didn't want to spend time circling in the target area before we went down to attack. We normally operated in sections of four, and would fly to the target at 10,000 feet in finger-four battle formation."

When the raiding force neared the target area, the Spitfires closed up and moved into loose echelon formation to starboard of the leader. David Green continued:

"As the target came into view I would position it so that it appeared to be running down the line of my port cannon. As the target disappeared under the wing, I would hold my heading. When the target emerged from under the trailing edge I would pull the aircraft up to kill the forward speed, roll it over on its back and let the nose drop until the target was lined up in the gunsight graticule. That way, one got the Spitfire to go down in the correct angle of dive of 60 degrees. It was a pretty steep dive, it felt as if one was going down vertically. The other aircraft in the section, Nos. 2, 3, and 4, would be following me down still in echelon."

When the leader's dive took him to an altitude of 4,000ft (1,219m) above the ground, he released his bombs.

"I would let go my bombs and call 'Bombs gone!'; the other chaps in the section would then release theirs. If there had been little or no flak the desire to see the results of the bombing was usually so

> **"It was a pretty steep dive, it felt as if one was going down vertically."**

great that I would pull hard on the stick to bring the aircraft out of the dive and into a slight climb, so that I could look over my shoulder to see where the bombs had gone. But if we were being fired at, we would use our high forward speed to get us down to ground level where there was cover."

During the final months of the war, almost every attack launched by the

British army received strong fighter-bomber support. The example above shows the scale of air support for the British advance on the Montone River in Italy, on 10 November 1944. That morning, during a two-hour period, two RAF and four South African Air Force Spitfire squadrons flew 54 sorties to soften up the German defences. Air operations continued in the same vein throughout the rest of the day.

■ VERSATILITY ■

Given the ability of the Spitfire in the fighter-bomber role, the reader should remember that attacks on ground targets were far from everyone's thoughts when the Spitfire was conceived. As so often with this aircraft, it was a case of the very good basic design proving very good at a wide range of different roles.

The Spitfire remained in front-line service in the RAF for nearly a decade after the end of the war. In the next chapter, we shall observe the final stages of its lengthy career in that service and also in foreign air forces.

At the end of the war, just over 1,000 Spitfires were serving with RAF front-line units. About two-thirds of those were Mark IXs (or the essentially similar Mark XVIs). For a 'stop-gap' fighter put into production in a hurry, this had been a remarkably successful variant.

SPITFIRE MARK XXII

Type Single-seat interceptor fighter

Armament Four Hispano 20mm cannon with 150 rounds each for the inner weapons and 175 rounds each for the outer weapons

Power plant One Rolls-Royce Griffon 61 liquid cooled V-12 engine with two-stage supercharger developing 2,035hp

Dimensions Span 36ft 1in (11.25m); length 32ft 11in (10.03m)

Weight Maximum loaded weight 10,086lb (4,574kg)

Performance Maximum speed 449mph at 25,000ft (723km/hr at 7,622m); service ceiling 45,500ft (13,872m)

The Spitfire force was rapidly run down after the war as the RAF reduced its strength and many units converted to jet fighters. During the early post-war period, the Mark XVIII was the main fighter variant to equip fighter units in the Middle East and the Far East. Externally similar to the late production Mark XIV with bubble canopy and additional fuel tanks in the rear fuselage, this variant also featured a redesigned and strengthened wing. Production ran to some 300 aircraft, and the variant equipped six front-line squadrons.

The Mark XVIII saw action with Nos. 28 and 60 Squadrons in Malaya, engaging in bombing and strafing operations against Communist guerillas in that country. Serving in the Middle East with Nos. 32 and 208 Squadrons, this variant became involved in clashes during the Arab-Jewish conflict leading up to the establishment of the state of Israel.

As mentioned earlier, the Mark XXI had been intended as the 'definitive' fighter variant of the Spitfire. At the peak more than 1,800 were on order, but with the end of the war most of these were cancelled. In the event, production ended at 120 aircraft, and this variant served with only four front-line squadrons.

Main left: A Spitfire XXI tips its wing to show the revised wing shape of this and later variants. Note also the fairing doors covering the main wheels and the armament of four 20mm cannon introduced as standard with this version.
Above right: After the war, Spitfires served in several second-line units. This Mark XVI operated with the Central Gunnery School.
Inset left and right: Spitfire XVIIIs of No. 208 Squadron based at Fayid in the Suez Canal Zone in 1947.

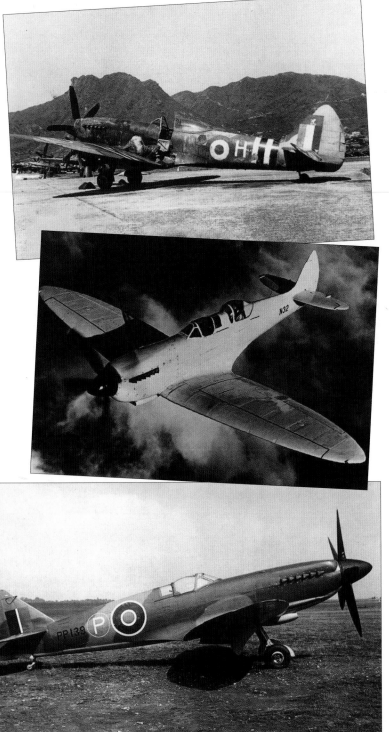

Left: Mark XVIIIs of No. 28 Squadron pictured at Kai Tak, Hong Kong, late in 1950. The aircraft carries the black and white identification bands on the rear fuselage and above and below the wings, introduced soon after the start of the war in Korea.
Middle left: Spitfire made for two. After the war, small numbers of Spitfire XVIIIs and IXs were converted into two-seat trainers with dual controls. Trainer variants served with the Indian, Dutch, Egyptian and Irish air forces, though the type was not adopted by the RAF.
Below left: Spitfire PP139 served as a development prototype for the Mark XXI, and incorporated several new features. The enlarged fin with the straight leading edge and the windscreen with revised contours were not incorporated into production aircraft.

During the post-war period, the Mark XVIII was the main fighter variant to equip fighter units in the Middle East and Far East

The next major production fighter variant, the Spitfire XXII, was essentially a Mark XXI with a bubble canopy and the new enlarged tail assembly. The majority of Mark XXIIs went to Royal Auxiliary Air Force squadrons, reserve units manned by the so-called 'weekend pilots'. During 1948, 12 of the 20 RAuxAF squadrons re-equipped with Spitfire XXIIs.

■ FINAL VARIANT ■

The final Spitfire variant, the Mark XXIV, looked little different from the Mark XXII. Its main points of difference were two additional fuel tanks fitted in the rear fuselage, and wing fittings to carry six 60lb (27kg) rockets. Supermarine built 54 Mark XXIVs and converted 27 Mark XXIIs on the production line to this configuration. The final Mark XXIV, the last of more than 20,000 Spitfires built, left the factory at South Marston near Swindon in February 1948.

Right and below right: Mark XXIs serving with No. 41 Squadron based at Luebeck in Germany shortly after the end of the war. (Adamson)

The majority of Mark XXIIs went to Royal Auxiliary Air Force squadrons

Only one front-line unit received the Spitfire XXIV, No. 80 Squadron based in Germany in January 1948. In July 1949, after the start of the Korean War, the unit moved to Hong Kong to provide air defence for the colony. The last RAF unit to operate Spitfires in the fighter role, it re-equipped with Hornets in January 1952. Photographic reconnaissance Mark XIXs continued in front-line service for a further two years, before this variant also ended its front-line career in the Far East. In April 1954, No. 81 Squadron in Malaya exchanged its trusty Spitfires for Meteors.

Although the Spitfire had passed out of front-line service, it would continue to perform second-line tasks in the RAF for three more years. The last full-time RAF unit to operate Spitfires was the civilian-manned Temperature and Humidity (THUM) Flight based at Woodvale in Lancashire. The unit's Mark XIXs, carrying meteorological measuring equipment, made daily flights to 30,000ft (9,144m) to record the weather conditions in each altitude band. These flights continued until June 1957, when the unit disbanded. Even then, the Spitfire's career in the RAF was not at an end. After the THUM Flight disbanded, one of its redundant Mark XIXs went to the Central Fighter Establishment at West Rayneham to serve as a gate guardian. Service engineers lovingly maintained the aircraft in flying condition, however, and when the unit transferred to Binbrook, the Spitfire went too.

During 1963, Indonesia launched its claim to parts of Malayan territory, and threatened to use force to secure it. To meet the threat, the RAF sent reinforcements to the area, including detachments of Lightning fighters. The Indonesian Air Force operated Second World War Mustang fighters, and there was uncertainty on the best tactics for the Mach 2

Left and above: A few Spitfires were fitted with the contra-rotating propeller, comprising two three-bladed units rotating in opposite directions. Although this made the fighter easier to fly and a more steady gun platform, it came too late for general service use.

Above: The Mark XXII was similar to the Mark XXI, but featured a bubble canopy as well as a larger tailplane, fin and rudder.

fighters to engage these. To discover the answer, the CFE ran a combat trial using the Spitfire XIX as a stand-in for the Mustang. Mock combats between the two aircraft revealed that the older fighter stood little chance in a wartime encounter. The Lightning was almost invulnerable while it maintained high speed and did not enter a turning fight with the more nimble opponent. The best tactic for the Lightning was to position itself a few thousand feet below the piston-engined fighter, and make a steep climbing attack from there. This gave a good chance of getting into a missile-firing position on the Spitfire (or Mustang) without being seen. The trial at Binbrook took place

27 years after the maiden flight of the Spitfire, and probably represented the final warlike act in the aircraft's long and distinguished career.

Also during the years following the Second World War, several foreign air forces operated Spitfires. The largest such operator was the French Air Force, which took delivery of more than 500 Mark Vs, VIIIs, IXs and XVIs. Some went to Vietnam and flew against Communist guerillas during the initial stages of the long conflict in that country.

■ SPITFIRES INTERNATIONAL ■

The Royal Dutch Air Force received 76 Mark IXs, some of which saw combat over what was then the Dutch East Indies. That conflict ran from 1947 to 1949, and ended with the foundation of the modern state of Indonesia.

Other major post-war Spitfire users were the Turkish Air Force, which received 273, the Royal Greek Air Force with 242, and the Royal Belgian Air Force with 203. The Indian Air Force received 159, the Italian Air Force 140, and the Czechoslovak Air Force 77.

Over a century has elapsed since Orville Wright made the first manned flight in a heavier-than-air flying machine. In the turbulent history of military aviation, no aircraft has carved a deeper niche than Mitchell's little fighter – which somebody else chose to call 'Spitfire'.

Above: Spitfire XXIIs formed the main equipment of the Royal Auxiliary Air Force units during the late 1940s. These aircraft belonged to No. 613 (City of Manchester) Squadron based at Ringwood, which converted to the variant in the summer of 1948.

Left: Spitfire XXII of No. 607 (County of Durham) Squadron. The '4' painted on the fin, fuselage and wing was the aircraft's racing number for the Cooper Trophy air race in 1948.

Above: Mark IX of the Royal Dutch Air Force, which received 76 examples of this variant.

Left: From its external appearance, the final variant of the Spitfire, the Mark XXIV, was little different from the Mark XXII. The main changes were that it carried two additional fuel tanks in the rear fuselage, and wing fittings to carry six 60lb (27kg) rockets. Only No. 80 Squadron was equipped with this variant, and after a brief spell in Germany, the unit took its Mark XXIVs to Hong Kong.

Above: One of 77 examples of Mark IX passed to the Czechoslovak Air Force.
Left: The French Air Force was the largest foreign operator of Spitfires after the war, when that service took delivery of some 500 Mark Vs, VIIIs, IXs and XVIs.

Above: Three Spitfire PR Mark XIs of the Royal Norwegian Air Force, which also received 71 Mark IXs.
Left: The Italian Air Force received 140 Spitfire IXs after the war.
Right: Spitfire XIVs of the Royal Belgian Air Force, which received 134 examples of this variant, in addition to 69 Mark IXs and Mark XVIs.

Above and below: Partners in war, and also in peace. A Hurricane pictured with a Spitfire XIX of the Royal Air Force Battle of Britain Memorial Flight. These aircraft are firm favourites at present-day airshows.
Left: The Southern Rhodesian Air Force received 22 Spitfire XXIIs from surplus RAF stocks in 1951.

APPENDIX
THE SPITFIRE FAMILY

The main driving force for the development of the Spitfire came from the progressive increases in power from the Merlin, and later the Griffon, series of engines. In developing the extra power, the engines guzzled fuel faster, requiring larger capacity (and therefore heavier) fuel tanks to restore the fighter's range. Also, the more powerful engines required propellers with more blades to convert that rotational power into thrust. During its life, the Spitfire progressed from a two-bladed propeller to a three-blader, then to a four-blader, and finally to a five-bladed propeller. The greater the number of propeller blades, the greater the weight and also the greater the twisting forces they exerted on the airframe when the engine ran at full power. At the end of the fighter's career, it was necessary to fit an entirely new and larger tail assembly, to overcome these twisting forces.

Application of the hard-won lessons of air combat led to other problems. The RAF demanded the installation of armour to protect the pilot and vulnerable parts of the aircraft's structure, as well as additional equipment and more powerful (and therefore heavier) weaponry.

When the fighter sat on the ground, these increases in weight did not matter much, but in the stress of combat it was an entirely different matter. If the pilot pulled 6G in the turn, every part of the aircraft weighed six times as much. If the wings and the rest of the

THE PRICE OF SUCCESS

"I loved the Spitfire, in all of her many versions. But I have to admit that the later Marks, although they were faster than the earlier ones, were also much heavier and so did not handle so well. You did not have such positive control over them. One test of manoeuvrability was to throw the Spitfire into a flick roll and see how many times she rolled. With the Mark II or the Mark V one got two and a half flick rolls, but the Mark IX was heavier and you got only one and a half. With the later and still heavier versions one got even less.

"The essence of aircraft design is compromise, and an improvement at one end of the performance envelope is rarely achieved without a deterioration somewhere else."

ALEX HENSHAW, CHIEF TEST PILOT AT THE CASTLE BROMWICH SPITFIRE FACTORY

structure were not strong enough to withstand these increased forces, the airframe would be overstressed and weakened. In extreme cases, the structure might collapse altogether. So, to cope with each major increase in the fighter's weight, the airframe was continually being redesigned to increase its strength and maintain a safe load factor. In addition, and inevitably, each such redesign brought with it a further increase in weight. Thus, every improvement in performance, fire power, range or capability gave a further twist in the spiral of increased weight. And that in turn led to a further deterioration in the fighter's handling characteristics.

K 5054 Prototype Spitfire, first flew in March 1936. Only one aircraft built.

Mark I Similar to the prototype but with some revisions to the structure, this was the first production fighter version. The Mark I made its maiden flight in May 1938, and entered service in the following September.

Mark I Recon Variants Mark Is modified for the reconnaissance role, designated from IA to IG depending on the reconnaissance configuration of the cameras and fuel tanks carried. First such aircraft entered service in November 1939.

Mark II Fighter version similar to the Mark I, but fitted with the more powerful Merlin 12 engine. Entered service in September 1940.

Mark III Fighter version similar to the Mark I but with a redesigned internal structure and fitted with a retractable tail wheel. This variant did not go into production. In September 1941, the prototype Mark III served as a test bed for the Merlin 61 engine with two-stage supercharger.

Mark IV Designation initially applied to the prototype Griffon-engined Spitfire. In 1941, the designation system was revised, and the Griffon aircraft became the Mark XX for a short time, before finally ending up as the Mark XII. The Mark IV designation was then re-allocated to reconnaissance versions.

Mark V Fighter version similar to the Mark I, but fitted with the more powerful Merlin 45-series engine. The Mark V entered service in February 1941, and was built in very large numbers. It was the first variant to be fitted with bomb racks, and operated in the fighter-bomber role.

Mark VI High-altitude interceptor fighter, similar to the Mark V but fitted with a pressurized cabin and longer-span wing. The Mark VI was built in small numbers and entered service in April 1942.

Mark VII High-altitude interceptor fighter, similar to the Mark VI but powered by the Merlin 61-series engine with two-stage supercharger. Built in moderate numbers, the first squadron equipped with this variant became operational in April 1943.

Mark VIII General-purpose fighter similar to the Mark VII but without the pressurized cabin. Entered service in the summer of 1943. Built in large numbers, all Mark VIIIs went to units based outside the United Kingdom. This variant also operated in the fighter-bomber role.

Mark IX General-purpose fighter version based on the Mark V, but fitted with the Merlin 61-series engine. Entered service in June 1942. This variant was intended as a stop-gap, pending large-scale production of the Mark VIII. In the event, the Mark IX remained in production until the end of the war. With the externally similar Mark XVI, it was built in greater numbers than any other variant. Late-production aircraft were fitted with bubble canopies. This variant also operated in the fighter-bomber and fighter-reconnaissance roles.

Mark X Photographic reconnaissance variant generally similar to the PR ID, but fitted with the Merlin 61-series engine and a pressurized cabin. Entered service in May 1944, and was built in small numbers.

Mark XI Photographic reconnaissance variant similar to the Mark X but without the pressurized cabin. Entered service in December 1942, and became the most-used photographic reconnaissance variant.

Mark XII Fighter version based on the Mark V but fitted with the early Griffon 2 engine with a single-stage supercharger. Originally it was designated the Mark IV, and then it was redesignated the Mark XX, before finally receiving this designation. Built in moderate numbers as a low-altitude fighter, all production aircraft had clipped wings. Entered service in February 1943.

Mark XIII   Low-altitude fighter-reconnaissance variant fitted with vertical and oblique cameras, and armed with four .303in (7.7mm) machine-guns. With only 26 examples produced, it entered service in the summer of 1943.

Mark XIV   Fighter version similar to the Mark VIII but fitted with the Griffon 61-series engine with two-stage supercharger. It entered service in February 1944. A fighter-reconnaissance version of the Mark XIV also appeared. The variant was built in large numbers, and the final production aircraft had bubble canopies.

Mark XV   Designation not applied to the Spitfire.

Mark XVI   Fighter version similar to the Mark IX but powered by the Merlin engine produced under licence by the American Packard Company. The two variants were produced side by side at the Castle Bromwich plant, and their external appearance was almost identical. The Mark XVI entered service in September 1944, and late-production aircraft were fitted with bubble canopies. This variant also operated in the fighter-bomber role.

Mark XVII   Designation not applied to the Spitfire.

Mark XVIII   Fighter-bomber version similar in external appearance to the late-model Mark XIV fitted with the bubble canopy, this variant featured a redesigned and strengthened wing, and carried additional fuel tanks in the rear fuselage. A fighter-reconnaissance version of the Mark XVIII also appeared. Built in moderate numbers after the war, it entered service in January 1947. All Mark XVIIIs went to units based outside the United Kingdom.

Mark XIX   Photographic reconnaissance variant which combined the Griffon 61 engine, the fuel tank layout of the Mark XI, and a pressurized cabin that was a marked improvement over that fitted to the Mark X. It entered service in the summer of 1944, and became the most-used reconnaissance variant during the final year of the war. The Mark XIX remained in front-line service in the RAF until 1954.

Mark XX   Designation applied to the prototype Griffon-powered Spitfire, alias the Mark IV, following the re-allocation of Mark numbers. After a further re-allocation of Mark numbers, this aircraft was redesignated as a Mark XII, and the Mark XX designation fell vacant.

Mark XXI   Fighter version with a redesigned and strengthened wing and fuselage, fitted with the Griffon 61-series engine. The Mark XXI entered service in April 1945, and saw some action before the war ended. Following the end of the conflict, several large contracts for the Mark XXI were cancelled, and the variant was built in only moderate numbers.

Mark XXII   Fighter version similar to the Mark XXI, but with a bubble canopy. Production aircraft fitted with enlarged tailplane, fin and rudder. The Mark XXII entered service in November 1947, and became the main post-war production variant. It remained in service with Royal Auxiliary Air Force squadrons until March 1951.

Mark XXIII   A projected fighter version that was to have been fitted with laminar-flow wing; not built.

Mark XXIV   Fighter version based on the Mark XXII, but with two additional fuel tanks in the rear fuselage and wing fittings to carry six 60lb (27kg) rockets. Only one squadron operated this variant. The type remained in front-line service in the RAF until January 1952.

PROLOGUE

Bielefeld, western Germany, 14 March 1945. The Lancaster B.1 (Special) heading towards its target had been unable to reach more than 14,000ft (4,250m). Beneath it bulked the outline of the largest and most destructive bomb ever used in war – the Grand Slam, weighing more than 22,000lb (10 tonnes). In the nose lay the bomb-aimer, holding the graticule of his sight on the target. The seconds ticked away interminably until at last the computer automatically released the huge bomb.

The pilot, Squadron Leader Calder, felt the bomber lift as the weight came off, and the wings, which previously had taken on a distinct upward curve, resumed their normal shape.

Lying prone in the nose, the bomb aimer watched as the huge weapon plunged downwards, dwindling in size as it did so, spinning as it went for greater accuracy. At first it appeared that it was going to fall short, but this was illusory. In the final seconds of its fall it seemed to sweep forward and hit about 90ft (30m) from the target.

■ TARGET COLLAPSED ■

The impact was not very spectacular; from that altitude there was just a tiny splash of mud as the Grand Slam, travelling faster than sound, penetrated something like 75ft (25m) into the earth. After an 11-second delay, however, a gigantic underground explosion erupted, flinging earth and mud some 500ft (150m) into the air, and forming an enormous cavity into which a large section of the target, a rail viaduct that was vital to German communications during the closing months of the war, collapsed.

Above: The Bielefeld Rail Viaduct had survived previous raids, but succumbed to the first Grand Slam dropped.

The Lancaster had not been flying alone – that would have been far too risky, even at this late stage in the war. It was accompanied by 14 others, each armed with a Tallboy, a smaller (12,000lb/5.4 tonnes) version of the Grand Slam. Even as the huge bomb went off, Tallboys were falling around the viaduct, their combined effect destroying several more arches of the now sadly battered target, and ensuring that it would never again be used to carry German reinforcements to where they were most needed.

The Lancaster had, in the space of three short years, become the backbone of RAF Bomber Command. A total of 7,366 were built, of which almost half were lost on operations. They carried out something like 156,000 operational sorties, an average of about 21 sorties each, which says much about the hazards they faced, and dropped more than 600,000 tons of bombs; an average of more than 81 tons each. They carried greater bomb loads farther than any other wartime bomber.

■ VERSATILITY ■

Lancasters formed the main equipment of the Pathfinder Force – they pioneered low-level marking and precision attacks, and, far more than any other heavy bomber type before or since, they proved amenable to modification to carry special weapons. With all this, the Lancaster retained its docile handling, even when badly damaged, which undoubtedly saved the lives to many crewmen. Long after the war, the Lancaster retains a mystique unequalled by any other bomber, and the affection of those that flew to war in it remains even today.

Above: Grand Slam, the largest bomb of all. Only 41 were dropped, all by Lancaster Specials of No. 617 Squadron.

Above: 1,000lb (450kg) bombs in storage. Lancasters dropped no fewer than 217,640 of these between 1942 and 1945.

AVRO LANCASTER MK III

1 Two .303in (7.7mm) Browning machine-guns
2 Frazer-Nash power-operated nose turret
3 Nose blister
4 Bomb-aimer's panel (optically flat)
5 Bomb-aimer's control panel
6 Side windows
7 External air temperature thermometer
8 Pitot head
9 Bomb-aimer's chest support
10 Fire extinguisher
11 Parachute emergency exit
12 F-24 camera
13 Glycol tank/step
14 Ventilator fairing
15 Bomb-bay doors forward actuating jacks
16 Bomb-bay doors forward actuating jacks
17 Control linkage
18 Rudder panels
19 Instrument panel
20 Windscreen sprays
21 Windscreen
22 Dimmer switches
23 Flight-engineer's folding seat
24 Flight-engineer's control panel
25 Pilot's seat
26 Flight-deck floor level
27 Elevator and rudder control rods (underfloor)
28 Trim tab control cables
29 Main floor/bomb-bay support longeron
30 Fire extinguisher
31 Wireless installation
32 Navigator's seat
33 Canopy rear/down-view blister
34 Pilot's head armour
35 Cockpit canopy emergency escape hatch
36 D/F loop
37 Aerial mast support
38 Electrical services panel
39 Navigator's compartment window
40 Navigator's desk
41 Aircraft and radio compass receiver
42 Wireless-operator's desk
43 Wireless-operator's seat
44 Wireless-operator's compartment window
45 Front spar carry-through/fuselage frame
46 Astrodome
47 Inboard section wing ribs
48 Spar join
49 Aerial mast
50 Starboard inboard engine nacelle
51 Spinner
52 Three-blade de Havilland constant-speed propellers
53 Oil cooler intake
54 Oil cooler radiator
55 Carburettor air intake
56 Radiator shutter

57 Engine bearer frame
58 Exhaust flame-damper shroud
59 Packard-built Rolls-Royce Merlin 28 liquid-cooled engine
60 Nacelle/wing fairing
61 Fuel tank bearer ribs
62 Intermediate ribs
63 Leading-edge structure
64 Wing stringers
65 Wingtip skinning
66 Starboard navigation light
67 Starboard formation light
68 Aileron hinge fairings
69 Wing rear spar
70 Starboard aileron

71 Aileron balance tab
72 Balance tab control rod
73 Aileron trim tab
74 HF aerial
75 Split trailing-edge flap (outboard section)
76 Emergency (ditching) exit
77 Crash axe stowage
78 Fire extinguisher
79 Hydraulic reservoir
80 Signal/flare pistol stowage
81 Parachute stowage box/spar step
82 Rear spar carry-through
83 Bunk backrest
84 Rear spar fuselage frame

85 Emergency packs
86 Roof light
87 Dinghy manual release cable (dinghy stowage in starboard wingroot)
88 Mid-gunner's parachute stowage
89 Tail turret ammunition box
90 Ammunition feed track
91 Emergency (ditching) exit
92 Flame floats stowage
93 Sea markers stowage
94 Roof light
95 Dorsal turret fairing
96 Frazer-Nash power-operated dorsal turret

157 Flap tube connecting link
158 Rear spar
159 Split trailing-edge flap (inboard section)
160 Split trailing-edge flap (outboard section)
161 Aileron control lever
162 Aileron trim tab control cable linkage
163 Aileron trim tab
164 Aileron balance tab control rod
165 Aileron balance tab
166 Aileron hinge fairings
167 Port aileron
168 Port wingtip
169 Port formation light
170 Port navigation light
171 Retractable landing lights (port wing only)
172 Cable cutters
173 Fuel vent pipe
174 Aileron control rod
175 Port outer (No. 3) fuel tank (114 gal/518 litres)
176 Outboard engine support frame/rear spar pick-up
177 Fuel booster pump
178 Fire extinguisher
179 Engine sub-frame
180 Filler cap
181 Outboard engine oil tank
182 Firewall/bulkhead
183 Carburettor air intake
184 Outboard engine support frame
185 Port mainwheel
186 Undercarriage oleo struts
187 Flame-damper shroud
188 Outboard engine support frame/main spar pick-up
189 Undercarriage retraction jacks
190 Oleo strut attachment pin
191 Undercarriage support beam (light-alloy casting)
192 Centre-section outer rib/undercarriage support
193 Location of port intermediate (No. 2) fuel tank (383 gal/ 1,741 litres)
194 Mainwheel well
195 Emergency retraction air valve
196 Retraction cylinder attachment
197 Port inner (No. 1) fuel tank (580 gal/2,637 litres)
198 Oxygen bottle stowage
199 Rest bunk
200 Main spar
201 Hinged inboard leading-edge
202 Cabin heater installation
203 Air intake
204 Inboard engine support frame
205 Inboard engine oil tank
206 Carburettor intake anti-ice guard
207 Port inner nacelle
208 Flame-damper shroud
209 Detachable cowling panels
210 Bomb shackles
211 Bomb-bay doors (open)
212 8,000lb (2,532kg) bomb

97 Two .303in (7.7mm) Browning machine-guns
98 Turret mounting ring
99 Turret mechanism
100 Ammunition track cover plate
101 Turret step bracket
102 Header tank
103 Oxygen cylinder
104 Fire extinguisher
105 DR compass housing
106 Handrail
107 Crew entry door (starboard)
108 Parachute stowage
109 First-aid pack
110 Starboard tailplane
111 Rudder control lever
112 Starboard tailfin
113 Rudder balance weights
114 Starboard rudder
115 Rudder datum hinge
116 Rudder tab actuating rod
117 Rudder tab

118 Starboard elevator
119 Elevator balance tab
120 Roof light
121 Tail main frame
122 Parachute stowage
123 Fire extinguisher
124 Tail turret entry door
125 Frazer-Nash power-operated tail turret
126 Four .303in (7.7mm) Browning machine-guns
127 Cartridge case ejection chutes
128 Rear navigation light
129 Elevator trim tab
130 Fin construction
131 Rudder balance weights
132 Port rudder frame
133 Rudder trim tab
134 Rudder tab balance weight
135 Rudder tab actuating rod
136 Rudder horn balance
137 Trim tab actuating jack

138 Tailplane construction
139 Elevator torque tube
140 Tailplane carry-through
141 Non-retractable tailwheel
142 Elsan closet
143 Ammunition track cover plate
144 Elevator and rudder control rods
145 H2S (radar-bombing) ventral antenna fairing
146 Dorsal turret step
147 Ammunition feed track
148 Tail turret ammunition box
149 Bomb-bay aft bulkhead
150 Bomb-bay doors
151 Bomb-bay doors aft actuating jacks
152 Reserve ammunition boxes
153 Main floor support structure
154 Flap operating hydraulic jack
155 Flap operating tube
156 Flap toggle links

THE MANCHESTER

The origins of the Lancaster lay in Air Ministry Specification P13/36, issued in September 1936, but it was some time before the definitive aircraft emerged. The requirements included a maximum bomb load of 8,000lb (3.63 tonnes), a six-man crew, which included a ventral gunner, and the ability to operate from existing 4,500ft (1,375m) long grass strips. Power was to be provided by two Rolls-Royce Vultures, a 24 cylinder liquid-cooled engine which was expected to develop about 2,000hp.

The Handley Page Company had early doubts about the Vulture, and switched to the proven Merlin, for what was to become the Halifax. At A.V. Roe, chief designer Roy Chadwick persevered with the bomber, with Napiers Sabre as a fall-back engine.

Two prototypes of the Avro Type 679, later to be named the Manchester, were ordered within

AVRO 679

Dimensions
Wing span 80ft 2in (24.43m)
Tailplane span 22ft 0in (6.70m)
Length 70ft 0in (21.33m)
Height 19ft 6in (5.94m)

Weights
Maximum take-off 45,000lb (20,400kg)
Maximum bomb load 10,000lb (4,500kg)

Power
Two Rolls-Royce 24 cylinder
Vulture I liquid-cooled engines
rated at 1,720hp each.

Performance
Maximum speed 256mph (412km/hr)
at 12,500ft (3,800m)
Range with maximum bomb load
c1,200 miles (1,930km) Service ceiling
c18,000ft (5,500m)

Armament
Two .303 Browning machine
guns in each of three Nash and
Thompson power-operated turrets,
nose, tail, and a retractable
ventral 'dustbin'. None fitted on
first flight.

a week of Specification P13/36 being issued, and the first flight took place at Ringway Airport on 25 July 1939. It was a large aircraft, with the wing in the mid position, and with twin fins and rudders. Handling problems were

immediately apparent; the controls were heavy, and lateral stability left much to be desired. The take-off run was far longer than anticipated, with no bomb load, with the gun turrets omitted and their positions faired over. Meanwhile the second prototype, already well advanced, was modified to try to cure these faults. The outer wing sections were redesigned, extending the span to 90ft 1in (27.46m); the control surfaces (ailerons and elevators) were improved, and larger fins and rudders fitted.

In the expectation that the faults of the first prototype would soon be overcome, contracts were placed for the production of 1,200 Manchesters. The first flight of the second prototype took place on 26 May 1940, handling had improved but directional stability, especially at low airspeeds, was still far from adequate. It was then decided to fit a central fin, which went some way towards improving matters.

Left: The Lancaster Mk I, originally known as the Manchester III, was developed around the Manchester fuselage and wing centre section.

Below: The twin-engined Manchester was the forerunner of the Lancaster. This No. 61 Squadron aircraft failed to return from a raid on Hamburg in April 1942.

Above: **The Manchester IA left off the central fin, but the span of the tailplane was greatly increased.**

There were problems with the Vulture whose design had been started in 1935. It had two V-12 engines on a common crankcase, one upright, with the other inverted beneath it. With a capacity of 42.48 litres, it was expected to deliver over 2,000hp at 3,000rpm for take-off, and 1,710hp at an altitude of 15,000ft (4,570m).

The Vulture was just that bit too clever for the time

Lubrication, excessive wear, metal fatigue and overheating all gave cause for concern. But with the build-up of RAF Bomber Command, it was decided to continue with the Manchester, in the hope that the problems would be solved.

▪ DEFENSIVE ▪

The gun turrets were installed in the second prototype; two .303 Brownings in the nose, tail, and in a retractable ventral 'dustbin' arrangement. These also gave rise to handling problems. When rotated, they interfered with the slipstream. The nose turret caused the aircraft to veer to one side, while the rear turret caused vibration in the elevators.

Battle experience in 1939 led to a rethinking of the defensive armament for bombers. The ventral turret was deleted and a twin-gun mid-upper turret installed. The armament of the tail turret was to be doubled to four machine guns, but various weight restrictions prevented this being put into practice for some considerable time.

Despite the problems, the Manchester had many good points. The layout of the spacious cabin was highly praised, while the bomb bay could hold either four 2,000 pounders (900kg) or four sea mines; or one of the new 4,000lb (1,800kg) bombs together with six 1,000 pounders (450kg). The structure was sturdy, and adjustments to the flight control system resulted in an aircraft that was quite pleasant to fly.

Continuing problems with the Vulture engines limited it to 52,000lb (23.59 tonnes) and to 12,000ft (3,660m) with maximum bomb load and 50 per cent fuel.

■ STOP GAP ■

Further testing revealed an average of only 76 flying hours between engine failures, and generally the Manchester was only able to maintain height on one engine at fairly light all-up weights. The Manchester was rushed into service even though it would be only an interim type with Bomber Command.

The first operational Manchester squadron was No. 207, formed at Waddington late in 1940. Composed mainly of experienced crews, conversion on to type proceeded, and the Manchester was released for short-range operations with a reduced bomb load.

The target was the German cruiser Admiral Hipper

The first operation was flown by six aircraft on the night of 24/25 February 1941 with six aircraft. The target was the German cruiser *Admiral Hipper*, which was in the French port of Brest. None of these early aircraft were fitted with the mid-upper gun turret, and the ventral dustbin remained unmanned for the raid. The bomb load consisted of twelve 500lb (225kg) semi-armour piercing bombs. Only moderate flak was encountered, and all aircraft returned safely. *Admiral Hipper* was not hit, which was only to be expected in those early days of the night-bombing war.

The first Manchester lost to enemy action came over England on 13 March, when a No. 207 Squadron aircraft was caught shortly after take-off.

The Vultures claimed their first victim exactly a week later, when a Manchester crashed shortly after take-off following an engine fire. On 13 April, all Manchesters were grounded for engine changes. Several aircraft were now entering service with the mid-upper turret, while the grounding period allowed others to have this fitted.

The Manchester still continued to be plagued by engine problems. The summer of 1941 saw the introduction of the Manchester 1A, which had a tailplane of increased span, taller twin fins and rudders, and no central fin.

■ LANCASTERS ■

The Manchester was being overtaken by events. The first Lancasters reached the squadrons late in 1941, and the fate of the twin-engined aircraft was sealed. It was finally withdrawn from Bomber Command operations after a raid on Bremen on 25/26 June 1942.

MANCHESTER SQUADRONS

Sqn No.	Bases	1st Operation	Last Operation
207	Waddington	24 Feb 1941	
	Bottesford		11/12 March 1942
97	Waddington	8/9 April 1941	
	Coningsby		9/10 Jan 1942
61	N. Luffenham	14/15 Aug 1941	
	Syerston		1/2 June 1942
83	Scampton	28 Jan 1942	1/2 June 1942
106	Coningsby	20 March 1942	25/26 June 1942
50	Skellingthorpe		8/9 April 1942
	Swinderby		25/26 June 1942
49	Scampton	2/3 May 1942	25/26 June 1942

The operational careers of the last four squadrons listed were very short, partly due to the fact that the similarities between the Lancaster and the Manchester allowed for an easy switch over.

MANCHESTER 1A

Dimensions
Wingspan 90ft 1in (27.46m); Tailplane span 33ft 0in (10.06m);
Length 70ft 0in (21.33m); Height 19ft 6in (9.54m).

Weights
Maximum take-off 56,000lb (25,400kg);
Maximum bomb load 10,350lb (4,700kg).

Power
Two Rolls-Royce 24 cylinder Vulture II liquid-cooled engines rated at 1,845hp each.

Performance
Maximum speed 265mph (426km/hr) at 17,000ft (5,200km/hr);
Range with maximum bomb load 1,200 miles (1,930km);
Service ceiling 19,200ft (5,850m).

Armament
Two Browning .303 machine guns in nose and dorsal turrets; four .303 Browning machine guns in tail turret.

THE LANCASTER DESCRIBED

It has often been said that the Lancaster arose from the failure of the Manchester. This is not entirely true – as early as the autumn of 1938, long before the first flight of the Manchester prototype, A.V. Roe's design office considered the possibility of a four-engined variant of the Type 679. But with other priorities in the design offices, only the most basic work was done at this stage on what was to become the Avro Type 683.

Above: The first four-engined bomber to enter service with Bomber Command was the Short Stirling. It was inferior to the Lancaster in both performance and load-carrying.

Early in the following year, a new specification was issued: B.l/39. Its ultimate purpose was to produce a heavy bomber which would start to replace the four-engined Stirlings and Halifaxes (neither of which had yet flown), and the Manchester itself in four to five years' time.

The requirements were stringent: a cruising speed of 280mph (450km/hr) at 15,000ft (4,570m) while carrying a bomb load of 9,000lb (4.08 tonnes), only slightly less than the maximum of 10,000lb (4.54 tonnes) specified. Range under these conditions was to be a

Left: As a safeguard against a shortage of Merlins, the Mk II Lancaster was powered by Bristol Hercules radial engines. Only 300 were built.

minimum of 2,500 miles (4,000km). This was pushing the state of the art very hard, and was not helped by the requirement for defensive armament, which was to consist of tail and ventral turrets each carrying four 20mm cannon. These turrets did not even exist at that time, and the complexity, weight and drag of such monsters eventually ensured that they never would. Prototype aircraft were ordered from both Handley Page and Bristol, but neither got past the mockup stage. The Air Ministry was however interested in A.V. Roe's proposal for a four-engined bomber developed from the Manchester, even though it would retain the same defensive armament as the latter. But with war looming, the twin-engined aircraft naturally had first priority, and initial

progress with the four-engined machine was slow. Not until the production Manchester was finalized could serious work start on its derivative.

With hindsight, the advantages of four-engined bombers seem glaringly obvious. Because they were bigger than their twin-engined counterparts, they could carry heavier loads of fuel and weaponry, which translated into larger bomb loads carried further. In 1939 this was less obvious, and in fact the twin-engined Manchester could carry a 40 per cent greater bomb load than the

BRITISH BOMBER COMPARISONS 1941

Aircraft type	Cruise speed at altitude	Bomb load for maximum radius	Radius with maximum bomb load
Wellington	170mph (273km/hr) at 11,300ft (3,450m)	2,500lb (1,130kg) for 1,100 miles (1,770km)	560 miles (900km) with 4,500lb (2,040kg)
Stirling	208mph (335km/hr) at 13,800ft (4,200m)	3,500lb (1,590kg) for 855 miles (1,375km)	285 miles (460km) with 14,000lb (6,350kg)
Halifax	203mph (327km/hr) at 15,100ft (4,600m)	5,800lb (2,630kg) for 910 miles (1,465km)	580 miles (930km) with 8,000lb (3,630kg)
Manchester	205mph (330km/hr) at 13,650ft (4,160m)	8,100lb (3,675kg) for 885 miles (1,425km)	500 miles (805km) with 10,350lb (4,700kg)

From this table it can be seen that the payload/range of the twin-engined Manchester was significantly better than either of its four-engined contemporaries, whether judged by maximum radius or maximum bomb load. It totally outclassed the earlier twin-engined Wellington in both departments.

Above: **The Rolls-Royce Merlin XX engine installation package for the Beaufighter IIF was adapted for the Lancaster.**

four-engined Halifax over a comparable distance, although, it must of course be said, this was provided that its Vultures kept running. There were other factors, although these were often rather problematical. Two engines required fewer systems, less installation weight, less maintenance, and lower costs for spares and replacements than four engines. Aerodynamically, with only two engines instead of four, there was the further advantage of having less drag to overcome in flight. The difficult bit was producing an engine that gave sufficient power to do the job, without it becoming too complex to be reliable. Rolls-Royce

was far from the only company to have problems with over-complex engines at this time. The Napier Sabre was scheduled to power the Manchester II, but delays in development ensured this aircraft variant was never built.

The overall wingspan was increased to accommodate engines

The Merlin was the obvious choice for the Type 683, but demand for this engine for Spitfires and Hurricanes, to say nothing of the Whitley and Halifax bombers, was high. As a backup, the

more powerful but heavier and draggier Bristol Hercules radial was selected. Ironically, increased demand for the Hercules caused by Stirling production eventually led to the Beaufighter, originally powered by the Bristol engine, being fitted with Merlin XXs, in its Mk IIF variant. For this, Rolls-Royce had developed an engine installation package, or power egg, which, with minor changes, proved eminently suitable for the new bomber.

Type 683, known in the design office as the Lancaster from a very early stage, was developed around the Manchester fuselage and wing centre section. The crew cabin had been highly praised, while the cavernous bomb bay met all current and not a few future requirements. The overall wingspan was substantially increased to accommodate the outboard engines, which also had the effect of improving take-off performance, while various other detail modifications were made.

■ FOUR ENGINES ■

A turning point came at the end of August 1940, when the decision was taken that Bomber Command's strategic force would be entirely equipped as soon

Left: **The Avro Type 683 prototype was initially known as the Manchester III, and only later renamed the Lancaster I.**

Above: The second Lancaster prototype introduced a ventral turret that was fitted to early production aircraft.

as possible with four-engined bombers. In retrospect this decision seems extraordinary, if only because the Stirling had barely started reaching its first squadron, while the service entry of the Halifax was still three months in the future, as was that of the Manchester. The four-engined heavy bomber had yet to prove itself, but there remained one sound operational reason for the decision. Even reliable engines failed occasionally, and all were vulnerable to flak and fighters. The failure of one engine in a four-engined type was much less serious than the same case in a twin, in which a full 50 per cent of the available power was lost, and asymmetric handling problems, with all the remaining power on one side, were far more extreme.

> ## Trials at Boscombe Down showed good handling qualities but directional stability was lacking

The decision to proceed with the four-engined Avro bomber was taken, although as a security measure the name Lancaster was dropped and the Type 683 became known as the Manchester Mark III, the Mark II designation having been reserved for the Napier Sabre-powered aircraft, which in fact was never built. The prototype used a Manchester I air-frame powered by Merlin Xs, and retained the short-span tailplane and triple fin layout of that aircraft. The first flight took place on 9 January 1941.

Trials at Boscombe Down showed good handling qualities although, as was only to be expected, directional stability was lacking. This was cured by a new tailplane of almost double the span of the original, and very much larger twin fins and rudders, with the central fin removed. With the new Merlin XXs fitted, the prototype reached a maximum speed of 310mph (500km/hr) at 21,000ft (6,400m) – an outstanding performance for a heavy bomber of that era. A new production contract was issued, limiting the output of Manchesters to 200 before switching to the Lancaster, as it had inevitably become known. The use of Manchester sub-assemblies speeded up this process.

■ SECOND PROTOTYPE ■

The second Lancaster prototype, which made its maiden flight on 13 May 1941, was rather nearer to the production machine standard, stressed for an all-up weight of 60,000lb (27.22 tonnes), and

---

LANCASTER

Dimensions
Wingspan 102ft (31.09m); Length (tail up) 69ft 6in (21.18m); Height (tail up) 20ft 6in (6.25m); Wing area 1,297sq ft (120.45m²).

Weights
Empty 36,900lb (16,740kg); Normal loaded 53,000lb (24,040kg); Maximum overload 65,000lb (29,480kg) (B.I Special with 22,000lb (9,980kg) Grand Slam 70,000lb (31,750kg); Maximum internal bomb load 14,000lb (6,350kg).

Power
Four Rolls-Royce Merlin 12-cylinder liquid-cooled engines each rated at 1,460hp (variable depending on type) driving a three-bladed variable-pitch, constant-speed propeller. Lancaster B.III powered by four Bristol Hercules 14-cylinder air-cooled radial engines each rated at 1,650hp.

Fuel and oil
Total fuel 2,154 gal (9,790 litres) in six wing tanks. 580 gal (2,637 litres) in each inboard wing tank; 383 gal (740 litres) in each intermediate wing tank, and 114 gal (518 litres) in each outboard wing tank. One or two overload 400 gal (1,818 litre) tanks could be mounted in the bomb bay. Oil tank capacity 150 gal (682 litres) carried in four wing tanks.

Performance
Maximum speed 270mph (434km/hr) at 19,000ft (5,800m); Cruise speed 210mph (338km/hr); 19.3 min to 11,000ft (3,350m); 43.5 min to 20,000ft (6,100m); Service ceiling 21,500ft (6,550m); Range with 14,000lb (6,350kg) bomb load 1,160 miles (1,870km); with 7,000lb (1,795kg) bomb load and one overload fuel tank 2,230 miles (3,590km).

Armament
Two .303 Browning machine-guns with 1,000rpg in a Frazer-Nash power-operated turret in the nose; ditto in the mid-upper position, and four Browning machine-guns with 2,500rpg in a Frazer-Nash power-operated turret in the tail. A few aircraft retained the ventral gun position, while many others had the mid-upper turret removed. Others were fitted with a Rose Rice tail turret with two .50 Browning heavy machine-guns.

with a dorsal gun turret fitted. It retained the ventral turret for the time being. This was followed into the air by the third prototype on 26 November of that year, which was powered by Hercules VI radials, and as such became the prototype Lancaster Mark II. But long before the radial-engined machine took to the air, production Mark Is were rolling off the lines.

The production aircraft still showed their Manchester origins, but had been refined in many ways. All-up weight had been increased to 65,000lb (29.48 tonnes) maximum, although this could be exceeded in an emergency; maximum bomb load had been increased to 14,000lb (6.35 tonnes); two extra fuel tanks had been fitted in the wings, and the ventral turret had been deleted as being of no earthly use at night. A collar fairing had been added around the mid-upper turret to prevent the guns being depressed enough to damage the aircraft, and a four-gun turret was standard in the tail position. The crew consisted of seven men: the pilot, who was also the aircraft captain, regardless of rank; a second pilot, who was quickly replaced by the new category of flight engineer; a bomb-aimer, who also manned the front turret; a navigator; a wireless operator; and mid-upper and tail gunners.

■ THE LANCASTER ■
CLOSE UP

The Lancaster is a lady, and for that reason is never described as 'it', but always as 'she'. No empty-headed glamour queen this, frivolous and shallow, but very much the

Above: The standard camouflage scheme was dark green and dark earth disruptive pattern above, and matt black below.

grand dame, the indomitable dowager, yet with a twinkle in her eye to hint at a racy past in her younger days. Her attire is sombre, a staid dull black on undersides of wings and tail and fuselage sides complemented by a tasteful camouflage scheme on top. Guns protrude from turrets in her nose and tail and mid-way down her upper fuselage, saying, as they said to many a German night fighter during the war 'Do not trifle with me, young man!' There she sits on the ground, nose high, seemingly sniffing at the sky, eager to take once more to the element for which she was designed.

As we walk towards her, the first imp ression is that she is big. Her huge main wheels, suspended on sturdy legs beneath the inboard engine nacelles, are almost shoulder-height, while the front fuselage towers high above us. Her mid-mounted wings spread 50ft (15m) to either side, carrying the four sleek cowlings which house the Rolls-Royce Merlin engines with their shrouded exhausts, fronted by large three-bladed propellers.

We draw nearer. Right in the front of her nose is a hemispherical transparent dome, with a round optically flat panel looking downwards. This is where the real business is done; through this the bombs are aimed. Above is a turret from which project the muzzles of two .303

Below: Figures on the ground give scale to the first production Lancaster, seen prior to delivery to Boscombe Down for type testing.

LANCASTER GUN TURRET

Type	FN 5	FN 50	FN 20	FN 64
Position	Nose	Mid-upper	Tail	Ventral*
Guns	2 x .303 Browning Mk II	2 x .303 Browning Mk II	4 x .303 Browning Mk II	2 x .303 Browning Mk II
Rounds per gun	1,000	1,000	2,500	500
Gunsight	Mk III Reflector	Mk IIIA Reflector	Mk III Reflector or Gyro Mk IIe	Periscopic
Traverse	+/-95°	360°	+/-94°	+/-90°
Elevation	60°	20°	60°	0°
Depression	45°	2°	45°	60°

Rarely used, mainly on early aircraft.

Browning machine-guns. Immediately behind the turret is a glazed cabin for the pilot and his flight engineer, but we see little of this as we walk beneath the giant bird.

What we do see is the huge bomb bay, which starts almost immediately beneath the front of the cabin and reaches back beyond the wing trailing edge to a point almost level with the dorsal turret. As is usual before engine start-up, the bomb bay doors are open, revealing the sinister outlines of the contents. In the centre is a large, dark green cylinder, a 4,000lb (1,800kg) high explosive 'cookie'. It is surrounded by twelve SBCs (Small Bomb Containers) filled with incendiaries. This is the most usual Lancaster bomb load.

We climb up and in, then it's down on to the central catwalk

Astern of the bomb bay is a teardrop-shaped fairing. This houses the scanner for H_2S, the latest radar bombing and navigational aid. We enter the Lancaster through a small hatch in the starboard side, just ahead of the leading edge of the tailplane. A short metal ladder hooks on to the sill, and we climb up and in, on to an inner step, then it's down on to the central catwalk.

■ REAR GUNNER ■

Once inside, it is difficult to see much until our eyes accustom themselves to the gloom. Not that there is a lot to see; to one accustomed to travel in modern airliners, the interior of a Lancaster is bleak indeed. The structure, fuselage formers and longerons are bare, showing the metal skin. Running the length of the fuselage walls are pipes, rods, all manner of plumbing and wiring. These are for carrying hydraulic fluid and power to where it is needed.

At this point, the first member of the crew leaves us. He turns left and vanishes.

He passes the primitive Elsan toilet to his right, scrambles over the tailplane spar structure, pauses for a moment to stow his parachute, then squeezes into his cold and cramped position, shutting the armoured doors behind him. He is the rear gunner, and his job is arguably the most dangerous, and certainly the coldest, the most lonely and isolated of any Lancaster crewman.

From now until the end of the mission, his only human contact will be the disembodied voices of other crew members over the intercom. His brief is unceasing vigilance for however many hours the mission takes. The German night fighters almost always attack from astern. Yet his task is thankless; if he is lucky enough to survive a complete tour of operations, he may well do so without once so much as seeing a night fighter, but knowing that the one he doesn't see may well kill him and his crew. He is proud of his skills; his party piece is probably putting a pencil in the barrel of one of his guns, then using his power controls to sign his name on a piece of card held up by an obliging ground crewman. But the chances are that he will never get the opportunity to use these skills. Even if he does, his four rifle-calibre machine-guns are far outranged by the cannon of the German night fighters which, if visibility is good enough,

Below: The open doors give some idea of the vast size of the bomb bay. The bombs were released in a preset sequence.

Above: **Up the ladder and in. A crew from No. 9 Squadron board their Lancaster ready for a mission.**

about in flight. Next to reach his station is the mid-upper gunner. After stowing his parachute in its place high on the right, he climbs into his turret via a step on the left of the fuselage. Access is not easy, however, due to the seat design which forces him to squeeze past it before he can enter.

The mid-upper gunner has only two machine-guns, although his turret can be traversed through 360 degrees, giving him a grandstand view all round. His field of fire is obstructed, however, to the rear by the tailplane and fins, on each side by the wings, engines and propellers, and straight ahead by the navigator's astrodome. The turret is surrounded by a fairing which contains a cam track. By restricting the movement of the guns, this ensures that he cannot damage his own aircraft when firing. When the guns are elevated at 20 degrees or more, turret traverse is fast and smooth, but below this it is much slower. This is to avoid damage to the turret fairing at full

can stand off and shoot at him. Otherwise they can slip in below where, against the dark backdrop of the ground, they are difficult to see, and pull underneath the bomber where his guns cannot reach and pick it off with their upward-firing guns.

Even in defeat, with his aircraft going down in flames or out of control, the rear gunner's fate is a lonely one. The call to bale out is 'Abracadabra Jump, Jump! Abracadabra Jump, Jump!'. It sounds silly, but it has one advantage. It cannot possibly be misunderstood. Nevertheless, it was often not used, and the order given in plain language. On hearing the command to bale out, the rear gunner opens his armoured doors at the rear of his turret, reaches back for his parachute and clips it on to his chest harness. He swivels his turret right round until the open doors are facing outwards, then does a backward roll out into the night sky above a hostile country. This is of course presupposing that his parachute has not been burnt or shot to pieces, that he is still able to turn his turret to the escape position, and that the centrifugal forces exerted by his out-of-control bomber will allow him to make these necessary moves.

The rest of the crew turn to the right along the catwalk. On the far wall is a handrail, very necessary for moving

LANCASTER BOMB LOADS

Bombing, and especially night bombing, was a very imprecise art in the Second World War. Even finding the target was difficult enough; hitting it often seemed next to impossible. The solution adopted was to saturate the target area with bombs – high explosive to demolish buildings, and incendiaries to set the ruins on fire. It was crude, but it was the only practicable means available to Bomber Command. There were, of course, specialized weapons which called for greater accuracy, but these were less common.

AREA BOMBING LOADS

Blast and demolition
1) 1 x 8,000lb (3,630kg) HE plus 6 (max) 500lb (225kg) HE.
2) 14 x 1,000lb (450kg) HE.

Blast, demolition and fire
3) 1 x 4,000lb (1,800kg) HE plus 3 x 1,000lb (450kg) HE plus up to 6 SBCs (Small Bomb Containers) each holding either 236 4lb (2kg) or 24 x 30lb (14kg) incendiaries.
4) 1 x 4,000lb (1,800kg) HE plus up to 12 SBCs. The most common Lancaster load.

Maximum incendiary
5) 14 SBCs.

Deployed tactical targets
6) 1 x 4,000lb (1,800kg) HE plus up to 18,500lb (225kg) HE, some with delayed action fuses.

Low-level attacks
7) 6 x 1,000lb (450kg) HE with delayed action fuses.

Hardened targets, naval installations, ships etc
8) 6 x 2,000lb (900kg) armour piercing with very short delay fuses.

Minelaying
9) Up to six 1,500lb (680kg) or 1,850lb (840kg) mines.

Above: Emergency escape from the rear turret was made by turning it sideways, as seen here, then rolling out backwards. *Left:* The mid-upper turret, showing the fairing which prevented the gunner from damaging his own aircraft. *Below:* H2S position in the Lancaster. Top left is the curtain which shuts out light; to the right is the flight engineer's position, with his seat folded. (Alfred Price)

depression, but in action it is a serious disadvantage as it makes tracking a fast-moving enemy fighter very difficult.

In an emergency, the mid-upper gunner must squirm out of the turret, retrieve his parachute from stowage, and depart through the door by which he entered. Just ahead of the mid-upper turret is an escape hatch in the fuselage roof, which is used in the event of a crash landing or a ditching at sea. In the latter event, a dinghy is housed in the upper surface of the starboard wingroot, which hopefully can be released manually from inside the aircraft, and which should then inflate automatically if the Lancaster comes down in the 'drink', as it is generally known. The walls in this area of the fuselage are cluttered with fire extinguishers and flame float and sea marker canisters.

Further up the fuselage is an obstacle, the rear wing spar carry-through, with a step on the far side which contains more parachute stowage. To the left of this is the rest bunk, which is normally used only for casualties.

A few feet along is yet another obstacle, the main wing spar carry-through. Larger than the rear spar, it has probably been the cause of more bad language by Lancaster crewmen than any other feature of this remarkable aircraft, being of a height to make their eyes sparkle. But once this has been negotiated, we arrive at the main crew positions via a 7mm-thick armoured door. Situated on the left is the wireless operator's post. He sits at a small table with his radio and his pencils and pads. He has a small window which is level with the leading edge of the wing, but at night keeps a curtain drawn across it. This is mainly because he needs artificial light by which to work, and this must not be allowed to betray the presence of the bomber to any roving fighters which might be in the area. In any case, over blacked-out enemy territory there is little to see, while above a heavily defended area the view can sometimes be a little too exciting for someone who has no immediate task to occupy him. The wireless operator has the warmest place in the aircraft; often he is overheated while other crew members are freezing.

H2S, a blind bombing aid which shows a radar picture of the ground

In front of the wireless operator sits the navigator, sideways on. He also has a table, but larger than that of the wireless operator, on which he spreads out charts, pencils, protractors, computer (not quite like our modern variety), and all the other paraphernalia needed to find a specific location in a blacked-out and hostile Europe. Almost overhead is an astrodome, through which the navigator can 'shoot' the stars to arrive at a very approximate position, but in this machine he has something better and very different.

This is H2S, a blind bombing aid which shows a radar picture of the ground below on a television-type screen. It needs a fait bit of interpretation to get good results, and like all electronic aids of this era, it can be temperamental. But it helps. Like the wireless operator, the navigator has a window, out of which he rarely looks, and he is partitioned off from the pilot by another curtain which keeps light out of the main cabin.

■ THE PILOT ■

Up front, his seat on a raised floor section to the left of the main cabin, is the pilot, who is also the aircraft captain.

Above: The H2S scanner housing supplanted the ventral turret position on many aircraft. This is a late-war model.
Above right: Lancaster pilot's position, showing the sliding hatch through which escape was barely possible. However, the extensively glazed cabin gave a good all-round view.

He has a good all-round view through the framed canopy, albeit slightly restricted to the rear and to starboard. There is a direct-vision panel on either side of the windshield, and in the canopy roof is an escape hatch, for use in a crash-landing or ditching. Behind him is a 4mm-thick sheet of armour, the top part of which can be folded down.

Straight in front of the pilot is the control column, topped with a wheel-type yoke. The column moves backwards and forwards to control the elevators in the tail, causing the aircraft to climb or dive, while the yoke moves like a car steering wheel, controlling the ailerons in the wings to make the aircraft bank to left or right. At his feet are the rudder pedals, which are used for flat turns to either side.

Low to the pilot's left is the compass, but to allow him to steer without constantly having to glance inside the cockpit a compass repeater is mounted on the centre strut of the divided windshield. On the dash in front of him are many dials and switches, which include the essential flying instruments – air speed indicator, artificial horizon, turn and bank indicator and rate of climb/descent indicator among them – while the throttle levers and propeller speed controls are mounted on a central console where they can be reached by both the pilot and the flight engineer.

The flight engineer sits to the right of the pilot. He has a folding seat, which is necessary to allow access to the bomb aimer's and front gunner's positions, and a tubular footrest which pulls out from under the raised floor section beneath the pilot's position. His task is to look after the engines, throttle settings and propeller pitch settings, fuel flow, and generally act as the pilot's assistant.

He has two panels to monitor. The first is on the starboard side, and this contains oil and fuel gauges, booster pump switches, fuel pressure warning lights, fuel tank selector cocks, and many other things. The second is part of the main dash, which can also be seen by the pilot. This contains revolution counters, boost gauges, ignition switches, engine fire extinguisher buttons and propeller feathering buttons, plus much else. All in all, the flight engineer is a pretty busy man.

■ BOMB AIMER ■

Squeezing past the flight engineer's station, we clamber down into the nose. Down, because this is the first time that we have been ahead of the bomb bay, and the amount we clamber down gives us some idea of its depth. This is the territory of the bomb aimer, who usually mans the nose turret when not actually on the bombing run, although he can also be called upon to assist the navigator by map-reading, always assuming that the ground is in sight.

The bomb aimer lies prone, his chest propped on an adjustable support. Beneath him is the forward escape hatch, which may also be used by the flight engineer and the pilot, in the latter case if he can reach it in time before the aircraft goes completely out of control.

To the right of the bomb aimer is the bomb fusing and selection panel. It is essential that the bombs are released in a predetermined order from the long bay if unwanted changes of trim are to be avoided. For this, a selector box is used. The bombs themselves are released by a hand-held 'tit', which has a small guard above the button to prevent accidents. Also featured are camera controls and photo-flares, which enable a picture to be taken of the aim point.

■ BOMBS GONE ■

The bomb sight itself is of the vector type, into which the aircraft speed and altitude are set, together with the ballistic data for the type of bombs carried, and the estimated wind speed and direction. The sight is gyro-stabilized, which allows banked turns to be made during the run-up to the target. Two lines of light on a reflecting screen form a cross which indicates where the bomb will drop at any given moment. Over the intercom, the bomb aimer guides the pilot to a

Left: Bomb release switch in hand, the bomb aimer lies prone facing his Mk XIV vector sight.
Below left: All late-production Lancasters, regardless of mark, were fitted with an enlarged nose transparency.

position where the extension of the vertical line passes through the aim point. When the bomber is lined up correctly, the aim point appears to slide gradually down the vertical line. Then when the cross touches the target, the bomb aimer presses the button and down go the bombs, bringing destruction to the target below. When not engaged in dropping the bombs, the bomb aimer occupies the nose turret, with its two machine-guns. At night he will probably have little to do; rarely is visibility clear enough to allow the night fighters to attack from head-on. In daylight or at low level, the situation may well be different, and it may even be that the turret must be occupied even on the bombing run. This gives rise to a problem: the gunner has no footrest, and in moments of excitement may well tread on the bomb aimer's head, to say nothing of showering him with hot 'empties' when he fires.

This, then, is the Lancaster, a bomber in which many thousands of men went to war, and for which many thousands of crewmen had affection, and faith that she was the best.

Below: When not actually on the bombing run, the bomb aimer normally manned the front gun turret. This Lancaster was visiting the USA on a goodwill mission in 1942.

The first unit to receive the Lancaster was No. 44 (Rhodesia) Squadron at Waddington. To provide initial experience, the first Lancaster prototype arrived in mid-September 1941, while several Manchester pilots were transferred to the squadron to ease the task of conversion. Not until Christmas Eve did the first three operational aircraft arrive, followed by four more on 28 December.

Above: This former No. 44 Squadron aircraft flew the Atlantic to Canada to serve as a pattern aircraft for Lancaster production there.

Far left: Fitters swarm all over the port inner engine of this Lancaster Mk II of No. 408 'Goose' Squadron, RCAF.

No. 44 Squadron had previously flown Hampdens, but from January 1942, seven Manchester squadrons were progressively re-equipped with the Lancaster. Unusually, three of the seven had not even started to receive the Manchester at this time, but this decision was not as strange as it seems. Brand new Manchesters, with their excellent payload/range capability, were still coming off the production lines, and Lancaster production was not yet in full swing. Also, the similarities of the two aircraft made it relatively easy to convert Manchester crews to the Lancaster; the latter could therefore be introduced into service faster by bringing more Manchesters on stream. The first Lancasters reached No. 97 Squadron in January, and No. 207 Squadron in March 1942.

The first Lancaster operation took place on the night of 3/4 March 1942. Four Lancasters of No. 44 Squadron, led by Squadron Leader John Nettleton, laid mines (an operation codenamed 'Gardening') off the German coast. All returned safely. The first excursion over Germany was made a week later, two aircraft of the same squadron joining a raid on Essen, again without loss. This run of good fortune was not to last; the first Lancaster to be lost in action failed to return from another Gardening sortie on 24/25 March.

■ THE AUGSBURG RAID ■

In the Spring of 1942 U-boat production facilities became priority targets, and one of the most important was the MAN works at Augsburg, where their diesel engines were made. Augsburg was not far from Munich, a round trip of some 1,250 miles (2,000km), mostly over enemy territory. The works was little bigger than the average football pitch, which ruled out a night attack. The attack would have to be in daylight.

On the afternoon of 17 April, 12 Lancasters took off for Augsburg. The first wave of six, flying in two Vics of three, was from No. 44 Squadron, led by John Nettleton. Two miles (3km) astern and about 3 miles (5km) to starboard was the second wave, six Lancasters from No. 97 Squadron led by Squadron Leader John Sherwood. Each aircraft carried four 1,000lb (450kg) bombs with 11-second delayed action fuses.

Leaving the English coast near Selsey Bill, they flew low over the Channel to cross the French coast near Trouville, and continued hugging the ground southwards for about 100 miles (160km) before turning east.

Diversionary attacks were planned to keep German fighters occupied, but

AUGSBURG RAID REPORT, EXTRACT

Aircraft attacking	Bombs dropped	Release height	Time at target	Results observed
8	14.3 tons	50/400ft (15/122m)	1955/2015	Huge red flames seen. One aircraft claimed hits on main building; two others claim bombs in target area.

"Owing to poor light and low altitude, photographs lacked all essential detail. No bomb bursts are shown, but a large fire is seen probably in the city of Augsburg, and it is clear that at least one and probably all the aircraft passed directly over the target. A PR photograph taken on 25/4 reveals severe damage chiefly to the S end of the works. The main Diesel Assembly Shop has suffered heavy damage."

Above: **Squadron Leader John Nettleton led the daring daylight raid on the U-boat engine factory at Augsburg, for which he was awarded the Victoria Cross.**

LANCASTER SQUADRONS, OPERATION MILLENNIUM

Squadron	Base	Date of first operation
144	Waddington	3 March 1942
97	Woodhall Spa	20/21 March 1942
207	Bottesford	24/25 April 1942
83	Coningsby	29/30 April 1942
61	Syerston	5/6 May 1942
106	Coningsby	30/31 May 1942
50	Skellingthorpe	30/31 May 1942
		(one aircraft only)

these miscarried. Between 20 and 30 Messerschmitt 109s of JG.2 returning to base encountered the rear Vic of Nettleton's wave. Attacking, they quickly shot down all three before turning their attention to the leading trio. One more Lancaster went down and the others were damaged before the Germans, by now low on fuel and ammunition, broke off the running battle. The second wave, although only a few miles away, was not spotted.

At this point Garwell's aircraft was hit by flak

Nettleton and Flying Officer J. Garwell, the other survivor of the first wave, bored eastwards on track for Munich until over the Ammer lake they swung north towards Augsburg, followed at a distance of about 10 miles (16km) by the No. 97 Squadron formation.

Augsburg finally hove into sight, and the two remaining Lancasters of No. 44 Squadron detoured around some tall factory chimneys and commenced their bombing run. At this point Garwell's aircraft was hit by flak and, shortly after releasing his bombs, he had to slide the burning Lancaster on to the ground. Four of the seven crewmen aboard survived, to be taken prisoner. Nettleton's Lancaster alone escaped into the gathering gloom.

Minutes later, the first Vic of the second wave from 97 Squadron arrived to find a thoroughly alerted defence. Unlike Nettleton, Sherwood did not attempt to dodge around the factory chimneys, but climbed above them, his two wingmen pulling into line astern behind him. All three

aircraft bombed accurately, but Sherwood's Lancaster was mortally hit by ground fire, and crashed in flames shortly after. By some miracle, Sherwood himself survived with only minor injuries.

Meanwhile, the final Vic, which had dropped back still further, now came racing in from the south. They were met by a storm of anti-aircraft fire, and all three were badly damaged. One blew up just as its bombs fell clear, but the other two got through. Wearily the survivors climbed into the darkening sky, one

Below: **Wellingtons were the most numerous bombers participating in Operation Millennium. However, they were soon to be phased out in favour of the Avro Lancaster. (via Flypast)**

Above: No. 83 Squadron Lancasters took part in the 1,000 bomber raid on Cologne. This unit was also the first Lancaster Pathfinder squadron.

Right: Cologne at the end of the war, showing the devastation around the cathedral. Wrecked bridges block the Rhine.

with only three engines operative, and straggled back to base, where one of the surviving 97 Squadron aircraft was struck off charge.

Seventeen bombs hit the factory buildings, inflicting extensive damage on them. Nettleton was awarded the Victoria Cross for his exploit, and many other survivors were decorated for this, the first Lancaster raid to be made public. But with a loss rate exceeding 50 per cent it was not, by the very nature of things, repeatable, even though the interception by German fighters which had caused such havoc to the first wave had largely been a matter of ill fortune.

■ OPERATION ■ MILLENNIUM

By the end of May 1942, seven squadrons had Lancasters on strength. This was just in time for them to take part in a raid which for Bomber Command was a turning point in the night air offensive.

The strategic bombing of the Third Reich was, in its early days, an extremely haphazard affair, with individual crews plotting their own courses and timings. Navigation was inexact, and only one crew in three managed to place their bombs within 5 miles (8km) of the target. Any damage caused was a mere pinprick. To make matters worse, the German night fighter defences had taken the measure of this form of attack, and losses were steadily rising. Bomber Command's future looked increasingly uncertain. This was the situation when Air Marshal Arthur Harris assumed command in February 1942.

Harris realized that only a spectacular success could save his command from being broken up. Previous raids had neglected the cardinal principle of concentration of force. This had to be corrected. An unprecedentedly heavy raid on a single target was needed, concentrated in time and space. A raid by 1,000 bombers would be the biggest raid ever attempted; the magic number of 1,000 would attract interest and demonstrate that RAF Bomber Command was truly a force to be reckoned with.

The target chosen was Cologne. The city was within range of a new radio navigational device called Gee, and on a moonlit night the serpentine coils of the Rhine made it easily identifiable from

All aircraft would follow the same route from a merge point off the coast

the air. To achieve concentration of force, all aircraft would follow the same route from a merge point off the coast (the first use of the bomber 'stream'), and the entire attack was to last just 90 minutes, an average of more than 11 aircraft bombing every minute! The German defences would

Above: **Mk I R5609 flew with No. 97 Squadron on the Cologne and Essen thousand-bomber raids. Later it took part in the Battles of the Ruhr, Berlin, Hamburg and Peenemunde. It survived the war. (Alfred Price)**

be saturated by weight of numbers, minimizing losses.

The Cologne raid took place on the night of 30/31 May 1942. The attack was in three waves, the first consisting of Gee-equipped Wellingtons and Stirlings with selected crews; their task was to locate the target and start fires to guide the main force in. The second wave consisted of the remaining Stirlings and Wellingtons, and the other twin-engined types – Hampdens, Whitleys and Manchesters. The third and most concentrated wave consisted of the new heavy bombers; more than 125 Halifaxes and about 75 Lancasters were scheduled to be over the target during the final 15 minutes of the attack. It has been suggested that this was to maximize the devastation in an already hard-hit city, but the fact is that operationally it was the best place for them. As the fastest and most heavily armed aircraft in the force, they were the least vulnerable to German night fighters, and equally were least likely to straggle on the homeward leg. This was borne out by events; losses to the third wave amounted to a mere 1.9 per cent, compared with 4.8 per cent to the first wave and 4.1 per cent to the second.

Post-war analysis by German generals described the Cologne raid as 'alarmingly effective'. For Bomber Command, it opened a new era in strategic bombing, with marked targets and highly concentrated attacks. Within three years, Lancasters would make up virtually the whole of the raiding force, and the damage they wrought upon German industry and communications was incalculable. From the Cologne raid onward, the history of the Lancaster was inextricably bound up with the development of Bomber Command's strategy and tactics.

The secret of success for Operation Millennium had been the ability to find the target and mark it for the following crews. While Gee was a useful navigation aid, it not only lacked the accuracy needed for blind bombing, but was too short-ranged to cover many important targets. The idea was mooted of a special target-finding force, and this was eventually formed in July 1942.

■ **THE PATHFINDERS** ■

Competition promotes increased efficiency, and Bomber Command introduced this in the form of a photographic ladder. It became standard procedure for each bomber to photograph its aim point, and each squadron's position on the ladder was determined by the accuracy of these. The ladder indicated which squadrons (and also which crews) were consistently finding their targets.

The first proposal was to form one or more elite units with selected crews.

For various reasons this was abandoned, and Path Finder Force (PFF) was formed, commanded by Group Captain Don Bennett, an Australian navigation expert and pre-war trailblazer.

Bomber Command was divided into operational areas called Groups. The squadron heading the photographic ladder in each of the four Bomber Groups was transferred to the newly formed No. 8 Pathfinder Group, based on Huntingdon. Inevitably, one Lancaster squadron was among them, No. 83. The others flew aircraft representative of the Groups in which they normally operated, but this was not to last. No. 156 Squadron traded its Wellingtons for Lancasters in January 1943; No. 7 Squadron its Stirlings in July of the same year; and finally No. 35 Squadron its Halifaxes in April 1944. By the end of the war, there were 14 Lancaster-equipped PFF Squadrons. But this was still three years in the future.

The first loads to go down contained a high proportion of incendiaries

Regrettably, PFF did not manage to bring about an instant improvement in bombing effectiveness. This had to wait for new navigational devices, for special pyrotechnic markers, and the development of methods which made the best use of them.

The former duly arrived in the shape of Oboe, an accurate but range-limited radio bombing device carried by Mosquitos. Dependent on signals from ground transmitters in England, it took in the highly industrialized Ruhr area, but not much else.

The heavy bombers were fitted with H2S, a radar navigation and blind bombing aid, although initially only a few aircraft carried it. It was much less accurate than Oboe, but as it was not dependent on external aids, it was not range-restricted.

Parachute flares had long been used as an aid to target finding. They had,

Above: **Flak bursts punctuate the night sky over Germany as Pathfinder markers go down on a target. Two other bombers are just visible.**

however, two drawbacks. Unless visibility was good, they would not light up the ground sufficiently well for crews to visually identify a target, or even pinpoint their own location. Then, of course, unless the flares were released in the right area, they simply illuminated a strange and often unrecognizable area of Germany, which was not a lot of help. Used in conjunction with Oboe or H2S, flares became far more effective.

In Operation Millennium, the first loads to go down contained a high proportion of incendiaries to start fires that would lead the following bombers to the target area. Something more accurate was needed, and this duly arrived in the form of markers, known as Target Indicators, or TIs.

Each TI contained 60 pyrotechnic candles. A barometric fuse preset to operate at low altitude blew the TI open, cascading the candles on to the ground, igniting as they went. Seen from above, the contents of each TI would appear as an intense pool of light, about 900ft (275m) in diameter. Burning time was about three minutes, so they needed to be replenished at frequent intervals.

By now the Germans had started to produce dummy targets to mislead the bombers. Their obvious reaction to TIs was to copy them and, when a raid was imminent, set them off on a dummy target. To circumvent this, TIs were produced in a combination of colours; red, yellow, green etc, and used in a predetermined order which varied from raid to raid.

When cloud covered the target, sky markers were used. These were parachute flares in a variety of colours, and sometimes throwing off coloured stars. Dropped by Oboe or H2S aircraft, they demanded a rather complicated offset bombing technique. While skymarking was nowhere near as accurate as ground marking, it gave accuracy far superior to the early years of the war, when 'agricultural bombing' – the accidental bombing of fields – was a common occurrence.

With the new equipment available, all that remained was to find the best methods of employing it. Oboe Mosquitos were used for the initial marking of all targets within its range. Outside Oboe reach, H2S was used. Tactics were roughly as follows. The first aircraft to arrive, typically five minutes before the main attack was scheduled to start, were the Finders, backed by a few Supporters. The Finders dropped flares where they thought the aiming points were likely to be. Having visually identified the aim point, they would drop further flares directly above it.

The Finders would be followed by the Illuminators, who would drop sticks of flares directly across the aim point. Then would come the Primary Markers, to put TIs on the aim point itself. Backers-Up would continue to drop TIs at intervals, to give the Main Force an aiming point throughout the attack.

This form of visual marking was code-named Newhaven. When, due to poor visibility or broken cloud, the marking was carried out using H2S, it became Parramatta, while skymarking was dubbed Wanganui.

Below: **Flak damage sustained by a Lancaster of No. 50 Squadron over Leipzig. Miraculously, nothing vital was hit.**

As with all new methods, teething troubles occurred, mainly due to the precise timing required. The first real success achieved by PFF came during the Barmen-Wuppertal raid on 29/30 May 1943. The target was accurately marked, and the subsequent bombing highly concentrated. How was this done?

■ BARMEN/WUPPERTAL ■

A total of 719 aircraft were despatched. Of these, 272 were Lancasters (the force had been building up rapidly, and a further 12 squadrons now operated the type). Of these, 20 aircraft were Lancaster Is and IIIs of PFF, and the attack was spearheaded by 11 Mosquito IVs fitted with Oboe.

Main Force, following on behind, included 31 Lancaster Is and IIIs of No. 8 Pathfinder Group; 76 Lancaster Is and IIIs of No. 1 Group; 16 Hercules-engined Lancaster IIs of No. 3 Group; and 129 Lancaster Is and IIIs of No. 5 Group. Loads consisted of a mixture of high explosives – 4,000lb (1,800kg) cookies in the case of the Lancasters, and incendiaries.

The bombing was heavy and concentrated

Visibility in the target area was poor, due to industrial haze and smoke, but the first Mosquitoes marked accurately at 00.47 hours, with red target indicators. They were followed by PFF backers-up with green TIs, and PFF 'fire-raisers' with incendiaries. Four of these, equipped with H_2S, also marked with yellow TIs. Main Force aircraft were

Above: Incendiary bomb containers are loaded. Fires on the ground drew other bombers like moths to a candle.

instructed to aim at the reds if visible; otherwise at the centre of the greens.

The bombing was heavy and concentrated; 611 aircraft claimed to have bombed the primary target. A total of 33 aircraft were lost on this raid, about 4.6 per cent. Lancaster losses amounted to seven, or about 2.6 per cent of those despatched; barely half the average losses for the raid.

A factor common to all forms of warfare is confusion, and the Pathfinder-led attacks on Germany were no exception. If a Pathfinder put down his TIs in the wrong place, for whatever reason, inevitably a proportion of Main Force would use them as an aim point. In addition, the Germans, by dint of much practice, grew adept at decoys. A third factor was creep-back; the tendency of crews over a heavily defended target to release their bombs at the earliest possible moment, with the result that the Main Force bomb pattern would extend further and further back from the original aim point until in extreme cases it ended in open countryside. What was

needed was a raid controller to direct the marking, giving a continuous running commentary on which TIs were to be used for aiming and which should be ignored; which was the real target and which a decoy; and generally keeping the bombing pattern tidy.

A possible solution appeared to be that pioneered by Wing Commander Guy Gibson for Operation Chastise, the destruction of the Mohne and Eder Dams in the Ruhr. He controlled his force, albeit a small one, very effectively using VHF voice radio to communicate. Possibly a Master Bomber could control an orthodox raid in the same way. There was only one way to find out – lay on a small-scale experiment.

■ OPERATION ■ BELLICOSE

An easy target would have proved little; in the event, the one chosen called for a high degree of precision. Friedrichshafen lies on the north shore of the Bodensee (Lake Constance), the south shore of which is in Switzerland. In the 1914–18 war it had been notorious as the home of the Zeppelin factory, a building complex about 1,500ft (460m) long by 1,050ft (320m) wide. In 1943, it was the largest production centre for radar parts in the whole of the Third Reich, and its destruction would be a severe blow to the German air defences, and much else.

> ## EXTRACT FROM BOMBER COMMAND NIGHT RAID REPORT NO. 340
>
> "611 aircraft, out of a force of 719, attacked the Barmen district of Wuppertal with very great success. The fire-raising technique was effectively employed, as a complement to ground marking, resulting in the best concentration yet achieved by the Pathfinder Force. Immense damage was caused in the town, covering over 1,000 acres and affecting 113 industrial concerns, as well as totally disrupting the transport system and public utilities."

Left: Laden with equipment, a crew strolls out to its No. 61 Squadron Lancaster. Normally transport would be laid on.

Continuous marking of such a small target was next to impossible. Special tactics were needed. Main Force crews were to orbit the target at between 4 and 6 miles (6–10km), with no more than two aircraft at the same altitude. The instant a TI landed on the target, the Master Bomber would issue a special signal, and as many aircraft as possible would attack immediately. It was of course possible that the target could quickly become obscured by smoke; in this case, the crews were to make their attack run from a certain point, sighting on a second point, but delaying bomb release long enough for the aircraft to cover 6,000ft (1,800m) to the actual target.

This raid was sufficiently different for special training and picked crews to be needed. No. 5 Group supplied 56 Lancaster IIIs with experienced crews drawn from 12 squadrons. No. 8 Group provided four hand-picked Pathfinder crews from 97 Squadron, based at Bourn, also with Lancaster IIIs. Piloted by Flight Lieutenants

Rodley, a survivor of the Augsburg raid, and John Sauvage, and Pilot Officers D.I. Jones and Jimmy Munro, the latter a Canadian, they were flown north to Scampton for two days' intensive training.

It was perhaps significant that for this trial mission the Master Bomber was not a Pathfinder, but the very experienced Group Captain Leonard Slee. His deputy was the Australian squadron commander, Wing Commander G.L. Gomm. In addition, there were two controllers, either of whom could take charge in the event of an emergency. The force took off late in the evening of 20 June 1943 and headed south, crossing the Channel at maximum altitude. Once over France, they progressively lost height down to 10,000ft (3,050m) as they passed Orleans, then lower still to between 2,500 and 3,000ft (750–900m). After crossing the Rhine they began to climb to attack altitude, which was 5,000ft (1,500m) for the Pathfinders and 10,000ft (3,050m) for the Main Force. At about this time, Group Captain Slee's

Lancaster lost an engine and was unable to keep its place at the head of the stream. Wing Commander Gomm, of No. 467 (Australian) Squadron, took over as Master Bomber.

Exactly on time, Munro and Jones released a string of flares parallel to and on either side of the target. The gun defences opened up at once, more strongly than expected, and Gomm ordered all aircraft to gain another 5,000ft (1,500m). Realizing that this would make visual identification very difficult, the four Pathfinders stayed at their original altitude.

The Master Bomber ordered all aircraft to attack at once

Sauvage put down a green TI just north of thee Zeppelin sheds. He was followed by Rodley, who dropped a green TI accurately. On seeing this, the Master Bomber ordered all aircraft fitted with the Mk XIV bombsight to attack at once. An attempt to renew this marker failed. Jones later commented that he had to abandon one run because it was impossible to hold his aircraft steady in the concussions from the bombs. More flares were dropped along the shoreline

Below: Prototype Lancaster Mk III. Externally indistinguishable from the Mk I, the main difference was American-built Packard Merlins with Hamilton propellers.

Above: Aircraft of No. 50 Squadron at Swinderby. The nearest was struck off charge when it crashed at Thurlby, Lincolnshire, on 19 September 1942.

around the two predesignated points in order to enable the remainder of Main Force to bomb indirectly.

After the attack, all 59 Lancasters (one had been driven off track by thunderstorms) orbited the target to form up before heading for Maison Blanche and Blida airfields in Algeria, where they arrived safely.

For 'Rod' Rodley, however, it was an eventful trip. Unknown to him, a TI had hung up. When, far out over the Mediterranean he lost height, the barometric fuse operated and the candles ignited. The first intimation that all was not well came when an evil red glow suddenly appeared beneath his Lancaster. Thinking he was under attack from a night fighter, Rodley took evasive action, while Sergeant Duffy, his flight engineer, checked for damage. The bomb bay was a mass of flames, but the cause was obvious. A quick pull on the jettison toggle and the blazing remnants of the TI fell clear, leaving the Lancaster damaged but flyable.

Considerable destruction was caused to the target, and the Master Bomber concept was rated a success. Six of the Lancasters were damaged by anti-aircraft fire, one beyond repair. The 'shuttle'

concept of flying on to North Africa was also rated a success, and was later used by both Bomber Command and the USAAF. As a footnote, intercepts of German night fighter radio traffic revealed that patrols were flown in the Florennes/Juvincourt area, presumably waiting for the bombers to return. They did of course, several nights later, bombing La Spezia on the way for good measure.

As the strategic bombing of the Third Reich continued, PFF methods became ever more sophisticated, with contingency plans for almost every eventuality. At the same time, the proportion of Lancasters to other heavy bomber types grew ever greater. Moving forward in time to just over a year later, on 23/24 July 1944, a force of 619 heavy bombers was sent against the German naval base at Kiel. Of these, no fewer than 84 per cent were Lancasters.

■ PATHFINDER ■ PROGRESS

By this time, the concept of the Master Bomber was tried and proven. His function was to check on the accuracy of the marking, call by radio for adjustments or back-up where necessary, and, while loitering in the area until the bombing was completed, do everything possible to ensure that the munitions went down exactly where they were intended to go.

Whereas in the Friedrichshafen raid the Master Bomber had flown a Lancaster, loitering over heavily defended targets for extended periods in a four-engined bomber could not be considered a good insurance risk. It was not long before the standard aircraft for this purpose became the fast and agile twin-engined Mosquito. This was the case

BOMBER COMMAND AIRCRAFT IN RAID ON KIEL, 23/24 JULY 1944

Group	Type	No.	Missing
8	Mosquito IX	1	–
	Mosquito XVI	6	–
	Mosquito XX	3	–
	Lancaster III	89	1
1	Lancaster I	85	1
	Lancaster III	104	1
6	Lancaster II	14	–
	Lancaster X	28	–
5	Lancaster I	46	1
	Lancaster III	53	–
3	Lancaster I	59	–
	Lancaster II	14	–
	Lancaster III	27	–
4	Halifax III	100	–

TOTAL
10 Mosquitos, 519 Lancasters, 100 Halifaxes

Top: To assist target identification, detailed models were made by the Central Intelligence Unit. Seen here is Kiel harbour.

Above: Lancaster Mk I of No. 83 Squadron. After a distinguished career with PFF, this aircraft came down in Holland after raiding Essen on 3/4 April 1943.

for the Kiel raid, in which the Master Bomber and his deputy flew two of the 10 Mosquitos allocated for primary marking. Some idea of PFF progress can be given by quoting the Plan of Attack in full.

"The method employed for the raid on Kiel was controlled Newhaven marking. Blind Illuminators, 21 Lancasters, were to drop red TIs at H-6 (six minutes before zero hour), and white flares if the weather was suitable. If there was more than 6/10ths cloud, they were to retain their white flares, and drop green flares with red stars instead. If their H_2S should prove

unserviceable, they were to retain their markers and act as Main Force. These were to be followed by the Primary Visual markers, 6 Lancasters, at H-4, who were to drop red and green TIs using the red TIs dropped by the Illuminators as a guide, but only after definite visual identification. If they could not identify the target visually they were to retain their markers and act as Main Force. Visual Centerers, 16 Lancasters, distributed throughout the attack, were to aim green TIs with one second overshoot at: 1) the centre of mixed red and green TIs; 2) the centre of red TIs; 3) the centre of green TIs; in that order of priority. If no TIs were visible, they were to act as Main Force. The marking was to be kept up during the attack by the Secondary Blind Markers, 7 Lancasters at H+10 and 4 at H+II. They were to drop red TIs by H_2S. If there was more than 6/10ths cloud they were to release skymarking

flares green with red stars. If their H_2S was unserviceable they also were to act as Main Force. 28 Lancasters of 8 Group were to act as supporters, bombing at H-6 on H_2S, or if that was unserviceable, visually or on a good dead reckoning."

■ KIEL ■

The Main Force was scheduled to attack in four very concentrated waves, putting 516 heavy bombers over the target in the space of just 15 minutes. Scattered among them would be 15 ABC (Airborne Cigar) Lancasters of No. 101 Squadron, each carrying an extra crewman whose function was to jam the German night fighter radio frequencies. Bombing instructions were, in order of priority: 1) centre of mixed red and green TIs or red TIs; 2) centre of green TIs; 3) centre of skymarking flares.

Rarely does anything go precisely according to plan, and the raid on Kiel was no exception. The target was covered with 10/10ths cloud. No contact could be made with the Master Bomber, and his deputy assumed control of proceedings. Marking was checked by H_2S and considered accurate, although rather scattered in the early stages. Main Force bombed on the glow of TIs as seen through the cloud, but both marking and bombing appeared to become more concentrated towards the end of the attack, and many explosions and fires were reported.

Severe damage was caused to the north-east portion of the Deutsche Werke shipyards, and hangars at the Holtenau airfield were partially destroyed. A considerable amount of damage was done to the facilities and barrack area near the Torpedo Boat Harbour, and moderate damage to a torpedo components and electrical signalling works. Sixteen medium-sized buildings in the Marine Artillery Depot were partially destroyed. Only four Lancasters were lost on this mission; a mere 0.7 per cent of the total.

PFF led the way to the targets, but Main Force, huge and largely anonymous, was the mighty sledgehammer that came crashing down on them.

MAIN FORCE

For all practical purposes, Main Force was Bomber Command. Main Force delivered the greatest weight of bombs against the war machine that was the Third Reich, and Main Force took the greatest number of casualties. Nor should it be forgotten that Main Force was the training ground for those who became Pathfinders or who smashed the Ruhr Dams and sank the *Tirpitz*. Although it was occasionally diverted to tactical aims, by far the greatest effort was strategic.

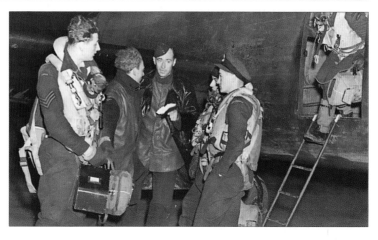

As the war continued, the Lancaster progressively became the backbone of Main Force. In numbers of sorties flown and tonnages of bombs delivered, it outstripped all other bombers in service by a considerable margin.

The strategic bombing of Germany, and to a lesser extent its Axis partner Italy, consisted of a number of what amounted to protracted set-piece battles, interspersed with many highly individual actions. The thousand-bomber raids of May and June 1942 had only been achieved by milking training units of aircraft and crews, and pressing every possible reserve machine into service. This tremendous effort could not, by the very nature of things, be sustained. During the months following June 1942, Bomber Command restricted itself to raids of up to 300 aircraft against single targets roughly twice a week, weather permitting.

The number of Lancaster squadrons steadily grew. Prior to October 1942, conversion on to the new type was carried out by a specially formed third flight within each squadron. This allowed squadrons to operate old and new types side by side until conversion was complete, with them thus remaining fully operational. After this, conversion flights were centralized and merged into Heavy Conversion Units.

Top: Squadron crew returns from a raid. Two are Canadians and one a New Zealander, reflecting an ever-increasing influx from the Dominions.
Above: Wing Commander Guy Gibson (right) led No. 106 Squadron to Gdynia, dropped the first 8,000 pounder, and took part in Operation Robinson before forming the Dam Busters.
Far left: The devastated oil refinery at Harburg, just to the south of Hamburg.

Special weapons often feature in the Lancaster story. One of these was the huge Capital Ship Bomb, which featured a shaped charge designed to cut through armour. This monstrosity was turnip-shaped, and possessed appalling ballistic qualities for a role where accuracy was essential.

FRIEDRICHSHAFEN, BOMB LOADS

Leader and Deputy Leader	2 x Lancaster III	1 x 4,000lb (1,800kg) 7 x 500lb (227kg)
97 Sqn PFF	2 x Lancaster III	3 x red TI; 3 x green TI 16 x white flares 2 x 500lb (227kg) 2 x red TI, 2 x green TI 32 x white flares 2 x 500lb (227kg)
9, 49, 50, 57, 61, 106 Sqns, No. 5 Grp	32 x Lancaster III	1 x 4,000lb (1,800kg) 7 x 500lb (227kg)
44, 207, 467, 619 Sqns, No. 5 Grp	Lancaster III fitted with Mk XIV bombsight	14 x 500lb (227kg)
44, 207 Sqns, No. 5 Grp	Lancaster III not fitted with Mk XIV bombsight	Full incendiary load

SEARCHLIGHTS

"One of my most anxious moments of the whole raid was when, during one of my five successful runs over the target, T-Tommy was caught in a cone of searchlights. I fought desperately to lose those probing beams of light which had caught my aircraft in their web. Shrapnel rattled along the fuselage like hailstones until, by diving at near maximum speed, I escaped into the friendly darkness. Poor Jack Hannah, my wireless operator, stationed at the astrodome on the lookout for enemy fighters, protested in vigorous terms as he was tossed about like a pea in a pod."

PILOT OFFICER D.I. JONES, NO. 97 SQUADRON

Targets for the Capital Ship Bomb were soon found. In August 1942, the German's only aircraft carrier *Graf Zeppelin* and the battle cruiser *Gneisenau* were reported at Gdynia in Poland. A raid was mounted on 27 August by Lancasters of No. 106 Squadron adapted to carry the special bomb. It was led by Wing Commander Guy Gibson, already possessed of a formidable reputation, with a specialist bomb aimer, Squadron Leader Arthur Richardson, for this mission only.

■ ANTICLIMAX ■

The result was, perhaps inevitably, an anticlimax. Visibility was poor, and the defences stronger than expected. Arriving over Gdynia, 106 Squadron was unable to locate *Graf Zeppelin*, but managed to find what was believed to be *Gneisenau*.

Top: To carry bombs of 8,000lb (3,600kg) or more, Lancaster bomb bay doors were bulged, as seen on this Mk II.

Above: A gaggle of Lancasters at low level. Not the Le Creusot raid, but these in Far Eastern finish show up much better.

PARTICIPANTS IN OPERATION ROBINSON

Squadron	Number of aircraft	Base
9	10*	Waddington
44	9	Waddington
49	10	Scampton
50	12	Skellingthorpe
57	10	Scampton
61	7*	Syerston
97	9	Woodhall Spa
106	12*	Syerston
207	15	Langar

* Denotes two aircraft to Montchanin.

Gibson made numerous runs over the harbour, and despite Richardson's best efforts, the bomb missed the battle cruiser by about 1,200ft (360m). The rest of the squadron fared no better. In the event, the German aircraft carrier never entered service.

Early in September, 8,000lb (3,600kg) bombs started to arrive on the squadrons. These needed bulged doors and other modifications to the bomb bay, and Gibson's squadron, its aircraft already adapted for the Capital Ship Bomb, pioneered their use. The following month saw another Bomber Command set-piece attack.

Left: Close examination reveals ice cream cornets among the bombs, denoting raids on *Dante's Daughter* of No. 103 Squadron. These symbolized Italian targets.
Below: Greetings from Canada! A tastefully decorated 8,000lb (3,600kg) bomb on its loading trolley in front of a Mk II of No. 426 Squadron RCAF.
Bottom: Lancaster Mk II of No. 426 Thunderbirds Squadron RCAF, one of the many Canadian Lancaster units. It was lost over Stuttgart on 7/8 October 1943.

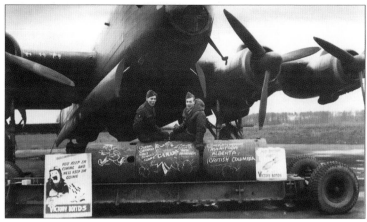

After take-off, on 17 October, some 96 Lancasters from 5 Group assembled in a loose gaggle over Upper Heyford in Oxfordshire, and from there proceeded to Land's End. Descending to 1,000ft (300m) over the sea to avoid radar detection, they gave Ushant a wide berth before turning south-easterly over the Bay of Biscay. When about 60 miles (95km) from the French coast, they dropped down to 300ft (90m) and turned almost due east.

Crossing the coast near the Isle d'Yeu, they swept over the sparsely populated Vendée, passed a few miles south of Tours, and picked up the River Cher at Montrichard. German fighters were absent, and unhindered by the defences, the low-level armada thundered on. The sole incident occurred as a Lancaster of No. 57 Squadron took a partridge through the windscreen, injuring the flight engineer.

4,000ft, the minimum release height for the 4,000lb cookies

Reaching the Loire near Nevers, the formation climbed to its briefed attack altitude of 4,000ft (1,200m), the minimum release height for the 4,000lb (1,800kg) cookies that were carried by 15 aircraft. As they climbed, they edged a few degrees southwards in the direction of Le Creusot and took up their attack formation.

Navigation and timing were spot on, and surprise

■ OPERATION ■ ROBINSON

Vital targets were not always in Germany. One such was the Schneider armaments factory at Le Creusot in south-eastern France, roughly halfway between Dijon and Lyon. Although it covered nearly 300 acres, the need to avoid civil casualties demanded a standard of accuracy that could only be attained in daylight. The nine Lancaster squadrons operational in

No. 5 Group began to practise low-level flying early in October.

The lessons of the Augsburg raid had been well learnt. As in that ill-fated attack, the bombers were scheduled to reach the target just before dusk, making their escape into the darkening sky. This time, however, the inbound route of the raiding force was carefully planned to minimize the possibility of fighter interception.

OVERSEAS LANCASTER SQUADRONS

Squadron	Nationality	First operation	Base
460	Australian	22/23 Nov 1942, Stuttgart	Breighton
467	Australian	2/3 Jan 1943, Gardening	Bottesford
426	Canadian	17/18 Aug 1943, Peenemunde	Linton-on-Ouse
405	Canadian	17/18 Aug 1943, Peenemunde	Gransden Lodge
408	Canadian	7/8 Oct 1943, Stuttgart	Linton-on-Ouse
432	Canadian	18/19 Nov 1943, Sea Search	East Moor
463	Australian	26/27 Nov 1943, Berlin	Waddington
75	New Zealand	9/10 April 1944, Villeneuve St George	Mepal
300	Polish	18/19 April 1944, Rouen	Faldingworth
419	Canadian	27/28 April 1944, Friedrichshafen	Middleton St George
428	Canadian	July 1944	Middleton St George
431	Canadian	December 1944	Croft
434	Canadian	2/3 Jan 1945, Nuremburg	Croft
424	Canadian	February 1944	Skipton-on-Swale
433	Canadian	1/2 Feb 1945, Ludwigshaven	Skipton-on-Swale
427	Canadian	11 March 1945, Essen	Leeming
429	Canadian	April 1945	Leeming

was virtually complete. The raiders arrived shortly after sunset, but the target was clearly visible despite the gathering dusk. In an attack lasting just nine minutes, over 200 tonnes of high explosive and incendiaries rained down.

At the same time, six Lancasters led by Guy Gibson broke away from the main force and attacked a transformer station at Montchanin, a few miles to the south-east. They carried ten 500lb (225kg) bombs each, and were briefed to attack from 500ft (150m). The transformer station was wrecked, but two of the pilots were over-enthusiastic and attacked from well below the minimum safe height. One aircraft was damaged and the other crashed, both victims of their own bomb explosions.

These were the only losses of the day, although one Lancaster forced to turn back with engine failure was intercepted by three Arado Ar 196 floatplanes of the Kriegsmarine. The flight engineer was killed in the attack, but the Lancaster gunners drove off the Germans, claiming two shot down.

In all, damage to the Lancasters was remarkably light, with just a few holes in some aircraft. Although limited production was resumed at Le Creusot after a period of about three weeks, major repair work was still in progress eight months later. Given the minimal casualties that were sustained, Operation Robinson must be reckoned an outstanding success.

The battle of El Alamein commenced just five days after the raid on Le Creusot, while Operation Torch, the Allied landings in north-west Africa, were scheduled for 11 November. Lancaster squadrons played an indirect part in these operations by bombarding targets in northern Italy, keeping the Italian Navy in port, and other reinforcements at home. Between 22/23 October and 11/12 December, 936 sorties were

Above left: **The projection at the bottom of the turret is the Monica aerial; the damage was caused by flak.**
Left: **Star of the Wings for Victory Week in Trafalgar Square, this No. 207 Squadron Lancaster was one of the first production aircraft. It survived the war.**

flown. Genoa was raided five times, Turin seven times, and Milan once, this last in daylight. Italian air defences were ineffective and losses were light, even though France was often crossed in daylight on the outbound leg. But the long distances involved, plus a double crossing of the Alps, all carried out in late autumn weather frequently with icing conditions, made raiding Italy a tremendous test of endurance for the Lancaster crews.

If the weather was too bad for the Alpine crossing to be attempted, German targets were substituted instead at the last moment, causing, as Guy Gibson recorded, "Last minute flaps, a new briefing, new maps, and bad tempers all round." Hamburg, Duisburg, Stuttgart and Mannheim were among the German targets attacked during this period.

Lancaster output soon reached the stage where squadrons from No. 1 Group, based in North Lincolnshire and South Yorkshire, could start equipping with the type. The first three to do so were No. 460 (Australian) Squadron at Breighton; No. 101 Squadron at Holme-on-Spalding Moor, the first operation of which was the long haul to Turin on 20/21 November; and No. 103 Squadron at Elsham Wolds.

The conversion of the Australian squadron on to the Lancaster highlighted a trend. Although No. 44 Squadron had been dubbed 'Rhodesia', there were not enough Rhodesians to man it fully. Of the 48 aircrew on the Augsburg raid, only eight were Rhodesians. Two, including Nettleton himself, were South Africans. Two Canadians, two New Zealanders and a single Australian completed the overseas contingent. The remaining 33 were British.

From the outbreak of war, volunteers from the British Empire, or Commonwealth, as it is now called, had hastened to the aid of the mother country. Their governments followed suit, and from

quite an early stage, squadrons with national affiliations were formed. It is doubtful whether the personnel of these units was ever drawn entirely from just one country, but a high proportion of Australians, Canadians or New Zealanders in one squadron gave it a uniquely national flavour. No. 460 was the first of many such Lancaster squadrons, but numerically the Canadians took pride of place; No. 6 Group was for all practical purposes an all-Canadian Bomber Group.

■ ELECTRONIC ■ WARFARE

The year of 1943 commenced with raids on Berlin, with the Pathfinders honing their marking techniques on the city. Electronic warfare took on greater significance with the introduction of new jamming and threat detection systems. Of these, Tinsel could be tuned to transmit engine noise on the German

fighter control frequencies; Monica was a tail warning radar; while Boozer could detect German radar emissions. Many other systems followed in the years to come.

Tinsel was initially successful, though the Germans gradually introduced measures to limit its effectiveness. Monica, in contrast, was a minor disaster from the outset. Quite unable to discriminate between friend and foe, it constantly gave false alarms as friendly aircraft in the bomber stream blundered into and out of its search area. Worse still, the Germans developed a detector codenamed Flensburg, which could home on Monica's emissions from very long ranges. Naxos-Z was another German detector, designed to home on H2S. The latter would have been no great problem had H2S been used intermittently for navigation, and for blind bombing in the target area, but many crews kept it switched on throughout the sortie,

Above right: Lancaster Mk 1 of No. 106 Squadron damaged by a night fighter during the Battle of the Ruhr in April 1943. *Right:* Danger came not only from the air. This Lancaster collided on the ground with an American B-17 Fortress.

Above: Hamburg, with the distinctive River Elbe running through it, showed up well on the H2S screen, as can be seen by comparing it with the map at left. (Alfred Price)

making the task of the night fighters much easier.

Boozer, however, was rather better; if the bomber was illuminated by ground radar, a red warning light came on in the cockpit. If fighter radar emissions were detected, an orange light glowed. There were two snags. Illumination by ground radar was too frequent for the warning to be of much value, while once a night fighter gained visual contact its radar was often switched to standby, upon which the warning light went out precisely at the moment of greatest danger.

WINDOW OVER HAMBURG

Many references to the difficulties caused by Window to the ground and fighter defences were overheard in intercepted wireless traffic. Some enemy aircraft reported interference. One very interesting remark was "it is impossible, too many hostiles". This indicates that the Window echoes, besides producing general interference of the (German) display tube, were also confused with true aircraft echoes.

"115 sorties by night fighters were overheard, 33 of which mentioned British aircraft. Our crews reported 49 interceptions, but only seven of these developed into attacks. Enemy aircraft frequently seemed unaware of the presence of bombers in their vicinity. Only two instances of fighter damage were reported, and all of the five bombers seen to be shot down in combat were at least 20 miles (32km) away from Hamburg."

BOMBER COMMAND NIGHT RAID REPORT NO. 383

Below: Centurion! This 550 Squadron Lancaster survived the war with a tally of over 100 sorties against targets, which included the Ruhr and Berlin.

■ THE BATTLE ■ OF THE RUHR

The Ruhr was the industrial heart of Germany, invariably heavily cloaked by industrial haze, making targets notoriously difficult to locate. However, with the introduction of Oboe it could be attacked accurately for the first time.

The Battle of the Ruhr opened on 5/6 March with a heavy raid on Essen, the home of the Krupps steelworks, one of the most important targets in Germany. It was marked by PFF, then bombed by Main Force in three waves. The final wave consisted of 145 Lancasters from 14 squadrons, about half the Main Force total. One-third of the Krupps works was heavily damaged, more than all previous raids on this target combined had achieved.

Raids on Munich, Nuremberg and Stuttgart followed, to avoid setting a pattern which would allow the defences to concentrate, then, just over a week later, Bomber Command returned to Essen. A third raid on Essen took place on 3/4 April, and a fourth on 30 April/1 May. Barmen/Wuppertal, described in the preceding chapter, also fell into this period. Another Ruhr target, Duisburg, had been raided twice. Dortmund and Dusseldorf were hit during May with over 300 Lancasters on each raid, the first time this figure had been exceeded. Raids on targets in the Ruhr continued until 14/15 June, culminating in a heavy attack on the steel and coal centre of Oberhausen.

The Battle of the Ruhr conclusively demonstrated Bomber Command's ability to hit targets in this area even in poor visibility, while taking only moderate casualties. But the Ruhr was within range of Oboe. The pressing need was to carry the battle deeper into Germany with similar results.

■ OPERATION GOMORRAH ■

Hamburg was the second largest city in Germany, and the largest port in Europe. Its strategic importance lay in its ship-building activities, most notably the manufacturing of U-boats. Situated close to the coast, and with a large and very easily recognizable river running through it, Hamburg was suitable for locating by H2S.

In addition, a new counter-measure codenamed Window was made available for the first time. It consisted of bundles of aluminium foil strips, which would each give the appearance of a heavy bomber on German radars, making tracking impossible.

On the night of 24/25 July 1943, 791 bombers set course for Hamburg. Of these, 347, or slightly less than half, were Lancasters, but they carried nearly three-quarters of the total tonnage of bombs. As they approached, they were monitored by German ground radar until the bomb aimers started to drop bundles of Window down their flare chutes at one-minute intervals.

Above: Time exposure of German flak over a defended area. This is what the Lancaster crews faced nightly.
Right: Flight Lieutenant William Reid VC of No. 61 Squadron. Twice wounded, his aircraft badly damaged and two crewmen dead, he continued the mission and bombed the target.

The result was complete chaos for the defenders. One minute they could see many contacts, indicating a heavy raid was underway. The next, the radar screens filled up, giving the appearance of a raid by 11,000 bombers! All semblance of control was lost, and fighters already airborne were ordered to the vicinity to hunt independently. They spent most of their time fruitlessly chasing clouds of Window, while the flak was reduced to firing at random, in the hope of scoring a lucky hit.

PFF marked accurately with New-haven, and Main Force, now virtually unhampered by the defences, sent their bombs whistling down. Bombing accuracy was marred only by an element of 'creepback' in the later stages, caused by over-eager crews releasing their bombs a fraction too early on the attack run. Cumulatively, this extended for 7 miles (11km).

The loss rate for Hamburg had previously been around 6 per cent, but on this night only 12 aircraft were missing, a rate of 1.5 per cent. Only four Lancasters failed to return, but three of these were

from the high-flying No. 103 Squadron, which had gained the least protection of all from Window.

■ FOLLOW-UPS ■

Hamburg's ordeal was far from over. Daylight raids by the USAAF 8th Air Force were made on 25 and 26 July, while on the night of 27/28, Bomber Command returned in force with 787 aircraft, 353 of them Lancasters. The same tactics were used, and losses were still very light at 2.2 per cent. A third raid followed on 29/30 July, and the fourth and final one on 2/3 August. The damage assessment report stated: "The city of Hamburg is now in ruins. The general destruction is on a scale never before seen in a town or city of this size."

The next event of note was a heavy raid upon the weapons research centre at Peenemunde. This was a high-risk mission; Peenemunde was a small target on the Baltic coast, and good visibility was needed for bombing accuracy, so much so that a full-moon night was chosen, 17/18 August. Deep penetrations were seldom made at this time of year, as the northern sky was never completely dark. Conditions were therefore ideal for the night fighters.

The force despatched consisted of 324 Lancasters, 219 Halifaxes and 54 Stirlings, with Group Captain John Searby of No. 83 Squadron as Master Bomber. The course to the target was planned to make it look as if the bombers were heading for Berlin. This impression was reinforced by eight PFF Mosquitos, which carried out a diversionary attack. It worked, and over 200 German fighters converged on the capital. But once bombs started going down on

Top left: Most Lancasters died in flames, as did this Heavy Conversion Unit aircraft following a training accident.
Left: Lancaster Mk I ME703 of No. 576 Squadron survived the holocaust of the Nuremburg raid in March 1944, only to receive a direct flak hit five weeks later.
Below: Chaos in the Juvissy marshalling yards after a raid by 200 Lancasters on 18/19 April 1944.

In what amounted to a short campaign, some 3,095 sorties were flown, 1,373 of them by Lancasters. In total, more than 8,600 tons of bombs fell on Hamburg, of which Lancasters alone contributed over 6,000 tons. Losses were 86 bombers, 39 of them Lancasters. Apart from the damage inflicted on the target, the German defence system, fire and rescue services had been left in complete disarray.

The defenders proved more resilient than expected. Measures taken included a looser form of fighter control, new airborne radar of a different wavelength, emission detectors as described earlier, and saturating the target area with 'cat's-eye' single seaters. Before long, bomber losses started to rise again.

Top: This Canadian Lancaster visited Berlin on at least seven occasions, flying with three different squadrons: Nos. 432, 426 and 408.
Above: Casualty! Shot down over Berlin, this Lancaster broke up in mid-air and its tail landed in a garden. (Alfred Price)

PFF marking was not up to scratch, and the bombing was scattered. The absence of a Master Bomber did not help matters. Four days later they tried again, this time with better results.

A further 11 heavy raids on the German capital were carried out by the middle of February, interspersed with other targets. Results were indeterminate; while at first losses were light, they gradually increased. In all, 6,209 Lancaster sorties were flown in this period, losing 321 aircraft in action. This represented an unsustainable loss rate of 5.2 per cent, which rose to 8 per cent for a final raid in March.

Peenemunde was heavily damaged, but the price was high

These figures do not include operational attrition. Fog and low cloud over England in the small hours of 17 December caused the loss of 28 Lancasters, in addition to 25 missing, while two more had collided after takeoff. The loss rate for this one mission was an appalling 11.4 per cent.

The success of Hamburg could not be repeated. Berlin was too large an area, too heavily defended, too far inland, and much harder to indentify with any precision. By this time, the advantages of Window were much less, as the German defences adapted themselves to it. While extensive damage was caused, the concentrated destruction of Hamburg was not repeated.

▦ NUREMBERG ▦
If the Battle of Berlin was a defeat for Bomber Command, the raid on Nuremberg on 30/31 March 1944 was a disaster. For Bomber Command, the Nuremberg raid was the night when it all went wrong.

Deception attacks on Kassel and Cologne were recognized early, which enabled the defences to concentrate on

Peenemunde, there was no disguising the real target, and those fighters with sufficient fuel stormed north to intercept, arriving in time to encounter the final two waves.

Peenemunde was heavily damaged, but the price paid for the raid upon it was high. Losses amounted to 40 aircraft, of which 24 were Lancasters. It is believed that the majority fell to fighters, but how much worse this could have been had the fighters not been lured elsewhere first. Diversions and feints became a standard tactic in Bomber Command's armoury, followed later as strength increased by simultaneous attacks on multiple targets.

▦ THE BATTLE ▦ OF BERLIN
The operations so far described were successful, but Bomber Command also had setbacks. The Battle of Berlin was one such. It commenced on 18/19 November 1943 with an attack by an all-Lancaster force, but on this occasion

half moon. The track of the bombers was visible from miles away, and the fighters needed no further invitation.

94 bombers failed to return that night, while 13 crashed on their return

An incredible total of 94 bombers failed to make the return journey from Germany that night, while 13 crashed on their arrival at base. Yet another was written off with battle damage, for an attrition percentage of 13.83. Seventy more aircraft returned with varying degrees of damage.

Most of the losses occurred on the outward leg. Night fighters accounted for 78 aircraft, including 55 Lancasters; flak claimed 11 (five of them Lancasters); two bombers collided and another was lost to an unknown cause. Of the 440 Lancaster crewmen who failed to return home, only 107 survived. Worst of all was that the raid was an almost complete failure.

Top left: The remains of the V-weapons site at Wizernes after a raid by Lancasters of No. 5 Group, 20 July 1944.
Left: Repair was a vital part of aircraft replacement. The nearest fuselage section belonged to an aircraft badly damaged by a night fighter in June 1944.
Below left and right: Before and after. A raid on the oil storage depot at Bec d'Ambes on 4 August 1944.

the main raid of 781 heavy bombers, of which 569 were Lancasters from 34 different squadrons. The twin-engined night fighters were scrambled and ordered to assemble over a certain radio beacon. Unfortunately, the course of the bombers took them towards this beacon, running them straight into the trap. Forecast winds were incorrect, and the bomber stream became spread out. Then, by mischance, atmospheric conditions were such that long condensation trails formed behind the bombers, shining white in the clear air under a

■ RETURN TO EUROPE ■

The outcome of the entire war in Europe hinged on the successful invasion of Normandy. From April 1944, the majority of Lancaster sorties were against targets in France and Belgium, mainly railway centres and airfields, radar stations and coastal gun batteries.

The weeks following D-Day saw Main Force heavily engaged in France and the Low Countries. Road and rail communications, enemy troop concentrations and fuel depots were all accorded priority, but meanwhile the V-1 and V-2 assault on London had begun, and a great deal of effort was diverted to their launching sites. Nor were targets in the Third Reich neglected; the Germans could be given no opportunity to move their home defence fighters forward.

This period saw a large-scale return to daylight operations for Bomber Command, made possible by Allied air superiority in the area, although the need to keep up the pressure around the clock made great demands on the bomber crews. Then, as the Allied armies pushed further inland, heavy attacks were made on German-held airfields in Holland. As the German defences were ground down, losses became progressively lighter; barely 1 per cent for December 1944.

During the concluding six months of the war, the Lancaster force grew to an

Above: Lancaster assembly line at Baginton. The wartime censor has rather clumsily airbrushed out the aircraft number.

enormous 57 squadrons; over 1,200 aircraft in all. As the area of occupied Europe shrank, so targets in Germany featured more and more. Concentrated attacks on synthetic oil plants were made during the winter of 1944/45, vastly reducing supplies. Dresden, at that time a key road and rail target, was attacked in strength on 13/14 February 1945; Essen by more

than 1,000 bombers in daylight on 11 March, and Kiel on 9/10 April. Berlin, once the most heavily defended area in Germany, was raided five nights later by more than 500 Lancasters, of which only two (0.4 per cent) failed to return. But by this time major targets were in short supply and the majority of raids were on a comparatively small scale, and as the Allied armies pushed into Germany, the strategic bombing war gradually drew to a close.

■ FINAL OPERATIONS ■

The Lancaster ended the war on more peaceful tasks. Operation Manna saw 17 Lancaster squadrons dropping containers of food to the population of Holland; Operation Exodus involved the repatriation of released British prisoners of war, with basic accommodation for 24 passengers in each aircraft. This was followed by Operation Dodge, the return of 8th Army veterans from the Mediterranean area. It was an honourable finish to a hard-fought campaign.

Left: Edith, veteran of 84 sorties during which she destroyed a German fighter, completed a further 14 trips dropping food and repatriating prisoners of war.

A heavily defended target could put up a storm of light flak, but most bombing was carried out at altitudes beyond its reach. Heavy flak could not be avoided by high flying, but it had a far slower rate of fire than the light automatic guns. Not only were far fewer shells coming up at any one time, but they took between 20 and 30 seconds to arrive at typical operational altitudes. Radar-predicted heavy flak was pretty accurate, but one method of avoiding it was to change course and altitude at frequent intervals. Hopefully the shells would then burst in the spot where the bomber would have been had it not evaded.

This improved the odds a bit, but if shells came up in the wrong place or burst at the wrong height, Lady Luck became the sole arbiter. Many pilots felt that the best course was to take no evasive action at all, but to drop the nose and accelerate out of the flak zone as fast as possible. It was also undesirable to make radical changes of course and altitude while on the attack run, if bombing accuracy was to be maintained. But having said that, the Lancaster's deadliest enemy was the fighter, whether met by day or by night. As the vast majority of Lancaster

sorties were made under cover of darkness, we will concentrate on the night fighter threat.

As we saw in the preceding chapter, countermeasures were widely used to hinder the defenders. While these were often very effective, what they could not do was prevent a fighter from searching visually. If a night fighter succeeded in working its way into the bomber stream, it was in a target-rich environment. Even with its radar and radio communications jammed solid, it was often possible for the fighter to make a visual sighting without these

Above: Radar-predicted heavy flak guns were mainly deployed along the coast or around cities.
Below left: Searchlights illuminated the bomber for flak or fighters; they could also dazzle the pilot and disorient him.
Opposite: Two .50 calibre machine-guns in the tail gave a mightier punch than the usual four .303 Brownings.

aids. And once the fighter was in visual contact, an attack usually followed.

Normal Lancaster defensive armament consisted of two machine-guns in each of nose and dorsal positions, and four more in the tail, all in power-operated turrets. The guns were Browning .303 calibre, with a high cyclic rate of fire. They could pour out a lot of rounds, but the bullets themselves were small and lacked hitting power. Four types of ammunition were in general use: ball, tracer, armour-piercing and incendiary.

The four guns in the rear turret were usually harmonized on a point at 750ft (225m) for night missions, and on a 7ft 6in (2.29m) square pattern at 1,200ft (365m) by day. The nose and mid-upper turrets were normally harmonized 5ft (1.52m) apart at 1,200ft (365m), although it was generally accepted that the maximum effective range of the .303 Browning was 900ft (275m). The main defence at night was the tail and

Left: The tail and mid-upper turrets were the Lancaster's main defensive armament. This example, from No. 15 Squadron, also carries G-H radar bombing equipment.
Below left: Mk I Lancaster used for traials of a periscopically sighted ventral turret in 1942. It was not a success.

into the effective range of the British machine-guns, which could to a degree compensate for their small projectiles by their high rate of fire.

From June 1944, a number of Lancasters were fitted with the Rose Rice tail turret, which mounted two .50 calibre Brownings. While the combination of a much heavier projectile and a slightly higher muzzle velocity gave a rather better effective range, the cyclic rate of fire of this weapon was at most 850 rounds per minute. The standard four-gun Lancaster turret could spew out no less than 306 bullets in a four-second burst, compared with just 113 for the Rose Rice turret. It must, however, be admitted that the weight of fire of the latter was about 50 per cent heavier provided that all bullets struck home, but the former was more likely to score multiple hits.

mid-upper turret, in that order. Rarely were the nights clear enough to allow fighters to make frontal attacks, and it was unlikely that a Lancaster would overhaul a fighter from astern, so the nose turret was of most use in discouraging the ground defences during low-level missions.

Wartime British bomber armament has often been criticized as inadequate, because it was both out-ranged and out-gunned by the German fighter weapons. There are, however, two factors to consider: British bombers were far more heavily defended than those of any other nation except the Americans, and that included their German counterparts. For example, the Heinkel He 111 typically carried a single rifle-calibre machine-gun in each of just five positions, with limited fields of fire and no power-operated turrets. Then at night, visibility was such that the German fighters often had to get very close before they could see the bomber clearly enough to identify it and take aim. This brought them well

The primary task of the Lancaster was to deliver bombs and return safely

Operationally, what were the implications? The primary task of the Lancaster was to deliver bombs on target and return safely. Given this, it was sufficient to foil the fighter's attack. Shooting it down was the cherry on the cake. On dark nights, when the fighters were forced to get in close, sometimes to less than 200ft (60m), the four-gun turret, with nearly triple the rate of fire of the Rose Rice, had much to commend it. Few German night fighter pilots would press home an attack while they were taking hits themselves. The final advantage of

LANCASTER, DEFENSIVE GUNS		
Browning machine-gun	.303 calibre	.50 calibre
Cyclic rate of fire	1,150rpm	750/850rpm
Weight	22lb (10kg)	64lb (29kg)
Muzzle velocity	2,660ft/sec (811m/sec)	2,750ft/sec (838m/sec)
Projectile weight	174 grains	710 grains

Above: The nose turret was rarely of use at night, but daylight raids became more frequent. No. 100 Squadron – 128 operations.

the standard four-gun turret was that it had no less than 130 seconds' firing time, compared with a mere 24 seconds for the Rose Rice. However, unless shooting up ground targets was on the agenda, this was rarely called for; against enemy fighters 24 seconds' firing time was usually adequate.

If, however, the object of the exercise was to shoot down German fighters, then the heavier gun was preferable. This was also the case on clear nights with good visibility, when the German fighters could stand off at long range and shoot. In daylight – and from late 1944 Lancaster carried out a surprising number of daylight operations – it was no contest; the heavier gun with its longer range was by far the most preferable. Among the squadrons equipped with the Rose Rice rear turret were Nos. 83, 101, 153 and 170.

The other major variation in Lancaster defensive armament was the Glenn Martin 250 mid-upper turret,

which also mounted two .50 calibre Brownings. This was carried by the Lancaster B.VII, of which a total of 150 were built. But as deliveries of this model did not commence until April 1945, it was just too late to see action.

■ GUNSIGHTS ■

Guns are not a lot of use unless they can be accurately aimed. The main gunsight used in Lancaster turrets was the Barr & Stroud G Mk III reflector sight. In use, this showed an illuminated orange circle with a central dot, both focused at infinity. A brightness control adjusted it according to conditions: bright in sunlight, dim at night. The radius of the circle was approximately equal to the wingspan of a single-engined fighter at a range of 1,200ft (365m), while the radius of the circle gave the deflection (the amount of aiming ahead) needed to hit a target with a relative crossing speed of 50mph (80km/hr).

In 1944, the Mk IIc gyroscopic sight entered service as a turret sight. This could actually predict the point of aim, although only if the approaching

fighter could be tracked for a short while, and its wingspan set on a dial. For this reason, it was very much a daylight sight, as it was rare for a gunner to have time to do such things at night. Finally, a gun-laying radar codenamed Village Inn was introduced in the final months of the war, which allowed opponents to be engaged from beyond visual range. While potentially devastating, the problem was obtaining positive identification of the radar contact as hostile. The means were to hand, but the war ended before unrestricted blind firing could be permitted as a general rule.

The essence of effective defence against fighters was always to see them first. At night this was far from easy.

ROSE RICE TURRET

2 x .50 Browning machine-guns
335 rounds per gun
Mk IIIA reflector sight
Traverse +/-94°
Elevation 49°
Depression 59°

Above: **Mk I fitted with an experimental arrangement of remote barbettes with the sighting position in the tail.**

As a general rule, they came from below, where they were masked by the dark ground and most difficult to see. By contrast, the bomber would be lined against the sky, which is always a fraction lighter, even on a starless night. Attacks generally came from astern, with the fighter swimming up from the depths and attacking in a slight climb with its fixed frontal armament. Its target was rarely the fuselage, as if the bombs detonated, the resulting explosion could quite easily destroy

Below: **Canadian-built Mk X, fitted with the small and neat Glenn Martin mid-upper turret.**

the night fighter too. Normally the wings, with the vulnerable engines and fuel tanks, were selected as the aiming point, although many a time silencing the rear gunner was a priority.

Later in the war, the German night fighters used Schrage Musik, cannon pointing upwards at an angle of about 60 degrees, aimed by a reflector sight mounted in the cabin roof. This allowed them to attack from almost directly underneath, out of the arcs of fire of all except those few Lancasters which had retained ventral turrets, and generally out of sight of the gunners also. All the fighter had to do was to formate beneath the bomber and take

careful aim at the fuel tanks between the engines. A short burst of fire was then usually sufficient.

■ SCHRAGE MUSIK ■

Because the German fighters did not use tracer in a Schrage Musik attack, Bomber Command was rather slow in identifying it. If a bomber set out, then failed to return, there was no one to tell the tale. Only those few aircraft that survived such attacks limped back bearing the tell-tale scars, and gradually the tactic became known.

Methods of dealing with night fighters varied. Often, if one was sighted that was not making any overtly aggressive moves, the policy was to leave it well alone, hoping that the bomber had not been seen. Other crews maintained that an aggressive attitude was best, opening fire even at long range in order to show the fighter the kind of welcome it could expect if it made an attacking move. Sometimes these ploys worked; at other times they didn't.

Flight Lieutenant Tony Weber's Pathfinder crew developed their own unique brand of defence against attack from below. The Lancasters of No. 405 Squadron had had their dorsal turrets removed to improve performance, which left the mid-upper gunner as a spare bod. A small viewing hole was cut in the fuselage floor aft of the bomb bay, fitted with safety straps, oxygen connection and power for a heated flying

Above: 'Village Inn' gunlaying radar was fitted to a few tail turrets towards the end of the war.

Left: The most widely used German night fighter was the radar-equipped Messerschmitt Me 110G.

suit. This position was then manned by the erstwhile mid-upper gunner. When a fighter was spotted coming in below, the pilot was warned. He immediately throttled back and lowered 10 degrees of flap, which killed a lot of speed and gave the aircraft greater manoeuvrability. As the Lancaster slowed, the fighter started to overshoot beneath it. Then, at the critical moment, Weber shoved the yoke fully forward, putting his huge bomber into a dive.

The result was a steep descent right on top of the offending fighter, accompanied by the fervent hope that the German pilot's reflexes were fast enough for him to get out of the way in time. Negative 'g' made the Merlins cut through fuel starvation, temporarily extinguishing the exhaust flames and probably adding to the German pilot's visual problems. One dose of this nerve-racking treatment usually convinced him to go and look for someone who didn't play so rough. No. 405 Squadron later adopted the ventral viewing hole on all its aircraft.

The other, official counter to fighter attack was the corkscrew. Few people (and fighter pilots are no exception) are

Above: **The upward slanting cannon instal-lation known as Schrage Musik allowed the night fighters to attack from the blind spot below the Lancaster. (Alfred Price)**

any good at deflection shooting, and the object of the corkscrew was to give the fighter a difficult target rather than a sitting duck.

It consisted of a steep turn of about 30 degrees combined with a dive of about 500ft (150m), followed imme-diately by a steep turn of about 30 degrees in the opposite direction com-bined with a climb of about 500ft (150m). These manoeuvres would be repeated as long as the fighter was in an attacking position. In this way, course and altitude could both be main-tained, at the expense of speed over the ground, while few German fighter pilots were good enough to follow a

corkscrewing Lancaster and still get into a good firing position.

Instructions for the corkscrew were given by the man best placed to see what was happening – usually the rear gunner, although the mid-upper gunner or the bomb aimer, from a position in the astrodome, could also act as controller for the engagement. On spotting a fighter moving into position, the man making the sighting would call over the intercom, "Prepare to corkscrew left [or right]", the rule being to break into the direction of the attack where possible. Then as the fighter moved into firing range, the exe-cutive order of "Go" would be given, launching the bomber into a series of wild gyrations. The controls had to be handled roughly, making the corkscrew violent, if it were to be really effective. The Lancaster could corkscrew very well

even with a 12,000lb (5,400kg) bomb on board, while unladen it was extremely manoeuvrable for such a large machine.

McLean was credited with five German fighters shot down plus one probable

Survival depended on teamwork – total co-operation and trust between pilot and gunners. A classic engage-ment occurred on 15/16 March 1944, following an abortive raid on an aero engine factory at Metz, near the Franco-German border.

The Lancaster was from No. 617 Squadron, the Dam Busters, and had a mainly Canadian crew. The rear gunner

THE CORKSCREW MANOEUVRE

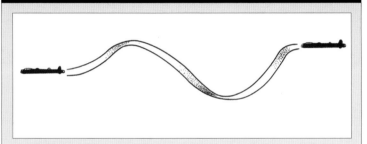

The corkscrew was a manoeuvre designed to make it very difficult for an enemy fighter to gain a firing position.

Above: Some Lancaster squadrons removed their dorsal turrets to improve performance.

up a contact to port at a range of about 3,600ft (1,100m). McLean strained his eyes, finally making out a dark shape which appeared to be four-engined. At first it was assumed to be another returning bomber. Gradually the shape closed, which was unusual, and when it was about 2,700ft (820m) away, McLean realized that it was actually two night fighters in close proximity to one another. Following standard procedure, he told his pilot: "Prepare to corkscrew port!"

■ THREE FIGHTERS ■

The next shock came quickly; a Messerschmitt 109 single-seater fighter was sighted, flying abreast of the Lancaster about 1,500ft (450m) distant with navigation lights burning! The only explanation for this behaviour seemed to be that it was trying to distract the gunners from the fighters astern. At this moment, one of the two broke towards the Lancaster with obviously aggressive intentions.

As it closed, McLean gave the order "Go!" and Duffy commenced a violent corkscrew just as the fighter opened fire at extreme range. The Lancaster was hit, but not seriously, and the German pilot broke away before lining up for another firing pass.

was a Scot with original ideas about defensive tactics, and only that morning the crew had been on a fighter affiliation exercise to try them out.

Men are born with differing abilities. Some have a natural flair for ball games; others play the piano outstandingly well. Flight Sergeant T.J. McLean's individual talent, and indeed his whole instincts, were for air-to-air gunnery. Credited with five German fighters shot down plus a probable on a previous tour of operations, he had volunteered to join No. 617 Squadron, widely regarded at that time as a suicide outfit, and had been assigned to Flying Officer Bill Duffy's crew as the tail gunner.

Past experience had convinced Tom McLean that the most effective loading

for his guns was 45 per cent tracer and 55 per cent armour piercing, rather than the ball, tracer, incendiary and armour-piercing mix laid down in regulations. On this trip he had unofficially arranged for his preferred mix to be loaded for the first time, to his rear turret only. Not even the crew knew about this; the nose turret and the mid-upper, which was manned by Canadian Red Evans, both had standard loadings.

All aircraft were recalled without bombing when it was found that the target was under heavy cloud, but on the return trip across France the sky was cloudless, the stars shone brightly, and visibility was exceptionally good.

The first warning came from Monica, the tail warning radar, which picked

Above: German night fighters were largely dependent on ground control to position them in the bomber stream.

Having drawn no return fire from the bomber, the Me 110 was more venturesome on its second attack, closing right in. Once again the big bomber corkscrewed, spoiling its aim, while McLean poured an angry burst of fire at it, hitting its port engine, then called "Drop" over the intercom. Immediately, the flight engineer throttled back all four engines and the Lancaster rapidly lost speed, reducing the range faster than the German pilot had expected, or was prepared for. McLean drew a bead on the cockpit and once more let fly. On hearing his guns, the flight engineer once more opened the throttles in what was a very well-rehearsed manoeuvre.

> ### The second fighter plunged earthwards, trailing a comet-like fiery tail

On fire, the first Me 110 fell away into the void, and after making sure that the second fighter still remained in its original position, the rear gunner passed the word "Easy" over the intercom. Upon hearing this, Bill Duffy relaxed the corkscrew manoeuvre.

They were not left in peace for long. The second night fighter, made cautious by seeing the fate of its partner, moved out to a position almost abeam of the Lancaster before commencing a curving attack from slightly below it. Again, a violent evasive corkscrew, again a torrent of fire from both rear and mid-upper turrets, and the second fighter plunged earthwards, trailing a comet-like fiery tail.

Still the Me 109 shadowed them, just out of range. A renewed visual search (Monica had been switched off) showed yet another Me 110 coming up behind, moving from port to starboard, then finally to almost dead astern.

At this point Duffy spotted some cloud ahead and below, and pushed over into a shallow dive towards it. As he did so, the 110 came in, and once more the Lancaster went into a hard corkscrew, this time to starboard. Almost immediately McLean called "Drop!" The combination of corkscrew and speed loss spoiled the German pilot's aim completely, and he came hurtling in, to be met by a barrage of tracer and armour-piercing bullets at close range. With pieces flying off, his aircraft nosed up with flames bursting from its port wing and starboard engine, before entering a jerky flat spin down into the abyss. A red glow lit the cloud layer below.

At this, the Me 109 switched off its lights and turned in for an attack from abeam of the Lancaster. The tail turret could not be brought to bear, but Red Evans in the mid-upper position returned fire, then, as the Me 109 passed beneath

Below: In March 1944, a Lancaster of No. 617 Squadron accounted for three Me 110 night fighters like these in a single action. (Alfred Price)

the bomber, quickly traversed his turret to speed it on its way on the far side. It never returned.

At this stage of the war, night fighters were encountered quite frequently. Sometimes, by dint of hard manoeuvring or escaping into cloud, the bomber managed to shake them off. At other times, the air gunners managed to beat off the attack, while just occasionally they shot one down. In the general scheme of things, four against one was impossible odds; to survive such an encounter, let alone shoot down three fighters and beat off a fourth, bordered on the miraculous.

There are several footnotes to this outstanding action. As noted in the preceding chapter, Monica could be homed on from very long ranges. It was almost certainly this which drew as many as four fighters to a single Lancaster.

The corkscrew saved the lives of hundreds of bomber crewmen

The role of the Me 109 was more mysterious. Was it a deliberate decoy, or had it left its lights on accidentally? It seems hardly likely that it was acting as a controller, and it is extremely doubtful that it was acting as a station-keeping aid for the twin-engined fighters; they had their radars, which they were using, and presumably Flensburg as well. The most probable explanation is that it was a day fighter on a night cross-country that had forgotten to switch off its navigation lights, that just happened to be in the right place at the right time.

Flight sergeant McLean's ammunition mix had much to commend it, inasmuch as the 'fright factor' of so much tracer, combined with the penetrative power of armour-piercing bullets, was potentially very effective. But not all bomber crews thought this way; some preferred to fire no tracer at all on the grounds that this merely demonstrated the inadequate range of the .303 Brownings, thereby encouraging the night fighters to stand

off and shoot back. In fact, McLean's idea would only be effective if the fighter could be lured in close, which of course was done.

There can be no doubt that the corkscrew saved the lives of hundreds of bomber crewmen. However, to be really effective it had to be violent, as if it was too gently executed, an experienced fighter pilot could simply follow the bomber through the manoeuvre. Properly carried out, it made the bomber a very difficult target, even by day.

In the closing months of the war, Lancasters carried out many daylight raids over Germany. Whereas American heavy bombers flew in tightly packed formations to take advantage of the massed firepower of their heavy machine-guns, the reach of the Lancaster guns was less. The latter therefore flew in loose gaggles rather than tight formation, and corkscrewed when attacked by fighters. The combination of fire and movement generally proved an effective defence.

RAF LANCASTER SQUADRONS FORMED NOV 1942–DEC 1945

Squadron	First operation	Base formed
101	20/21 Nov 1942, Turin	Holme-on-Spalding Moor
103	21/22 Nov 1942, Gardening	Elsham Wolds
12	3/4 Jan 1943, Gardening	Wickenby
156	26/27 Jan 1943, Lorient	Warboys
100	4/5 Mar 1943, Gardening	Grimsby
115	20/21 Mar 1943, Gardening	East Wretham
617	16/17 May 1943, Dams Raid	Scampton
619	11/12 June 1943, Dusseldorf	Woodhall Spa
7	8/9 July 1943, Cologne	Oakington
514	3/4 Sep 1943, Dusseldorf	Foulsham
166	22/23 Sep 1943, Hanover	Kirmington
625	18/19 Oct 1943, Hanover	Kelstern
626	10/11 Nov 1943, Modane	Wickenby
550	26/27 Nov 1943, Berlin	Grimsby
576	2/3 Dec 1943, Berlin	Elsham Wolds
630	18/19 Dec 1943, Berlin	East Kirkby

RAF LANCASTER SQUADRONS FORMED JAN 1944–MAY 1945

Squadron	First operation	Base formed
622	14/15 Jan 1944, Brunswick	Mildenhall
15	Jan 1944, not known	Mildenhall
635	22/23 Mar 1944, Frankfurt	Downham Market
35	April 1944, not known	Graveley
582	9/10 April 1944, Lille	Little Staughton
90	June 1944, not known	Tuddenham
149	17 Sep 1944, Boulogne	Methwold
218	Sep 1944, not known	Methwold
153	7 Oct 1944, Emmerich	Kirmington
227	11 Oct 1944, Walcheren	Bardney
186	18 Oct 1944, Bonn	Tuddenham
170	19/20 Oct 1944, Stuttgart	Kelstern
195	26 Oct 1944, Leverkusen	Witchford
189	1 Nov 1944, Homburg	Bardney
150	2 Nov 1944, not known	Fiskerton
138	29 Mar 1945, Hallendorf	Tuddenham

SPECIAL SQUADRONS

As a weapon of war the Lancaster was a bludgeon rather than a rapier. But circumstances alter cases, and when precision weapons were devised for special targets, the Lancaster became a scalpel.

Ruhr industry was dependent on hydro-electric power and water, supplied by several huge dams. The destruction of the largest of these would have a devastating effect on German armaments output. But no ordinary bomb was capable of smashing these concrete monsters. In the Weybridge offices of Vickers, a quiet genius called Barnes Wallis applied himself to the problem.

The solution he came up with was a large mine, which had to be placed with absolute precision against the inner face of the dams by flying at exactly 220mph (354km/hr) and 60ft (18m), releasing the weapon to an accuracy of less than one-fifth of a

second. This called for a special squadron, trained specifically for the task. To lead it, the very experienced and dynamic Wing Commander Guy Gibson was chosen, and his aircrews were hand-picked from the best that Bomber Command could offer. They were a mixed bag – predominantly British, but including 26 Canadians, 12 Australians, two New Zealanders and a single American. It is less widely known that the ground crews and support tradesmen were also hand-picked, which made for an exceptionally efficient unit. Thus was the birth of No. 617 Squadron at Scampton in March 1943.

The mine, codenamed Upkeep, was a large cylindrical weapon weighing 9,250lb (4,200kg), over two-thirds of which was high explosive. Aircraft were taken from squadrons in No. 5 Group, as it had been found that 'low mileage, one careful owner' machines had better serviceability rates than those fresh from the factory, and modified. The bomb bay doors were removed and special brackets fitted, together with an electric motor to get Upkeep rotating at 500 revolutions per minute before release. The bomb bay was faired to front and rear of the mine in order to reduce drag, and the mid-upper turret was removed.

Right: Provisioning Lancaster, with modified bomb bay for Upkeep, and dorsal turret removed.
Below: An inert Upkeep falls clear of the dropping aircraft during trials at Reculver.
Left: To mark the 34th anniversary of the raid on the dams, a Lancaster reflew the mission in 1977.

Diagram labels:
MANUAL RELEASE — MOUNTING OF MOTOR AND DRIVE — MOD TO TOP OF FLOOR FOR HYDRAULIC PIPES — MOUNTING OF HYDRAULIC FILTERS — LONGERON BRACKET ASSEMBLY — FAIRING PLATFORM — WINCH REACTION SOCKETS — REAR FAIRING — TOP COVER

POSITIVE LOCK — FRONT FAIRING — MOUNTING OF STOP VALVES — TRANSVERSE BEAM — MOD. TO FLOOR BOTTOM — MOD TO TRAILING FAIRING STRIPS — BOTTOM COVER AND GUN MOUNTING

ARRANGEMENT OF FUSING — SPEED INDICATOR — REV. COUNTER DRIVE — DRIVING BELT — SIDE ARMS WITH PIVOT BOLTS PULLEY AND RELEASE ARMS — GUNNERS KNEELING PAD

Above: Diagram of the modifications required to carry Upkeep. Surviving aircraft were converted back to original standard.

Transformed in this manner, Mk Is became Type 464 Provisioning Lancasters.

Other changes were made as they were found necessary. The entire raid was to be flown at low level, so bomb aimers assisted navigation using a specially prepared roller map. The nose turret had to be manned continually, which gave a role to the otherwise redundant mid-upper gunner, and stirrups were fitted to prevent him treading on the bomb-aimer's head in moments of excitement.

Achieving the exact height over water at night proved difficult, but was overcome by fitting Aldis lamps in the nose camera port and behind the bomb bay, angled so that the two spots of light touched at exactly 60ft (18m) and offset to starboard where they were easily seen by the navigator, who monitored height on the attack run.

> **This was the first use of the 'Master Bomber' technique, later to become standard**

Standard bombsights could not be used, but the Dann sight, rigged up from a plywood triangle, an eyepiece and a couple of nails, worked well in practice, while pilots had marks on the windshield to aid them in lining up on a target.

Close control of the operation was vital, and for this Gibson had all Lancasters fitted with fighter-type VHF radios. This was the first use of the 'Master Bomber' technique, later to become standard throughout Bomber Command.

At low level, the Lancasters might have to fight their way into and out of the target area, while the Mohne Dam at least was known to be defended. Three thousand rounds per gun was carried, giving 157 seconds of firing time. All of it was tracer, to keep the heads of the German gunners down.

■ OPERATION ■ CHASTISE

The attack on the dams was set for 16/17 May, when good weather was forecast, the moon was full, and the water level behind the dams was at its highest, Nineteen Lancasters took off in three waves. The first wave consisted of nine aircraft in three Vics of three, led by Gibson.

Left: Dr Barnes Wallis, creator of Upkeep, Tallboy and Grand Slam, pictured with the standard of No. 617 Squadron.
Below: Provisioning Lancaster at dispersal, showing the drive belt that rotated Upkeep at 500rpm before release.

Above: Gibson leads his crew aboard Lancaster ED932, AJ-G, prior to taking off on the Dams Raid. His aircraft survived the war, only to be scrapped.
Left: ED825, AJ-T, was the reserve aircraft for the Dams Raid, and was flown by Flight Lieutenant McCarthy when his own machine went unserviceable.

Its primary targets were the Mohne and Eder Dams. The second wave, of five Lancasters flying individually, took a more northerly route. Their target was the Sorpe Dam, of different construction to the first two and needing a different mode of attack, albeit with the same weapon. The third and final wave of five aircraft also flew individually. Taking off two hours after the others, it was a reserve to be used against the main targets if needed, otherwise to attack secondary dams in the area.

Opposition to the passage of the first wave was moderate, but Bill Astell's Lancaster fell to light flak. The remainder arrived over the Mohne Dam on time. Gibson later wrote, "In that light it looked squat and heavy and unconquerable; it looked grey and solid in the moonlight, as though it were part of the countryside itself and just as immovable. A structure like a battleship was showering out flak all along its length."

After circling to make an assessment of the situation, Gibson began his attack run, curving in down-moon, past the hills and low over the water. He had his spotlights on for height, and the light flak saw him coming and opened up with everything they had, answered by Deering in the front turret. Bomb Aimer "Spam" Spafford released the mine, and they swept low over the dam. From the air it looked like a perfect drop, but in fact the mine had fallen short. The dam remained standing.

Next came Hopgood. He was not so lucky. Hit by flak, his aircraft was set on fire and crashed, while his mine bounced

Above: Dams Raid debrief. Standing (left to right): Air Chief Marshal Arthur Harris, Air Marshal Cochrane. Seated: intelligence officer, Spafford and Taerum of Gibson's crew.

clear over the dam. Gibson then made a critical move. Ordering Australian Mick Martin to attack, he flew slightly ahead of him and to one side to draw the enemy fire, and to add his own guns to Martin's in suppressing the defences. Even so, Martin's Lancaster was hit, and its mine was released off course to detonate harmlessly.

Fourth to attack was Dinghy Young, and with both Gibson and Martin distracting the defenders, he made a perfect run unscathed, and deposited his Upkeep right against the dam wall. Still the dam stood, but even as Maltby made his run, the parapet crumbled and the dam burst. His mine added to the breach made by Young.

■ ON TO THE EDER ■

Martin and Maltby now set course for home, while Gibson and Young, the latter acting as deputy leader, led the three remaining armed Lancasters to the Eder Dam.

This was undefended, for the Eder was surrounded by steep hills, making an attack very hazardous. Australian David Shannon made three attempts at it without being able to line up correctly. Henry Maudslay then tried twice, with no better luck. Shannon's fourth attempt run was accurate; his mine exploded against the dam, causing a small breach.

Maudslay tried once more, but his mine hit the parapet with him just above it. For years it was assumed that he and his crew died in the explosion, but it appears that, badly damaged, he limped some 130 miles (210km) towards home before falling to flak.

Only one armed Lancaster remained, and on the second attempt its Australian pilot, Les Knight, made a perfect run. His mine punched a hole clean through the giant dam wall, and under the enormous pressure of water, the breach gradually widened.

The second wave of Lancasters had been less fortunate. The first aircraft to be lost during Operation Chastise was that of Byers, a Canadian, which was shot down by flak as it crossed the coast. In almost the same place, New Zealander Les Munro's Lancaster was damaged by flak and forced to abandon the mission, while Geoff Rice, flying as low as possible, hit the sea and lost his mine. Recovering by a hair's breadth, he also was forced to return. Barlow, an

OPERATION CHASTISE, PARTICIPANTS

PILOT	LETTERS	AIRCRAFT NO.
First wave		
Wg Cdr G.P. Gibson	AJ-G	ED 932/G
Flt Lt J. V. Hopgood	AJ-M	ED 925/G
Flt Lt H.B. Martin	AJ-P	ED 909/G
Sqn Ldr H.M. Young	AJ-A	ED 887/G
Flt Lt D.J.H. Maltby	AJ-J	ED 906/G
Flt Lt D.J. Shannon	AJ-L	ED 929/G
Sqn Ldr H.M. Maudslay	AJ-Z	ED 937/G
Flt Lt W. Astell	AJ-B	ED 864/G
Plt Off L.G. Knight	AJ-N	ED 912/G
Second wave		
Flt Lt J.C. McCarthy	AJ-T	ED 825/G
Flt Lt R.N.G. Barlow	AJ-E	ED 927/G
Flt Lt J.L. Munro	AJ-W	ED 921/G
Plt Off V.W. Byers	AJ-K	ED 934/G
Plt Off G. Rice	AJ-H	ED 936/G
Third and reserve wave		
Plt Off W.H.T. Ottley	AJ-C	ED 910/G
Plt Off L.J. Burpee	AJ-S	ED 865/G
Flt Sgt K.S. Brown	AJ-F	ED 918/G
Flt Sgt W.C. Townsend	AJ-O	ED 886/G
Flt Sgt C.T. Anderson	AJ-Y	ED 914/G

Note: McCarthy was originally scheduled to fly ED 923/G, but this aircraft developed a hydraulic leak.

Australian, was claimed by flak just inside the German border, and of the ill-fated second wave, only the American Joe McCarthy survived. After making nine runs against the Sorpe, he dropped his mine on the tenth, but without any visible results.

The final wave fared only slightly better. Burpee, a young Canadian from Gibson's previous squadron, went down over Holland, while Ottley lasted only a little longer. Both fell to light flak. Of the other three, all Flight Sergeants, Anderson was the least lucky. Last off, the fates conspired to force him to abandon the mission without attacking.

One Victoria Cross and no fewer than 33 other awards were made

Brown attacked the Sorpe after several attempts, like McCarthy with no visible result, while Townsend, on couse for the Mohne Dam, was diverted to the Ennerpe Dam instead. After several brushed with flak, he emerged into an area made unrecognizable by floods from the already breached Mohne and Eder. Finally, Townsend arrived at what appeared to be the Ennerpe and dropped his mine, but post-war evidence seems to indicate that he attacked the Bever Dam 5 miles (8km) away.

Although the entire German air defence system was by now alert to the events, losses were lighter on the run home. Apart from Maudslay, the only other loss was Dinghy Young. Hit by flak as he recrossed the coast, he went down into the sea. Others, including McCarthy, Brown and Townsend, had eventful return flights, but recovered safely to Scampton.

Success had been dearly bought. Eight Lancasters failed to return home; of the 56 men on board them, only three survived. Gibson was awarded the Victoria Cross, Britain's highest decoration, and no fewer than 33 other awards were made to participants in the raid.

Above: The Dortmund-Ems Canal, scene of the Dam Busters' worst disaster, was finally breached in 1944. (Alfred Price)
Below: Under the leadership of Group Captain Leonard Cheshire VC, No. 617 Squadron became the most accurate heavy bomber squadron of the war.

The Dams Raid had long passed into legend. No. 617 Squadron had established itself as an elite unit; truly a special squadron. Over the next two years, it would fully maintain this reputation.

The Dams Raid over, a new role was sought for No. 617 Squadron. The modified Lancasters were replaced by standard Mk IIIs, and the crews started intensive high- and low-level training. Wing Commander Guy Gibson was replaced by Squadron Leader George Holden. A few unexciting trips to Italy followed; then, on 30 August 1943, the squadron was ordered to Coningsby to concentrate on low-level attacks.

■ DORTMUND-EMS ■

The next target was the heavily defended Dortmund-Ems canal, a strategic artery in the German transport system. Bomber Command had often attempted to breach its banks, but without success. Now 617 was to try, using the new 12,000lb (5,440kg) high-capacity bomb.

Low cloud in the target area caused the first attempt to be recalled, minus Maltby, who went into the sea after hitting someone's slipstream at low level. On the following night they tried again. It was a disaster. Heavy mist in the target area foiled all attempts to bomb

Above: **No. 9 Squadron, pictured here with its famous W4964** *Johnny Walker***, was something of an elite outfit. Its total of 106 operations took in the Ruhr, Hamburg, Berlin and Peenemunde and** *Tirpitz.*

accurately, while the defences claimed five Lancasters, among them those of Holden and Les Knight. The squadron rapidly gained the reputation of being a suicide outfit. This notwithstanding, six aircraft, in company with six more from No. 619 Squadron, went out again the following night to attack the Antheor Viaduct in southern France at low level. This was another failure, and the squadron was withdrawn from operations while changes took place.

One was the introduction of the extremely accurate Stabilizing Automatic Bomb Sight, or SABS, introduced by

Arthur 'Talking Bomb' Richardson, whom we last saw over Gdynia with Guy Gibson. No. 617 was now to become a medium- and high-level 'sniper' squadron. The other was the arrival of Wing Commander Leonard Cheshire to command on 11 November.

A more exacting test came on the night of 8/9 February

Cheshire was an enigma. Introspective and unconventional, he was arguably the most inspirational bomber leader of the war. Always leading from the front, he has been described by David

Shannon as a pied piper; people followed him gladly. He now set out to make the squadron live, breathe and eat bombing accuracy.

Several missions followed against pinpoint targets, but they were not a great success. Oboe marking was too inaccurate against small targets. Cheshire and Martin worked out between them that only low-level marking in a dive would be good enough, and on 3/4 January 1944, they tried it against a flying bomb site at Freval. By the illumination of flares, they marked from 400ft (120m), and 12,000lb (5,440kg) bombs from the remainder of the formation obliterated the target.

A more exacting test came on 8/9 February, by which time No. 617 had moved to Woodhall Spa. The aero engine works at Limoges were almost totally destroyed after being marked at low level, while damage to French houses close by was minimal. Other raids followed with equal success, the only failure during this time being another attempt against the Antheor Viaduct.

To mark heavily defended targets, a smaller and faster aircraft was needed. The obvious choice was a Mosquito, which Cheshire duly acquired, bringing the low-level marking career of the Lancaster to an end. At the same time, 617 became pathfinders and Main Force leaders to No. 5 Group. But other plans for them were afoot.

■ D-DAY DECEPTION ■

The first of these was Operation Taxable, a deception ploy that was designed to make the Germans think that a vast invasion fleet was moving towards Cap d'Antifer, some 20 miles (30km) north of Le Havre. This was done by 16 Lancasters, flying precise speeds and courses, dropping Window at five-second intervals. Packed to the gills with Window bundles, they maintained the deception for some eight hours, until dawn broke to reveal only an empty sea to the expectant Germans.

The second was the introduction of the Tallboy, a new 12,000lb (5,440kg) bomb with exceptionally good ballistic qualities and penetrative power. Like Upkeep, Tallboy was the brainchild of Dr Barnes Wallis, and only the SABS-equipped Dam Busters could bomb accurately enough to make the best use of this new and devastating weapon.

Above: Lurking in the Norwegian fjords, the German battleship *Tirpitz* kept strong British naval forces tied down.

MOHNE DAM

"The gunners had seen us coming. They could see us coming with our spotlights on for over two miles away. Now they opened up and tracers began swirling towards us; some were even bouncing on the smooth surface of the lake. This was a horrible moment: we were being dragged along at four miles a minute, almost against our will, towards the things we were going to destroy. I think at that moment the boys did not want to go. I know I did not wat to go."

WING COMMANDER G. PENROSE GIBSON
VC, DSO, DFC

One of the few south-to-north rail routes still open in France at this time passed through a tunnel near Saumur, on the Loire. Shortly after midnight on 8/9 June the squadron arrived overhead, and Cheshire placed two red spot fires in the mouth of the tunnel. Nineteen Tallboy-armed Lancasters moved in, plus another six with more conventional loads. The result was a series of enormous craters that tore the line to pieces. One Tallboy, however, had impacted the hillside and bored its way down to explode actually inside the tunnel almost 60ft (18m) below, completely blocking it.

Other precision raids followed: concrete E-boat pens at Le Havre, and V-Weapon sites scattered around the Pas-de-Calais and elsewhere. Then, in July, command of the squadron passed from Cheshire to Wing Commander Willie Tait DSO DFC.

■ 617 VERSUS *TIRPITZ* ■

The German battleship *Tirpitz* had long been a thorn in the side of the Royal Navy. Lying in Alten Fjord in northern Norway, by its very existence it tied down British naval units which would have been better employed elsewhere.

Even from the most northerly of British airfields, Alten Fjord was outside Lancaster range. A deal was struck with the Russians, who made Yagodnik, near

EVADING RADAR

LEGEND

— *Tirpitz* at Tromsø

—— Bombers' route

⌒ 1,500ft (457m) radar cover

◎ Radar stations

TROMSO

NORTH SEA

NORWAY

SWEDEN

LOSSIEMOUTH

0   100
MILES

Evading the German radar cover by flying in over Sweden, Nos. 617 and 9
Squadrons achieved complete surprise in their third attack on the *Tirpitz*.

system proved equal to the task, and a smokescreen quickly obscured the battleship. This notwithstanding, a single Tallboy hit was scored, but *Tirpitz* was still afloat. The Kriegsmarine moved her south to Tromsø for use as a floating gun battery; she would never sail again, but this was not known either.

Calculations showed that fitting internal fuel tanks in the fuselage of the Lancasters would just allow the monster to be attacked from Lossiemouth. On 20 October, 40 aircraft of 617 and 9 Squadrons set out on the long haul to Tromsø. A combination of poor weather and enemy fighters made this attack a failure, and few crews even so much as saw the battleship.

They achieved complete surprise and scored multiple hits

The final attack on *Tirpitz* was mounted on 12 November, with 31 Lancasters from both squadrons. Approaching from the neutral (Swedish) side, they achieved complete surprise and scored multiple hits. The *Tirpitz* slowly turned turtle, but the water was too shallow for her to sink completely.

Below: "Twas a famous victory!" *Tirpitz* lies belly up in Tromsø Fjord, having capsized after multiple bomb hits.

Arkhangelsk, available as a refuelling stop. For this and subsequent anti-*Tirpitz* operations, No. 617 was joined by No. 9 Squadron, which, although fitted with the Mk XIV vector bombsight, was also something of an elite outfit. Of the 36 Lancasters detailed, 24 carried Tallboys; the others were loaded with 12 Johnny Walker Diving Mines each, an original but ineffective weapon.

The raid nearly ended in disaster as bad weather over Russia forced many Lancasters to land where they could. Six were abandoned in the marshes. When on 15 September the attack was finally mounted, the German early warning

Tait was now replaced by 617's final wartime commander, Group Captain John Fauquier, a Canadian. Tallboys now rained down on the U-boat pens at Bergen, and the Bielefeld Viaduct. In common with most bridges, the latter proved singularly hard to hit, and 54 Tallboys were aimed at it during February 1945 without result. But now Barnes Wallis' 22,000lb (10 tonne) Grand Slam was ready for use.

Only the Lancaster B.I Special could carry Grand Slam. This aircraft had strengthened main gear, nose and dorsal turrets deleted, and the bomb doors removed, plus other minor modifications. The crew was reduced to four.

The first Grand Slam raid took place on 14 March 1945, as related earlier. Five days later, six Grand Slams and 13 Tallboys were hauled to the rail viaduct at Arnsberg, where, incredibly, every bomb fell within a 600ft (180m)

radius. To underline the astounding level of bombing accuracy, when the bridge at Nienberg was attacked on 22 March, the first four aircraft sent in to bomb scored direct hits from a Grand Slam at one end and a Tallboy at the other, and lifted the entire centre span into the air, where it was hit straight in the middle by another Tallboy!

The final mission was against Berchtesgaden, Hitler's redoubt

One more bridge was smashed, then the U-boat pens at Farge were attacked. Two Grand Slams went clean through the 23ft (7m) thick reinforced concrete roof and exploded inside, while shock waves from 10 near misses shattered the foundation. 617 Squadron's final

Above: Lancasters of No. 101 Squadron were identifiable by their Air-borne Cigar masts. This one is unloading incendiaries.

mission was against Berchtesgaden, Hitler's southern redoubt, in the final days of the war.

There was one other special Lancaster squadron, No. 101, whose aircraft, aerials, carried the top secret ABC (Air-borne Cigar) from October 1943. ABC was a jammer working on the German night fighter frequency, and required an additional member of crew to operate it. Lancasters of No. 101 Squadron carried a full load of bombs and, scattered throughout the bomber stream, accompanied Main Force on nearly every raid. In the later stages of the war, with multi-pronged raids the norm, 101 became the biggest Lancaster squadron of all, with a final complement of 42 aircraft.

APPENDIX
THE LANCASTER FAMILY

Although built in large numbers and with many variants, the Lancaster's external appearance changed little during its production, and its overall dimensions not at all.

LANCASTER MK I

Basic data for the Lancaster given in tabular form in Chapter 2 applies to the Mk I Merlin XX or XXII engines. Production continued past the end of the war, and the final Lancaster ever built was a Mk I. Many were later fitted with H2S, others had bulged bomb bay doors to allow them to carry 8,000 and 12,000lb (3,600 and 5,440kg) HC bombs.

Above: Lancaster Mk I raided Nuremberg and Dresden while with No. 170 Squadron. It is seen here post-war, testing tyres for Dunlop.

LANCASTER MK I VARIANTS

Provisioning Lancasters used on the Dams Raid were converted Mk Is. Mk I Special was designed to carry 22,000lb (10 tonne) Grand Slam with a maximum overload weight of 70,000lb (31,750kg). No nose or mid-upper turret. Only 32 built. Mk I (FE) intended for the Far East against Japan, but the war ended before they could arrive. Internal fuel capacity was increased to 2,554 gallons (11,600 litres); range with 7,000lb (3,175kg) bomb-load 3,180 miles (5,100km); FN 82 rear turrets were standard.

Right: A saddle tank was designed to increase fuel capacity for Far East operations, but in high temperatures, take-off became marginal.

LANCASTER MK II

Powered by four Bristol Hercules VI or XVI 14 cylinder radial engines each rated at 1,735hp. Rate of climb was about five per cent less than that of the Mks I and III; service ceiling was lower at 22,000ft (6,700m); maximum and cruising speeds were rather lower, mainly due to the extra drag of the radial engines. Range with 12,000lb (5,440kg) was 1,000 miles (1,600km). Maximum overload weight was 63,000lb (28,600kg).

Right: Lancaster IIs of No. 408 'Goose' Squadron RCAF based at Linton-on-Ouse in October 1943.

LANCASTER MK III

Identical to the Mk I, the main difference being Packard-built Rolls-Royce Merlin 28s or 38s. These were popular with the engine fitters because of the lavish tool kits provided by the Americans. As with the Mk I, bulged bomb bay doors and H₂S were often fitted. Many late-build aircraft carried the Rose-Rice tail turret.

Above: The Lancaster Mk III was virtually indentical to the Mk I.

LANCASTER MK IV AND V

Essentially a stretched Lancaster, longer, with greater wingspan, and better performance, the Mks IV and V differed so much that they were renamed Lincoln B.1 and B.2

Below: The Lancaster Mk IV and V were so different from the original that they were renamed Lincoin B.1 and B.2.

LANCASTER MK VI

Nine aircraft only, converted from Mk Is and IIIs, used in the Pathfinder and ECM roles by No. 635 Squadron. Powered by Merlin 85s or 87s rated at 1,635hp enclosed in redesigned cowling, driving four-bladed propellers. Performance was significantly better than that of the Mk III. No production undertaken.

LANCASTER MK VII

Final production variant. Martin mid-upper and Rose-Rice tail turrets. Entered service April 1945. A few Mk VII (FE)s were built.

Above: The final production variant was the Mk VII, with .50in guns in mid-upper and tail turrets. This is a Mk VII (FE) intended for Tiger Force.

Above: The engine cowlings to the merlin 85/87s on the Mk VI differed from those of earlier models.

LANCASTER MK X

Above: The Mk X was a Canadian-built Mk III. This machine, seen at the Malton works still minus its mid-upper turret, served with No. 428 'Ghost' Squadron RCAF.

POSTWAR LANCASTER CONVERSIONS

ASR III, Mk III converted for air-sea rescue with an airborne lifeboat fitted to the bomb bay, and ASV radar. Dorsal turret was removed, and guns removed from rear turret. Small windows to both sides of rear fuselage. Re-engined with Merlin 224s.

Above: Conversion to ASR III standard, with paradroppable airborne lifeboat.

GR III/MR III, Mk III converted for general reconnaissance or maritime reconnaissance similar to ASR III, but no lifeboat.

PR I, Mk I converted for photo reconnaissance/survey work. All gun turrets were removed and faired over.

Above: Experimental ASV radar aerial mounting, intended for use in the anti-shipping role.

Above: Into the jet age. This Mk II spent its life at the RAE Farnborough as a test bed for early jet engines.

The end of the war saw dozens of Bomber Command Lancaster Squadrons disbanded and hundreds of aircraft scrapped, but this did not prevent another 21 squadrons from other RAF commands operating the type. Some other countries used them too; Canada took many of her Lancasters home, while the French Aeronavale acquired a considerable number for maritime reconnaissance and search and rescue, some of which remained in service up until the early Sixties. Other users were Argentina and Egypt.

In Britain the writing was on the wall. The Lincoln largely replaced the Lancaster in the few remaining front line bomber squadrons, and the last RAF Lancaster, an MR III, was retired in February 1954.

Above: Jet Age II; a Canadian Mk X-DC drone carrier, with Ryan Firebees beneath the wingtips.

Right: This propeller from a shot-down Lancaster of No. 12 Squadron makes a fitting memorial at Dronten in Holland.

PROLOGUE

Above: Me 109Es of Gerhard Schoepfel's unit, IIIrd Gruppe of Fighter Geschwader 26, pictured in their camouflaged dispersal points at Caffiers near Calais during the Battle of Britain.

Oberleutnant Gerhard Schoepfel was flying his favourite type of mission. He had eight aerial victories to his credit already, and was leading a free hunting patrol 4 miles (6.5km) high over southern England. It was the sort of mission that did not come his way often enough. With some 25 Me 109Es of IIIrd Gruppe of Fighter Geschwader 26 arrayed in battle formation behind and above him, he felt invincible. His task was to clear a path in front of raiding formations making for the important Fighter Command airfields at Kenley and Biggin Hill. The nearest bombers were some 20 miles (32km) behind him, and they were not his concern. Today, others had the frustrating task of flying close escort for the slow-flying Dorniers and Heinkels to ward off attacks by the Spitfires and Hurricanes. Schoepfel's role was

that of a hunter, pure and simple. His orders were to engage and destroy any British fighters he found, and he had complete tactical freedom to do so in any way he chose. Over enemy territory, the German pilot's practised eyes quartered the sky continually and systematically, seeking out his quarry.

■ COVER THE LEADER ■

"Suddenly I noticed a Staffel of Hurricanes underneath me. They were using the English tactics of the period, flying in close formation of threes, climbing in a wide

Above: Oberleutnant Gerhard Schoepfel. At the end of the war, he was credited with 40 aerial victories. (Schoepfel)

spiral. About 1,000m above them I turned with them and managed to get behind the two covering Hurricanes, which were weaving continually."

In deciding his tactics, Schoepfel knew it was important to retain the element of surprise for as long as possible. Several aircraft diving to attack would almost certainly be spotted. But a single aircraft might sneak unobserved into a firing position behind the enemy fighters. The German ace ordered his pilots to remain at high altitude and cover him, while he delivered a lone attack on the formation from out of the sun. The Hurricanes, belonging to No. 501 Squadron were climbing into position to engage the bomber formations nearing the coast. Picking up speed rapidly in the dive, Schoepfel remained unseen as he swung behind one of the two 'weaver' Hurricanes covering the rear of the formation. He placed his sighting graticule over the fighter, loosed off an accurate burst and saw it go down in flames. Then he pulled to one side and repeated the process with the second 'weaver'. Still the formation

continued on its ponderous way. The German pilot moved in behind the main formation, fired again and a third Hurricane fell out of the sky.

"The Englishmen continued on their way having noticed nothing. So I pulled behind a fourth machine and took care of him also. But this time I went in too close. When I pressed the firing button, the Englishman was such a short distance in front of my nose that pieces of wreckage struck my propeller. Oil streaming back from the fourth plane spattered over my windscreen and the right side of the cabin, so that I could see nothing. I had to break off the action."

Finally aware of their peril, the surviving Hurricanes broke formation and turned to engage the Messerschmitts diving to support their leader. There followed an inconclusive dogfight without loss to either side. Within a space of four minutes Gerhard Schoepfel, single-handed, had destroyed a third of a squadron of Hurricanes. One pilot was killed, and the other three jumped from their stricken aircraft and landed safely by parachute. In the summer of 1940, both the Luftwaffe and the Me 109 were at the peak of their effectiveness relative to the air forces and fighter types opposing them. Only the Spitfire was as fast as the German fighter, while all the other fighters it encountered in action were a good deal slower. It was a clear indication of Schoepfel's unbounded confidence in his aircraft and his ability that, alone and without hesitation, he took on an entire enemy squadron and emerged victorious from the encounter. Small wonder the very name of Messerschmitt was one that struck fear in Germany's enemies throughout the whole of the Second World War.

Right: The tail of Gerhard Schoepfel's aircraft photographed on the afternoon of 18 August 1940, including the victory bars for the four Hurricanes of No. 501 Squadron.

MESSERSCHMITT Me 109G-14

1   Starboard navigation light
2   Starboard wingtip
3   Fixed trim tab
4   Starboard Frise-type aileron
5   Flush-riveted stressed
    wing-skinning
6   Handley Page leading-edge
    automatic slot
7   Slot control linkage
8   Slot equalizer rod
9   Aileron control linkage
10 Fabric-covered flap section
11 Wheel fairing
12 Port fuselage machine-gun
    ammunition-feed fairing
13 Port Rheinmetall-Borsig
    13mm MG 131
    machine-gun
14 Engine accessories
15 Starboard machine-gun
    trough
16 Daimler-Benz DB 605AM
    12-cylinder inverted-vee
    liquid-cooled engine
17 Detachable cowling panel
18 Oil filter access
19 Oil tank
20 Propeller pitch-change
    mechanism
21 VDM electrically operated
    constant-speed propeller
22 Spinner
23 Engine-mounted
    cannon muzzle
24 Blast tube
25 Propeller hub
26 Spinner back plate
27 Auxiliary cooling intakes
28 Cooling header tank
29 Anti-vibration rubber engine
    mounting pads
30 Elektron forged engine bearer
31 Engine bearer support
    strut attachment
32 Plug leads
33 Exhaust manifold fairing strip
34 Ejector exhausts
35 Cowling fasteners
36 Oil cooler
37 Oil cooler intake
38 Starboard mainwheel
39 Oil cooler outlet flap
40 Wing root fillet
41 Wing/fuselage fairing
42 Firewall/bulkhead
43 Supercharger air intake
44 Supercharger assembly
45 20mm cannon
    magazine drum

46 13mm machine-gun
    ammunition feed
47 Engine bearer upper
    attachment
48 Ammunition feed fairing
49 13mm Rheinmetall-Borsig
    MG 131 machine-gun
    breeches
50 Instrument panel
51 20mm Mauser MG 151/20
    cannon breech
52 Heelrests
53 Rudder pedals
54 Undercarriage emergency
    retraction cables
55 Fuselage frame
56 Wing/fuselage fairing
57 Undercarriage emergency
    retraction headwheel
    (outboard)
58 Tail trim handwheel
    (inboard)

59 Seat harness
60 Throttle lever
61 Control column
62 Cockpit ventilation inlet
63 Revi 16B reflector
    gunsight (folding)
64 Armoured windshield frame
65 Anti-glare gunsight screen
66 90mm armourglass
    windscreen
67 Galland-type clear-vision
    hinged canopy

68 Framed armourglass
    head/back panel
69 Canopy contoured frame
70 Canopy hinges (starboard)
71 Canopy release catch
72 Pilot's bucket-type seat
    (8mm back armour)
73 Underfloor contoured fuel
    tank (88 imp gal/400 litres
    of 87 octane B4)
74 Fuselage frame
75 Circular access panel

134 Spar/fuselage lower pin
joint (vertical)
135 Flaps equalizer rod
136 Rüstsatz R3 auxiliary fuel
tank ventral rack
137 Undercarriage electrical
interlock
138 Wing horizontal pin
forward pick-up
139 Undercarriage retraction
jack mechanism
140 Undercarriage pivot-bevel
141 Auxiliary fuel tank
(Rüstsatz R3) of 66 imp gal
(3,000 litre) capacity
142 Mainwheel leg fairing
143 Mainwheel oleo leg
144 Brake lines
145 Mainwheel fairing
146 Port mainwheel
147 Leading-edge skin
148 Port mainwheel well
149 Wing spar
150 Flap actuating linkage
151 Fabric-covered control
surfaces
152 Slotted flap structure
153 Leading-edge slot
actuating mechanism
154 Slot equalizer rod
155 Handley Page automatic
leading-edge slot
156 Wing stringers
157 Spar flange decrease
158 Wing ribs
159 Flush-riveted stressed
wing- skinning
160 Metal-framed Frise-type
aileron
161 Fixed trim tab
162 Wingtip construction
163 Port navigation light
164 Angled pitot head
165 Rüstsatz R6 optional
underwing cannon gondola
166 14-point plug connection
167 Electrical junction box
168 Cannon rear mounting
bracket
169 20mm Mauser
MG 151 20mm cannon
170 Cannon front
mounting bracket
171 Ammunition feed chute
172 Ammunition magazine drum
173 Underwing panel
174 Gondola fairing
175 Cannon barrel

93 Tail trimming cables
94 Tailfin root fairing
95 Starboard fixed tailplane
96 Elevator balance
97 Starboard elevator
98 Geared elevator tab
99 All-wooden tailfin
construction
100 Aerial attachment
101 Rudder upper hinge bracket
102 Rudder post
103 Fabric-covered wooden
rudder structure
104 Geared rudder tab
105 Rear navigation light
106 Port elevator
107 Geared elevator tab
108 Tailplane structure
109 Rudder actuating linkage
110 Elevator control horn
111 Elevator connecting rod
112 Elevator control quadrant
113 Tailwheel leg cuff
114 Castoring non-retractable
tailwheel
115 Lengthened tailwheel/leg
116 Access panel
117 Tailwheel shock-strut
118 Lifting point
119 Rudder cable
120 Elevator cables
121 First-aid pack
122 Air bottles
123 Fuselage access panel
124 Bottom keel
(connector stringer)
125 Ventral IFF aerial
126 Master compass
127 Elevator control linkage
128 Wing root fillet
129 Camber-changing flap
130 Ducted coolant radiator
131 Wing stringers
132 Wing rear pick-up point
133 Spar/fuselage upper pin
joint (horizontal)

76 Tail trimming cable
conduit
77 Wireless leads
78 MW50 (methanel/water)
tank (25 imp gal/114 litres
capacity)
79 Handhold
80 Fuselage decking
81 Aerial mast
82 D/F loop
83 Oxygen cylinders (three)
84 Filler pipe
85 Wireless equipment packs
(FuG 16ZY communications
and FuG 25a IFF)
86 Main fuel filler cap
87 Aerial
88 Fuselage top keel
(connector stringer)
89 Aerial lead-in
90 Fuselage skin plating sections
91 U-stringers
92 Fuselage frames
(monocoque construction)

The story of the Messerschmitt 109 began in 1934, more than a year before the German government revealed the existence of the clandestine air force that it had built up. Early that year, the Air Ministry issued a requirement for an advanced monoplane fighter to replace the Heinkel 51 and Arado 68 biplanes then about to enter service, and invited aircraft companies to submit designs.

The early 1930s saw rapid advances in aviation technology, which revealed themselves most clearly in the design of fighter planes. The new generation of fighters was quite different in shape and performance from those that had gone before. Out went the fabric-covered strut-braced biplane with its open cockpit and fixed undercarriage. In its place came the sleek low-wing monoplane with an all-metal structure, enclosed cockpit and a retractable undercarriage. These new fighters were much faster than their predecessors in the climb, in the dive and in level flight. Also, in their developed versions, they were more heavily armed.

Chief designer Willi Messerschmitt had no previous experience of designing fighter aircraft

At that time, the Bavarian Aircraft Company (Bayerische Flugzeugwerke) at Augsburg was a little-known aircraft firm with about 500 employees. It had never built a military aircraft of its own design, though it was turning out small batches of planes built under licence for the Luftwaffe. Willi Messerschmitt, the company's brilliant young chief designer, had no previous experience of designing a fighter. He did have great flair and originality, however, and he was very ambitious. When he saw the Luftwaffe requirement he jumped at the chance to turn his hand to a state-of-the-art fighter plane.

Messerschmitt's new fighter employed almost every innovation of the period. It was a clean-lined all-metal low-wing monoplane with a retractable undercarriage and an enclosed cockpit. To keep the landing speed to reasonable limits, the small wing was fitted with retractable flaps and leading-edge slots. Messerschmitt designed the fighter around the new 610hp Junkers Jumo 210 engine. Work on the airframe advanced more rapidly than that on the power plant, however, and it was clear that the latter would not be ready in time. Messerschmitt had to look elsewhere for an engine to get his prototype into the air. Ironically, in view of later events, his choice of engine was a 695hp Rolls-Royce Kestrel imported from Great Britain.

Opposite: Ground crewmen pictured reloading the wing and engine-mounted 7.9mm machine-guns of a 'Caesar' of IIIrd Gruppe of Fighter Geschwader 51. Scrupulous cleanliness was necessary for this operation, since any grit or dirt on the rounds was liable to cause a stoppage during firing. *Below:* The first prototype Me 109 ground-running its Rolls-Royce Kestrel engine, at about the time of its maiden flight in September 1935. (via Ethell)

MESSERSCHMITT 109 B-1

Type Single-seat interceptor fighter

Armament Two Rheinmetall-Borsig 7.9mm machine-guns mounted on top of the engine and synchronized to fire through the airscrew (500 rounds per gun)

Power plant One Junkers Jumo 210 Da inverted V-12 liquid-cooled engine developing 635hp for take-off

Dimensions Span 32ft 4½in (9.87m); length 28ft (8.55m)

Weight Normal operational take-off 4,741lb (2,150kg)

Performance Maximum speed 289mph at 13,100ft (465km/hr at 4,000m); service ceiling 26,900ft (8,200m)

MESSERSCHMITT 109 C-1

Type Single-seat interceptor fighter

Armament Four Rheinmetall-Borsig MG 17 7.9mm machine-guns; two synchronized to fire through the airscrew (500 rounds per gun), two mounted in wings (420rpg)

Power plant Junkers Jumo 210 Ga inverted V-12 liquid-cooled engine developing 700hp for take-off; this and subsequent versions were fitted with direct fuel injection engines

Dimensions Span 32ft 4in (9.87m); length 28ft (8.55m)

Weight Normal operational take-off 5,060lb (2,295kg)

Performance Maximum speed 292mph (470km/hr) at 14,770ft (4,500m); service ceiling 27,570ft (8,400m)

Initially called the Bayerische Flugzeugwerke (Bf) 109, the new fighter made its maiden flight in September 1935. That was one month before the prototype Hurricane, and six months before the prototype Spitfire – its two main rivals during the early part of the forthcoming conflict.

The Arado, Heinkel and Focke Wulf companies also built prototypes of monoplane fighters for the Luftwaffe design competition. Messerschmitt's more ambitious design quickly demonstrated that it had a clear edge over the other three, however. Its maximum speed of 290mph (467km/hr) was 17mph (27km/hr) faster than that of its nearest rival, and its handling characteristics were also superior.

Below: Line-up of early-production Me 109 'Bertas' awaiting delivery at the Bayerische Flugzeugwerke factory at Augsburg early in 1937. At this time, this aircraft was the most potent fighter in service anywhere in the world. (via Schliephake)

Above: **An Me 109 'Caesar' of Fighter Gruppe 152.**

■ **INTO PRODUCTION** ■

Following the service trials, the Luftwaffe placed an order for ten more Me 109 prototypes. A second prototype, powered by the Jumo 210A engine, joined the test programme in January 1936. In the autumn of 1936, the Luftwaffe announced that the Me 109 was to be its standard single-engined fighter type. The Me 109B, the 'Berta', was the initial production variant. It was powered by the Jumo 210 engine and carried an armament of three (later four) 7.9mm machine-guns.

In February 1937, production Me 109Bs began emerging from the Augsburg factory. The first Luftwaffe unit to receive the new fighter was IInd

Gruppe of Fighter Geschwader 132 based at Jueterbog near Berlin.

Early in 1938, the next major version of the Me 109 appeared, the Me 109C 'Caesar'. This featured several detailed improvements, and its Jumo 210 engine was fitted with fuel injection. The initial version carried four machine-guns, two on top of the engine and one in each wing close to the root. The 'Caesar' was built in moderately large numbers, and the variant equipped several fighter units.

MESSERSCHMITT 109 D-1

Type Single-seat interceptor fighter

Armament Two Rheinmetall-Borsig MG 17 7.9mm machine-guns mounted on top of the engine synchronized to fire through the airscrew (500 rounds per gun); one Oerlikon MG FF 20mm cannon mounted under the engine and firing through the spinner (60 rounds)

Power plant One Daimler-Benz DB 600Aa inverted V-12 liquid-cooled engine developing 986hp for take-off

Dimensions Span 32ft 4in (9.87m); length 28ft 2in (8.60m)

Weight Normal operational take-off 5,336lb (2,420kg)

Performance Maximum speed 356mph (574km/hr) at 11,490ft (3,500m); service ceiling 32,800ft (10,000m)

Following hard on the heels of the 'Caesar' came the Me 109D 'Dora'. This was fitted with the new Daimler-Benz 600 engine which developed 960 horse power. The more powerful engine gave

The fine performance of the 'Dora' was undermined by difficulties with the DB 600 engine

greatly enhanced performance, and the 'Dora' could achieve a maximum speed of 356mph at 11,400ft (574km/hr at 3,500m). This variant also had greater fire power than its predecessors, with a 20mm cannon firing through the propeller spinner and two machine-guns mounted on top of the engine cowling. The DB 600 engine suffered serious teething troubles, however, and despite its fine performance, the 'Dora' was not

MESSERSCHMITT 109 E-1

Type Single-seat general-purpose fighter

Armament Four Rheinmetall-Borsig MG 17 7.9mm machine-guns in fuselage and wings; or two MG17 machine-guns and two MG FF cannon; some aircraft were modified to carry a rack for a single 110lb (45kg) bomb

Power plant One Daimler-Benz DB 601A inverted V-12 liquid-cooled engine developing 1,175hp for take-off

Dimensions Span 32ft 4in (9.87m); length 28ft 4in (8.64m)

Weight Normal operational take-off 5,535lb (2,510kg)

Performance Maximum speed 356mph at 13,130ft (573km/hr at 4,000m); service ceiling 34,450ft (10,500m)

Above: The Heinkel 51 biplane was the main fighter type serving with the Condor Legion during the early stages of the Civil War in Spain. It was outclassed by the Soviet-built fighter types that it came up against.

popular with pilots. Fewer than 200 were built before this variant passed out of production.

In September 1938, the so-called Munich Crisis broke, as a result of Adolf Hitler's claim that the Sudetenland area of Czechoslovakia should be incorporated into Germany. For a time, it seemed that Great Britain might go to war to help the Czechs retain this territory, but in the end the British prime minister Neville Chamberlain acceded to Hitler's demand. Several commentators have said that the move was necessary to allow Britain time to re-arm. They neglect the fact that the Luftwaffe, too, was in no state to engage in a major conflict. Its fighter force possessed 583 Me 109s of all versions, of which 510 were serviceable. Most of these aircraft were the 'Bertas', with smaller numbers

of the later 'Caesar' and 'Dora' variants. Eight fighter Gruppen had equipped or were in the process of re-equipping with the Me 109. The rest operated outdated biplane fighter types. The Luftwaffe bomber force was no better placed to fight a major war. At the time, many people were frightened by the barrage of misleading German propaganda regarding the size and invincibility of the Luftwaffe. Even now, in the present-day 21st century, these canards are still repeated.

The next version of the Me 109, the first built in really large numbers, was the 'Emil' powered by the new Daimler-Benz 601 engine. Based on the DB 600 engine that powered the 'Dora', the new engine was fitted with fuel injection and a more effective supercharger. Most important of all, it was far more reliable than the earlier engine. The initial batches of Me 109Es reached the Luftwaffe early in 1939. The main production version was armed with two 7.9mm machine-guns in the fuselage and two 20mm cannon in the wings.

■ MESSERSCHMITT AG ■

With the success of the new fighter assured, the management of the Bayerische Flugzeugwerke decided to capitalize on the international reputation won by its now-famous chief designer, and so they appointed Willi Messerschmitt to the posts of Chairman and Managing Director, and changed the company's name to Messerschmitt AG. The firm's two factories were turning out the fighter in large numbers, yet there were insufficient numbers to meet the needs of the expanding Luftwaffe. Four other aircraft companies, Arado, Erla, Fieseler and Focke Wulf, were producing the Me 109E under licence. Production of the fighter reached 130 per month, and it quickly replaced most of the earlier versions in front-line units.

■ IN ACTION IN SPAIN ■

In the summer of 1936, civil war broke out in Spain. General Franco, the Nationalist leader, appealed to Adolf Hitler for help in his revolt against the left-wing government. This was soon forthcoming, and the Luftwaffe dispatched a force, the Condor Legion, to fight alongside the Nationalists. Meanwhile, the Soviet Union had been supplying aircraft to Spain's Republican government. When the Luftwaffe began operations over Spain, its pilots found that the Soviet-built Polikarpov I-16 monoplane had a clear edge in performance over their Heinkel 51 biplanes.

The new 109s of the Condor Legion were operated from a primitive airfield near Seville

---

Generalmajor Hugo Sperrle, the commander of the Condor Legion, impressed on his superiors the need to get Me 109s into the theatre as rapidly as possible. To test the new fighter under combat conditions, late in 1936 the Luftwaffe shipped three Me 109 prototypes to Spain. These operated from a primitive airfied near Seville, and there were severe problems. Each of the handmade prototypes had components unique to itself, which made it difficult to keep

Below: **The Soviet Polikarpov I-16 was the best fighter operated by the Nationalist Air Force in Spain. It was clearly superior to the He 51, and came as a shock to the German pilots when they first met it over Spain.**

them serviceable. After a few weeks, and without seeing action, the fighters returned to Germany.

■ THE 109 TRIUMPHS ■

The trial highlighted the need for better ground support for the Me 109, if it was to perform effectively in action. Several Luftwaffe pilots flew the prototypes in Spain, and they had no doubt that the Me 109 was superior to any of the Soviet-built fighters opposing them.

As noted in the previous chapter, production Me 109 'Bertas' began to emerge from the Augsburg factory in February 1937. Sixteen of these machines were loaded in crates on a freighter which delivered them to the Condor Legion.

The first unit in Spain to re-equip with the Me 109B was the 2nd Staffel of Fighter Gruppe 88. When it became operational in April 1937 there was a lull in the ground fighting, and initially the new fighter saw little action. Then, in July, the Republican forces launched a powerful offensive near Madrid. The Me 109 Staffel joined the battle, escorting Junkers 52 bombers delivering attacks on Republican troop positions.

As predicted, the Me 109 proved greatly superior to the Soviet-built I-16. It was faster in level flight, had a higher operational ceiling and was much faster in the dive. For its part, the I-16 was more manoeuvrable, especially at altitudes below 10,000ft (3,048m). Republican fighter pilots tried to lure the Messerschmitts into turning fights below 10,000ft, but with little success. German fighter pilots soon learned that their machine's better performance at altitude gave them the advantage of being able to accept or refuse combat, as they chose.

The new German fighter carried radios which might have been very useful during air-to-air actions. The sets gave such poor reception, however, that many pilots flew with them turned off.

The Me 109s would deliver a series of high-speed diving attacks to break up the enemy

---

Normally the Me 109s would patrol at altitudes between 16,000ft (4,877m) and 20,000ft (6,096m), which gave them a substantial height advantage over their opponents. On sighting enemy aircraft, the German formation leader would usually move his force into an attacking position above the prey. The Messerschmitts then delivered a series of high-speed diving attacks, pulling up and zooming back to altitude after each. They repeated the process until the

Above: **The arrival of the Me 109B in Spain in the spring of 1937 gave German pilots a machine in which they could engage the I-16 with confidence. This example belonged to 2nd Staffel of Fighter Gruppe 88, and wears the markings carried by aircraft of the Condor Legion.**

enemy formation broke up, or the German fighters ran low on fuel or ammunition. Provided the Me 109s maintained their high speed and did not get drawn into turning fights, they were almost unbeatable.

Some of the fiercest aerial fighting over Spain took place early in 1938, during the Republican offensive near Teruél. By then both Staffeln of Fighter Gruppe 88 had re-equipped with the Me 109. On 7 February, Hauptmann Gotthardt Handrick, the Gruppe commander, was leading his unit during a bomber escort mission. Over the battle area he sighted a formation of 22 Soviet-built Tupolev SB-2 bombers moving in to attack a Nationalist troop position. Seeing no Republican fighters in the area, he led a concerted attack on the enemy bombers.

Several of the latter were shot down, and when I-16s finally arrived on the scene, they too suffered losses. The Me 109s destroyed ten enemy bombers and two fighters, without loss to themselves.

Elsewhere that day, another Me 109 pilot fought a noteworthy action.

Leutnant Wilhelm Balthasar shot down three bombers and a fighter within six minutes

Leutnant Wilhelm Balthasar delivered a succession of diving attacks on an escorted bomber formation and short down three bombers and a fighter, all within a space of six minutes.

The Me 109 achieved striking success over Spain, although the number of these fighters sent to fight in the conflict was never large. Up to December 1938, only 55 'Bertas', 'Caesars' and 'Doras' had reached Spain and only 37 were currently on the strength of Fighter Gruppe 88. However, such was the 109's superiority that these few aircraft had been sufficient to establish air supremacy over the entire country.

In March 1939, after suffering a succession of major reverses, the Republicans were forced to surrender. Following the cessation of hostilities, the Condor Legion returned home to Germany, leaving behind some 50 Me 109s for incorporation in General Franco's Air Force.

■ POISED FOR POLAND ■

By the summer of 1939, Adolf Hitler judged that he had gained as much as he could in Europe by bluff alone. To advance his aims further, he would have to demonstrate Germany's military might and commit its armed forces. Now his forces were poised to launch an all-out onslaught against Poland. In the next chapter, we shall observe how the Me 109 units fared during the early months of the Second World War.

On 1 September 1939, German ground forces invaded Poland, with powerful support from the Luftwaffe. At that time, the Me 109 force comprised 24 Gruppen and five independent Staffeln, with a total of nearly 1,100 fighters. More than two-thirds of the units flew the 'Emil'; the rest operated the older 'Berta', 'Caesar' and 'Dora' versions.

Only about one-fifth of the Me 109 force, five of the 24 Gruppen operating the type, was earmarked to take part in the campaign in Poland. The other units remained at their airfields in western Germany, ready to meet a possible onslaught from the Royal Air Force and the French Air Force. There was no large-scale Allied reaction, however, and the German fighters saw little action. The relatively small proportion of Me 109s assigned to support the attack on Poland proved quite sufficient to counter the meagre forces at the disposal of the Polish Air Force. The latter possessed only about 300 combat planes, almost all of them outdated types. The PZL 11, the most modern Polish fighter type then in service, had a maximum speed of only 242mph (389km/hr). It was no match even for the early versions of the Me 109. After a few days, the Polish Air Force was out of the fight, and unable to give any assistance to its hardpressed army. Two weeks into the campaign, the Luftwaffe felt sufficiently confident to move two Me 109 Gruppen from Poland to bolster the air defences in the west. On 28 September, the Polish forces laid down their arms and the campaign came to an end.

In the west, the aerial activity was on a small scale, as each side probed the other's strengths and weaknesses. On 30 September, the Royal Air Force learned a

Left: Instrument panel of an Me 109 'Emil'. Although the cockpit was cramped and the view of the outside restricted, pilots came to love the machine as a highly capable air superiority fighter.

Me 109 FRONT-LINE UNITS, 2 SEPTEMBER 1939

Unit	Aircraft total	Aircraft serviceable
Tactical Development Division		
Tactical Development (Lehr) Geschwader 2		
Staff Flight	3	3 Me 109E*
I. Gruppe	36	34 Me 109E*
10. Staffel	12	9 Me 109E
Air Fleet 1 (NE Germany)		
Fighter Geschwader 1		
I. Gruppe	54	54 Me 109E*
Fighter Geschwader 2		
II. Gruppe	42	39 Me 109E
10. Staffel	9	9 Me 109C, night-fighting unit
Fighter Geschwader 3		
Staff Flight	3	3 Me 109E
I. Gruppe	48	42 Me 109E
Fighter Geschwader 20		
I. Gruppe	21	20 Me 109E
Fighter Geschwader 21		
I. Gruppe	29	28 Me 109C and E*
Destroyer Geschwader 1		
II. Gruppe	36	36 Me 109B* (a)
Destroyer Geschwader 2		
I. Gruppe	44	40 Me 109D* (a)
Air Fleet 2 (NW Germany)		
Fighter Geschwader 26		
I. Gruppe	48	48 Me 109E
II. Gruppe	48	44 Me 109E
10. Staffel	10	8 Me 109C, night-fighting unit
Destroyer Geschwader 26		
I. Gruppe	52	46 Me 109B and D (a)
II. Gruppe	48	47 Me 109B and D (a)
III. Gruppe	48	44 Me 109B and C (a)
Air Fleet 3 (SW Germany)		
Fighter Geschwader 51		
I. Gruppe	47	39 Me 109E
Fighter Geschwader 52		
I. Gruppe	39	34 Me 109E
Fighter Geschwader 53		
I. Gruppe	51	39 Me 109E
II. Grupp	43	41 Me 109E
Fighter Geschwader 70		
I. Gruppe	24	24 Me 109E
Fighter Geschwader 71		
I. Gruppe	39	18 Me 109C and E
Destroyer Geschwader 52		
I. Gruppe	44	43 Me 109B (a)
Air Fleet 4 (SE Germany)		
Fighter Geschwader 76		
I. Gruppe	49	45 Me 109E
Fighter Geschwader 77		
I. Gruppe	50	43 Me 109E
II. Gruppe	50	36 Me 109E
Destroyer Geschwader 76		
II. Gruppe	40	39 Me 109B and C
Assigned to German Navy		
Traegergruppe 186		
5., 6. Staffeln	24	24 Me 109C (b)

(a) These units had been formed to operate the Me 110 twin-engined fighter, but until these became available they operated Me 109s.
(b) Unit operating standard Me 109Cs, formed to train pilots earmarked to operate the Me 109T from the aircraft carrier *Graf Zeppelin* when she was completed.
* Units marked with an asterisk took part in the campaign in Poland.

IN ACTION OVER FRANCE

"Relatively few Me 109s were lost in combat and only at the end of the campaign, during the Dunkirk evacuation, was there much in the way of fighter-versus-fighter combat. During the campaign in France it was difficult to compare our [Me] 109 with the French Morane or Curtiss fighters, because I never had a dogfight with either of them. I saw only one Morane during the entire campaign and it was disappearing in the distance. Our Geschwader had very little dogfighting experience until the Dunkirk action, where we met the Royal Air Force for the first time in numbers. Our pilots came back with the highest respect for the [new] enemy."

OBERLEUTNANT JULIUS NEUMANN, ME 109 PILOT, FIGHTER GESCHWADER 27

Above: Me 109 'Emil' of Fighter Geschwader 27 pictured early in the war. The oversized markings on the wings were to assist recognition, following a series of incidents when aircraft had been engaged in error by 'friendly' forces.

hard lesson when five Fairey Battle light bombers flew a daylight armed reconnaissance mission over the Saarbrucken area. Me 109s of Fighter Geschwader 53 intercepted the force and shot down four bombers without loss to themselves. Towards the end of the year, the Me 109 again showed its effectiveness as a bomber-destroyer. On 18 December 1939, a force of Vickers Wellingtons flew an armed reconnaissance mission off the coast near Wilhelmshaven, intending to attack any German warships located at sea. The 24 bombers flew in close formation and depended on their combined

crossfire to deter fighter attacks. Thirty-four Me 109s, drawn from Fighter Geschwader 26 and 77 and Destroyer Geschwader 1, engaged the bombers, together with 16 Me 110s. The German fighters pressed home their attacks despite heavy return fire, and shot down 12 of the Wellingtons. Two more bombers suffered such severe damage that they crashed on landing. For their part, the Wellingtons' gunners shot down only two Me 109s. After this action, the RAF made the policy decision that in future its attacks on targets in

Germany would take place almost exclusively at night.

On 10 May 1940, German forces launched their long-prepared offensive in the west. By that time there were 1,346 Me 109s serving with the front-line units, of which just over 1,000 were serviceable. Three-quarters of these aircraft were assigned to support

Everywhere the Me 109 reigned supreme, with no effective opposition

the offensive, while the rest remained in position to defend targets in Germany. The Luftwaffe quickly established air superiority over the Dutch, Belgian and French Air Forces, and over the Royal Air Force units based in France. Everywhere, the Me 109 reigned supreme, with no effective fighter opposition. Without hindrance from the air or the ground, Luftwaffe bombers and dive-bombers carried out destructive attacks on airfields and other targets ahead of the fast-moving Panzer thrusts.

At the end of May, the German advances pushed the battle front to within range of RAF fighter units flying from bases in southern England. Only during the Dunkirk evacuation was there any serious fighter-versus-fighter combat.

In the course of the evacuation, the Luftwaffe learned the

Right: A pilot boards his Me 109 'Emil' for a scramble take-off. The aircraft, which bears the 'Scalded Cat' insignia of Fighter Geschwader 20, was pictured during the summer of 1939.

FIRST PHASE OF THE BATTLE OF BRITAIN

Typical of the scrappy actions of the period was that on 13 July, when a convoy of freighters passed through the Strait of Dover. Half a dozen Junkers 87 'Stuka' dive-bombers were attacking the ships when they were engaged by 11 Hurricanes of No. 56 Squadron.

"Unfortunately for them [the Hurricanes], they slid into position directly between the Stukas and our close-escort Messerschmitts. We opened fire, and at once three Hurricanes separated from the formation, two dropping and one gliding down to the water smoking heavily. At that instant I saw a Stuka diving in an attempt to reach the French coast. It was chased by a single Hurricane. Behind the Hurricane was a 109, and behind that, a second Hurricane, all of the fighters firing at the aircraft in front. I saw the deadly dangerous situation and rushed down. There were five aircraft diving in a line towards the water. The Stuka was badly hit and both crewmen wounded, it crashed on the beach near Wissant. The leading Messerschmitt, flown by Feldwebel John, shot down the first Hurricane into the water, its right wing appearing above the waves like the dorsal fin of a shark before it sank. My Hurricane dropped like a stone close to the one that John had shot down."

Major Josef Foezoe, Leading Me 109s Of Fighter Geschwader 51 Escorting the Stukas

[No. 56 Squadron lost two Hurricanes destroyed and two damaged. On the German side, two Ju 87s were seriously damaged, but Fighter Geschwader 51 suffered no losses.]

same hard lesson as that impressed on the RAF earlier: bombers operating by day without fighter escort could expect heavy losses if they came under attack from well-handled enemy fighters. From then on, the Me 109 force would fly an increasingly large proportion of its missions in the fighter escort role.

■ BATTLE OF BRITAIN ■

The Battle of Britain was the first major action in which Me 109s confronted similar numbers of enemy fighters of comparable performance and flown by pilots with equal determination and skill.

During the Battle of Britain, Me 109 fighter units flew three types of opera-tion in support of German bombers. First, and most popular with the German pilots, was the free hunting sweep across enemy territory. Its purpose was to break up the defending fighter formations and chase them out of the area, to clear the sky for a bomber formation coming behind. German pilots assigned to this mission had full tactical freedom to engage and pursue RAF fighters as they wished. Second, and slightly less popular, were the 'intermediate escort' operations. In this case, the fighters stayed with their assigned bomber formation until enemy fighters approached their charges, and only then were they free to break away and go into action. Third, and least popular of all, were the close escort operations which occupied the greater part of the fighter force during any large-scale attack. German fighter units assigned to this role had to remain with their allotted bomber formation at all times. Frequently the Me 109s would drive the Spitfires or Hurricanes away from the bombers, but had then to break off the pursuit and return to positions close to their allocated bomber unit. The British fighters would then return to the

Below: **A pair of 'Emils' in factory markings, probably photographed during a delivery flight to a Luftwaffe aircraft park.**

Me 109 VERSUS SPITFIRE AND HURRICANE

"I cannot compare the Me 109 with the Spitfire or the Hurricane – I never flew either of those. We were told that there was no better fighter in the world than the 109 and we believed it. Why shouldn't we – it was certainly a very effective fighter. We knew that the Spitfire and the Hurricane were good fighters too and thought they might be closely comparable with our aircraft. So everything depended on the tactics used and how experienced and aggressive the pilots were. Of course, the RAF had some young and inexperienced pilots. But we had the feeling that there was a strong backbone of very well-trained and experienced pilots. The longer-serving RAF pilots had considerable flying experience. We in the Luftwaffe did not have this advantage. Very few of those who fought on our side in the Battle of Britain had more than four years' flying experience. Overall, we felt that we were dealing with an aircraft-pilot combination as good as our own."

OBERLEUTNANT JULIUS NEUMANN, ME 109 PILOT, FIGHTER
GESCHWADER 27

Left: Julius Neumann pictured in the cockpit of the Me 109 at the RAF Museum at Hendon in 1979. He recalled, "Immediately I sat in the cockpit I felt at home. Everything came easily to hand. Had the tank been full and there been enough room in front of me, I should have loved to have been allowed to take it up."

fray, and the frustrating process had
to be repeated. From these duels
between the two air forces, the
strengths and weaknesses of the 'Emil',
compared with the Mark I versions of
the Spitfire and the Hurricane, quickly
became evident.

At altitudes above 20,000ft (6,000m),
the 'Emil' was slightly faster in level
flight and in the climb than the Spitfire.
At all altitudes, the German fighter was
much faster than the Hurricane. Below
15,000ft (4,600m), the Spitfire was the

Both the British Spitfire and the Hurricane could out-turn the Messerschmitt 109

---

faster in level flight. Both British fighter
types could out-turn the Me 109 at any
altitude. Me 109 pilots found the fuel
injection system fitted to the Daimler-
Benz 601 gave a useful advantage when
they had a Spitfire or a Hurricane on their
tail. The Messerschmitt pilot would push
down the nose of his fighter and 'bunt'
away from his purser. If an RAF fighter
attempted to follow the manoeuvre, the
negative 'G' shut off the fuel supply from
the float carburetter fitted to the Merlin
engine. There would be an ominous

Me 109 FRONT-LINE UNITS, 7 SEPTEMBER 1940

Unit	Aircraft total	Aircraft serviceable
Air Fleet 2 (Holland, Belgium, NE France)		
Fighter Geschwader 1		
Staff Flight	4	3 Pas de Calais area
Fighter Geschwader 3		
Staff Flight	3	3 Samer
I. Gruppe	23	14 Samer
II. Gruppe	24	21 Samer
III. Gruppe	25	23 Desvres
Fighter Geschwader 26		
Staff Flight	4	3 Audembert
I. Gruppe	27	20 Audembert
II. Gruppe	32	28 Marquise
III. Gruppe	29	26 Caffiers
Fighter Geschwader 27		
Staff Flight	5	4 Etaples
I. Gruppe	33	27 Etaples
II. Gruppe	37	33 Montreuil
III. Gruppe	31	27 Sempy
Fighter Geschwader 51		
Staff Flight	5	4 Saint Omer
I. Gruppe	36	33 Saint Omer, Saint Inglevert
II. Gruppe	22	13 Saint Omer, Saint Inglevert
III. Gruppe	44	31 Saint Omer
Fighter Geschwader 52		
Staff Flight	2	1 Laon/Couvron
I. Gruppe	21	7 Laon/Couvron
II. Gruppe	28	23 Pas de Calais area
III. Gruppe	31	16 Pas de Calais area
Fighter Geschwader 53		
Staff Flight	2	2 Pas de Calais area
II. Gruppe	33	24 Wissant
III. Gruppe	30	22 Pas de Calais area
Fighter Geschwader 54		
Staff Flight	4	2 Holland
I. Gruppe	28	23 Holland
II. Gruppe	35	27 Holland
III. Gruppe	28	23 Holland
Fighter Geschwader 77		
I. Gruppe	42	40 Pas de Calais area
Trials Gruppe 210	26	17 Denain (fighter-bomber unit, also flew Me 110s)
Air Fleet 3 (NW France)		
Fighter Geschwader 2		
Staff Flight	5	2 Beaumont-le-Roger
I. Gruppe	29	24 Beaumont-le-Roger
II. Gruppe	22	18 Beaumont-le-Roger
III. Gruppe	30	19 Le Havre Fighter
Geschwader 53		
I. Gruppe	34	27 Brittany area
Tactical Development (Lehr) Geschwader 2		
II. Gruppe	32	27 Saint Omer (fighter-bomber unit)
Air Fleet 5 (Norway)		
Fighter Geschwader 77		
II. Gruppe	44	35 Southern Norway

WAR DIARY OF 1ST GRUPPE OF
FIGHTER GESCHWADER 3

Diary entry for 15 September 1940, now commemorated as Battle of Britain Day. At the time, this unit was part of Air Fleet 2, based at Samer near Boulogne under the command of Hauptmann Hans von Hahn.

"On 7 September the unit reported a strength of 23 Messerschmitt 109Es of which 14 were serviceable after four weeks of heavy fighting. 1200 [hours, take-off time] Escort (by 12 aircraft) of Do 17s against London. Obit Keller shot down a Spitfire, Leutnant Rohwer a Hurricane. Fw Wollmer dived into the Channel, the impact was seen by Lt Springer. This crash appears not to have been caused by enemy action. After a long dive Vollmer's machine rolled a quarter turn into a vertical dive and he did not succeed in bailing out. A motor boat detached from a German convoy near Cap Gris Nez and went to the scene of the crash. 1510 [hours] Operation by 9 aircraft to escort He 111s against London.

"At 1,500m there was almost total cloud cover. Over the Thames estuary and to the north of London there were gaps in the cloud. During the flight in there was contact with Spitfires. The bombers flew in loose formation to the north of London. Strong and accurate Flak. The Spitfires came from above, fired, and dived away. Hauptmann von Hahn shot down a Spitfire, Lt Rohwer probably destroyed a Hurricane. During an attack by Spitfires Oberleutnant Reumschuessel became separated from his wing man, Obfw Olejnik, and has not returned [this aircraft crashed near Charing, Kent; the pilot bailed out and was taken prisoner]. After he was separated from the formation Obfw Hessel was heard on the radio, but he failed to return [this aircraft crashed near Tenterden; the pilot bailed out and was taken prisoner]. Obfw Buchholz's aircraft was hit in the cooling system and forced down in the Channel. Obit Keller made contact with a rescue aircraft nearby, which picked up Buchholz. He had [minor] injuries and was taken to the military hospital at Boulogne. The body of Lt Kloiber has been washed ashore near St Cecile, and buried. Lt Meckel and 2 feldwebels attended the funeral. During the last few days news has been received from the Red Cross in Geneva that Obit Tiedmann, Obit Rau, Obit Loidolt, Lt Landry (these last two wounded) and Obfe Lamskemper have been captured by the British."

Scenes at the airfield at Caffiers near Calais, home of the Me 109 'Emils' of IIIrd Gruppe of Fighter Geschwader 26 during the Battle of Britain. The photos come from the personal album of Gerhard Schoepfel. *Top right:* **Engine change of a fighter in the open.** *Middle left:* **Ground crewmen constructing a sandbag blast pen to protect a fighter on the ground.** *Above left* **and** *middle right:* **Aircraft in their camouflaged blast pens.** *Right:* **Officers of IIIrd Gruppe of Fighter Geschwader 26 discussing the next mission. Seated second from left is the unit commander, Major Adolf Galland. To his immediate left is Gerhard Schoepfel.**

Above and right: 'Emils' loaded with 550lb bombs during attacks on England in the closing stages of the Battle of Britain.

warning splutter, and unless the RAF pilot restored positive 'G' immediately, his engine would stop dead. Several German pilots owed their survival to the Me 109's ability to bunt away from a pursuer.

■ RADIUS OF ACTION ■

While such marginal differences in performance and capability decided some actions during this critical period, it is important to view them in the overall context. Throughout the Battle of Britain, and particularly during its final phases when the capital was the target, the Me 109's limited radius of action was of crucial importance. During that contest, the Me 109, the Spitfire and the Hurricane each had an effective radius of action of about 100 miles (160km). For RAF fighters engaged in home defence operations, fighting over airfields where they could land to refuel, that distance

was adequate. However, for Me 109s flying in the bomber escort or support roles deep into enemy territory, it was inadequate. The German fighter pilots could not afford to spend long engaged in combat, their engines running at full throttle and guzzling fuel. If they were close to the limit of their radius of action, the Messerschmitts had to break off the action, often prematurely, and head for home. This factor greatly reduced the effectiveness of the German single-engined fighter force.

There is another point to consider. The cliché image of the Battle of Britain is that of a sky full of Me 109s, Spitfires and Hurricanes engaged in one-to-one turning fights with Me 109s. That might make for a spectacular painting or film shot, but it was far from the reality of air combat. Any pilot who fastened his attention too long on one enemy fighter ran the serious risk of setting himself up for a surprise attack by another.

PROVIDING CLOSE ESCORT FOR THE BOMBERS

"Sometimes we were ordered to provide close escort for a bomber formation, which I loathed. It gave the bomber crews the feeling they were being protected, and it might have deterred some of the enemy pilots. But for us fighter pilots it was very bad. We needed the advantages of altitude and speed so we could engage the enemy on favourable terms. As it was, the British fighters had the initiative of when and how to attack. The Heinkels cruised at about 4,000m [13,000ft] at about 300km/hr [190mph]. On close escort we flew at about 370km/hr [230mph], weaving from side to side to keep station on them. We needed to maintain speed, otherwise the Me 109s would have taken too long to accelerate to fighting speed if we were bounced by Spitfires. I hated having to fly direct escort. We had to stay with the bombers until our formation came under attack. When we saw the British fighters approaching we would want to accelerate to engage them. But our commander would call 'Everybody stay with the bombers.' We handed to the enemy the initiative of when and how they would attack us. Until they did we had to stay close to the bombers, otherwise their people would complain and there would be recriminations when we got back."

OBERLEUTNANT HANS SCHMOLLER-HALDY, ME 109 PILOT, FIGHTER GESCHWADER 54

Above: At the end of the Battle of Britain, the top-scoring pilot in the Luftwaffe was Major Werner Moelders, the commander of Fighter Geschwader 51. On 22 October 1940 he scored his fiftieth aerial victory.

On both sides, the really successful fighter pilots stalked their prey like hunters. They used the sun and cloud to remain unseen for as long as possible, as they edged into a favourable position before launching an attack. They then dived on their often unsuspecting prey, announcing their presence with a sudden and accurate burst of fire. There was no thought of chivalry. Usually the first thing the victim knew of the danger was when his aircraft shuddered under the impact of hits. A textbook example of this type of action appears in the Prologue (see page 139).

From the start of the Battle of Britain, one Gruppe operated the Me 109 in the fighter-bomber role, attacking targets in southern England. The fighter carried a bomb load of up to 550lb (249kg). In the final part of the Battle, from the end of September, several Me 109 units flew aircraft modified for the fighter-bomber role. The defending fighters found the fast, high-flying German fighter-bombers difficult targets to engage. As a result, the latter suffered minimal losses. On the other hand, the Me 109 carried only a small weight of bombs, and their scattered bombing meant that the attacks had only nuisance value.

■ REPUTATION INTACT ■

The Me 109 force emerged from the Battle of Britain with its reputation still intact. True, it had suffered losses at the hands of the RAF pilots. But during these hard-fought engagements, the Me 109 force had usually dealt out blows at least as hard as those it took.

Alongside the Spitfire Mark I, the 'Emil' was still a contender for the title of most effective fighter plane in the world. The new variant of the German fighter about to enter service, the Me 109 'Friedrich', would be even better.

Left: Hauptmann Horst Tietzen, the commander of 5th Staffel of Fighter Geschwader 51, with his personal 'Emil' with 18 victory bars on the tail. On the afternoon of 18 August 1940. when his victory score stood at 20, he was shot down and killed during an action with Hurricanes of No. 501 Squadron.

"THE MOST SERIOUS AND UNPARDONABLE ERROR"

"On 23 September our mission was a free hunting sweep in the triangle Ramsgate–Canterbury–Folkestone, where British fighter activity had been reported. With three of my pilots I took off at 10.27 and headed towards Ramsgate in a slow climb to 4,500m [about 15,000ft]. The weather was strange, with layers of cloud in which aircraft could easily hide. There were several flights of aircraft about which we saw for a moment before they disappeared, we never knew if they were British or German. It was uncanny. We flew in wide curves, always changing altitude, never flying straight for long. We had been flying for 60 minutes, I thought that was enough and we were turning for home when I suddenly observed a Hurricane squadron between Ramsgate and Dover, 12 aircraft in four 'pulks' flying one behind the other. They were about 1,000m (2,873ft) below us and climbing in wide curves, like a creeping worm. My impression was that it was a Hurricane squadron on a training mission. The Hurricane pilots had no idea that four 109s were above them following each of their movements, like an eagle looking down on its prey. The spectacle was so fascinating that we completely forgot what was going on around us. That is the most serious and unpardonable error a fighter pilot can commit, and catastrophe immediately followed. Four Spitfires, of which we had been unaware due to our carelessness, attacked us from out of the sun. They fired at us from behind, roared close over our heads at high speed and disappeared back into the sky. As we broke formation fearing another attack from the Spitfires, I saw a 109 going down in flames on my right. It was Oberfeldwebel Knipscher, we never heard what happened to him."

OBERLEUTNANT HANS SCHMOLLER-
HALDY, ME 109 PILOT,
FIGHTER GESCHWADER 54

Top: An 'Emil' crash-landed on a French beach. During the Battle of Britain, this fighter was not fitted with drop tanks, and lacked the range to penetrate far into southern England. Several were lost when they ran out of fuel on their way home following air combats or after encountering strong headwinds.

Above: Me 109E-7s of Fighter Geschwader 1, a unit that spent most of the war operating in the defence of the German homeland. (via Obert)

Right: Major Adolf Galland climbing out of the cockpit of his 'Emil' after a sortie over England during the Battle of Britain.

During 1940, the Messerschmitt company initiated a programme to clean up the airframe of the Me 109 and improve its fighting capability. The new variant became the Me 109 'Friedrich'. Compared with the 'Emil', the more obvious external changes were the more rounded spinner and nose contours, the rounded wing tips and the partially retractable tail wheel. The main production version was fitted with the new Mauser 15mm cannon, one of which fired through the propeller hub. This weapon had nearly twice the firing rate of the older 20mm Oerlikon cannon, and its far higher muzzle velocity made it a much more effective weapon than its predecessor.

Luftwaffe pilots who flew the 'Friedrich' remembered this variant with affection. It was faster than the 'Emil' and it handled rather better in the air. It was, in the truest sense of the expression, a 'fighter pilot's fighter'. The 'Freidrich' entered service in the spring of 1941, and by the middle of the year two-thirds of the Luftwaffe fighter force flew this type. Also at this time, the Royal Air Force introduced the Mark V Spitfire into its home defence squadrons, a move that restored the balance between the fighter forces of the two sides.

■ NORTH AFRICA ■

That balance existed only over north-west Europe, however. Until the spring

MESSERSCHMITT 109 F-2

Type Single-seat general-purpose fighter

Armament One Mauser 15mm cannon firing through the propeller spinner (200 rounds); two Rheinmetall-Borsig 7.9mm MGs synchronized to fire through airscrew (500 rounds per gun)

Power plant One Daimler-Benz DB 601N inverted V-12 liquid-cooled engine developing 1,200hp for take-off

Dimensions Span 32ft 6in (9.92m); length 29ft 4in (8.94m)

Weight Normal operational take-off 6,174lb (2,800kg)

Performance Maximum speed 373mph at 19,700ft (600km/hr at 6,000m); service ceiling 36,100ft (11,000m)

Top: A brand new Me 109 'Friedrich' in factory markings shows off its distinctive rounded wing form above the Alps.

Above: A 'Friedrich' of Fighter Geschwader 26 returning to its base at Liegescourt in northern France in the summer of 1941. (Schoepfel)

Opposite: Two 'Emils' of Fighter Geschwader 27 on patrol over the North African desert.

Top: 'Friedrich' wearing the personal markings of the commander of IIIrd Gruppe of Fighter Geschwader 2 based in northern France, photographed in 1941.
Above: An Me 109F of Fighter Geschwader 26 outside its camouflaged dispersal hangar in northern France.

of 1942, the Spitfire fighter units operated only from bases in Great Britain. Meanwhile, units equipped with the 'Friedrich' were heavily involved in the campaigns in North Africa and the Soviet Union, where the new fighter easily outflew the less modern types opposing it. For the German fighter pilots, this was a 'happy time' when many of them amassed large victory scores.

The foremost successful 'Friedrich' fighter pilot was Leutnant Hans-Joachim Marseille. He gained seven victories during the Battle of Britain while flying the 'Emil' before moving to the North African theatre to join Fighter Geschwader 27. From the beginning of

ATTACK ON RUSSIA

During the weeks following the invasion of Russia, packs of German fighters ranged far and wide over enemy territory. Close to the ground, the Polikarpov I-16, the main Soviet fighter type, was almost as fast as the Me 109F that equipped the majority of Luftwaffe fighter units. But the Type 24's radial engine was optimized for low-altitude operations, and as height increased its performance fell away steadily; at 20,000ft (6,096m) the I-16 was about 100mph (160km/hr) slower than the German fighter. Although the Soviet fighters were more manoeuvrable than their adversaries, in a fighter-versus-fighter combat that advantage did no more than allow a pilot to avoid being shot down, provided he saw his attacker in good time. For the most part, the Soviet fighter pilots had to dance to their enemies' tune. Typical of the scrappy actions taking place that morning was one near Brest-Litovsk, described by Unteroffizier Reibel of 1st Gruppe of Fighter Geschwader 53: "I was flying as wing man to Lt Zellot. We flew in the direction of Brest from Labinka. As my leader ordered a turn about, I saw two biplanes in front of us. I immediately reported them and we brought them under attack. When we were about 200m [61ft] from them they both pulled into a tight turn to the right. We pulled up high and then began a new attack, but though we both opened fire it was without success. Soon there were about ten other [enemy] machines in the area. My leader ran in to attack one of the planes while I remained high in order to cover him. Then an I-15 became separated from the others. I immediately prepared to attack it, but I had to break away when another enemy machine, which I had not seen, suddenly appeared 50m [15ft] in front of me. I opened fire with machine-guns and the cannon and it burst into flames and spun out of control. Apparently the pilot had baled out. Then I had to turn away, as I had two [enemy] machines behind me." Using their superior speed, the German fighters easily pulled away.

Above: Me 109 'Emils' of Fighter Geschwader 52 pictured at Kabaracie, Rumania, in the spring of 1941, shortly before the attack on the Soviet Union. The 'snake' marking on the rear fuselage indicated that these aircraft belonged to the IIIrd Gruppe.

1942, his victory total rose rapidly. With no Spitfires yet operating in that area, the 'Friedrich' was superior to the Hurricane and Tomahawk fighters flown by the RAF and its allies. During a remarkable action on 3 June 1942, Marseille shot down six Tomahawks in rapid succession. The action is well documented and the combat is confirmed in the records of the victim unit, No. 5 Squadron South African Air Force. By the time of his death in September 1942, Marseille's tally of 'kills' stood at 158.

Early on, the 15mm cannon fitted to the 'Friedrich' was replaced with a fast-firing 20mm Mauser cannon. With the two machine-guns mounted above the engine cowling, the closely grouped weapons gave

Me 109s IN NORTH AFRICA

Opposite:

1. Hauptmann Karl-Wolfgang Redlich of 1st Gruppe Fighter Geschwader 27 (left, holding papers), briefing pilots before taking off from Catania in Sicily to fly to North Africa. The 'Emil' in the background is fitted with a dust filter over the engine air intake. (Schroer)

2. Ground-running an 'Emil' at Catania, to warm the engine before setting out for North Africa. (Schroer)

3. Me 109 'Emils' of Fighter Geschwader 27 dispersed around the forward landing ground at Gambut in Libya. The photograph gives a good impression of the primitive conditions under which the unit had to operate. (Schroer)

4. Ground crewmen turning the handle for the inertia starter of the Daimler-Benz 601 engine. The handle rotated a heavy flywheel which, when it was turning fast enough, was clutched to the engine to turn it over and start it.

5. 'Emils' of Fighter Geschwader 27 on patrol over the desert.

6. Me 109F of Fighter Geschwader 27 preparing to get airborne. Note that this aircraft is missing its spinner.

7. Hauptmann Hans-Joachim Marseille of Fighter Geschwader 27, the most successful German fighter pilot in North Africa. At the time of his death in September 1942, his victory score stood at 158.

8. Fighter ace Leutnant Werner Schroer, adjutant of IInd Gruppe of Fighter Geschwader 27, with his personal aircraft. At the end of the war, his victory score stood at 114. (Schroer)

Above: **'Friedrich' of Fighter Geschwader 77 operating on the Leningrad front in 1942. (Pichler via Obert)**

passes. Under those conditions, only an exceptionally good shot could achieve the required number of hits using a single cannon.

Greater fire power was needed, and in answer to this problem the 'Friedrich' was modified to carry a blister under each wing containing an extra 20mm cannon and ammunition. The change trebled the fighter's fire power, but at no small cost in terms of its performance and general handling. It was the first ominous sign of a problem that would afflict the Me 109 and other German piston-engined fighter types for the remainder of the war. In short, any fighter that had sufficient fire power to engage Allied heavy bombers successfully would be too heavy and too unwieldy to engage Allied fighters on equal terms.

That critical shortcoming would become all too evident when the next variant of the fighter entered production, the 'Gustav', which is described in the next section.

a dense pattern of fire that proved very effective against enemy fighters and light bombers. Against the four-engined bombers, with their tougher structures, it was another matter however.

◼ FIRE POWER ◼

From mid-1942, the Me 109F units operating over western Europe and North Africa encountered the American B-17 Flying Fortress and B-24 Liberator heavy bombers with increasing frequency. On average, it needed about 20 hits with 20mm rounds to knock down one of these rugged aircraft. When in formation, the heavy bombers put up a powerful defensive cross-fire which forced the fighters to make high-speed firing

EASY TIMES IN RUSSIA

Initially, the German fighter pilots had an easy time over Russia, and the more talented of them built up huge victories scores. There were plenty of opportunities for everyone, however, even the inexperienced pilots. In the summer of 1942, Unteroffizier Walther Hagenah was posted from training to 1st Gruppe of Fighter Geschwader 3 operating the Me 109F. He flew as wing man to Oberfeldwebel Otto Wessling, a skilful and experienced pilot. Hagenah told this author: "Wessling was a superb leader who seemed to be able to score hits from ranges as great as 400m [1,312ft]. He would manoeuvre into a position of advantage above his enemy, dive on his prey and open fire from long range, hit his enemy and pull away without getting close to his foe. My first weeks as an operational fighter pilot were a disappointment. To be sure I fired at enemy aircraft, but all I seemed to hit was the air. I was beginning to get discouraged. One day Wessling took me to one side on the ground and said, 'Now it is time that you made your first victory!' On 12 August 1942, we were on patrol on the central Russian front and he spotted a pair of LAGG-3 fighters. He took us round into an attacking position on their tails and down we went. We came from out of the sun and achieved surprise. He hit one of them from about 400m [1,312ft] and down it went. Then he called me and said, 'Now you go ahead and hit the other one!' But the second Russian pilot had a lot of pluck and he really threw his aircraft about the sky in an effort to shake us off his tail. Then Wessling joined in the dogfight, but at the same time telling me what I had to do to get 'my' kill. Eventually he succeeded in manoeuvring both me and the Russian fighter into a position where I could open fire at it – just as a gamekeeper will chase a deer into a position where a wealthy man can hit it with his gun. All I had to do was follow Wessling's instructions and fire when he said, and I hit the enemy fighter. So I achieved my victory. I was very proud. Wessling was big enough to keep quiet about how I got it."

During the Second World War, the principal fighter types in the major warring nations underwent courses of development to improve their fighting capability. They were fitted with more powerful (and heavier) engines, more effective (and heavier) armament, larger (and heavier) fuel tankage and additional (and heavier) protective armour and items of equipment.

As the fighter steadily gained weight, from time the airframe had to be stiffened to restore its original strength factors. That added a further twist to the spiral of increasing weight. Since the fighter's wing area usually remained constant, each increase in weight led to increase in wing loading. And that, inevitably, led to a deterioration in the fighter's handling characteristics. Stalling speeds became higher, control forces heavier, turning performance worsened and, in many cases, the aircraft developed vicious traits.

No fighter design suffered more from this remorseless process than the Me 109. Even at the start of the war, it will be remembered, the Me 109 had already passed through several variants. By the spring of 1942, it had reached the end of its effective development, and ideally it should then have passed out of production. However, Messerschmitt's planned replacement fighter, the Me 209, was still on the drawing board.

The Me 109G-2 was 660 pounds heavier than its predecessor, the Me 109F

At that time, the war was still going well for Germany. Her leaders confidently expected that the campaign on the Eastern front would come to a victorious end in the autumn of 1942. Until a replacement fighter type was ready, the Luftwaffe opted to squeeze a little more speed from the Me 109 and keep the fighter in full production.

The new variant, the Me 109 'Gustav', was designed around the Daimler-Benz 605 engine. In essence, this was a DB 601 with the cylinder block rebored to increase the engine's capacity from 33.9 litres to 35.7 litres. The additional capacity gave an extra 175 horse power at full throttle, for no significant increase in the engine's external dimensions. That fact did not prevent the new variant of the Me 109 from putting on weight, however. The first major production version, the 'Gustav-2', was 660lb (300kg) or about 10 per cent heavier than the earlier 'Friedrich' and its handling charact-

Top: Me 109 'Gustav' of Fighter Geschwader 54 pictured at a forward airfield in Russia, showing the difficult conditions encountered during the spring thaw.
Above: Me 109 'Gustav' of Fighter Geschwader 53 pictured at a forward airfield in Sicily in 1943. (via Rigglesford)
Opposite: Pilots of Fighter Geschwader 53 at readiness snatching a quick meal beside one of their aircraft. (via Schliephake)

istics were correspondingly worse; compared with the Me 109 'Berta', the figures were 2,200lb (1,000kg) and 46 per cent respectively! During May 1942, a total of 234 Me 109s came off the production lines in Germany and Austria, most of them 'Gustavs'.

MESSERSCHMITT 109 G-2

Type Single-seat general-purpose fighter

Armament One Mauser 20mm cannon firing through the spinner (150 rounds); two Rheinmetall-Borsig 7.9mm MGs synchronized to fire through the airscrew (500 rounds per gun)

Power plant One Daimler-Benz DB 605A inverted V-12 liquid-cooled engine developing 1,475hp for take-off

Dimensions Span 32ft 6in (9.92m); length 29ft 0in (8.85m)

Weight Normal operational take-off 6,832lb (3,100kg)

Performance Maximum speed 406mph at 28,535ft (654km/hr at 8,700m); service ceiling 39,360ft (12,000m)

Soon after the 'Gustav' entered service with Fighter Geschwader 27, Hans-Joachim Marseille lost his life while flying the type. In September 1942, his victory score passed the 150 mark, making him the first fighter ace in history to achieve this total. On the final day of the month he flew a newly delivered 'Gustav-2' on a bomber escort mission over Egypt. There was no contact with the enemy and the flight was uneventful, until on the return flight the aircraft's engine started to smoke. Then it caught fire. The cockpit filled with fumes and, escorted by his comrades, Marseille stayed with the aircraft until he reached German-held territory. Then he jumped from the stricken fighter, but his luck had deserted him. As he left the Messerschmitt, it appears that his head struck some part of its structure and he was knocked unconscious. His parachute did not open and he was killed on hitting the ground. Subsequent examination of his parachute revealed that it was still in the pack, held closed by the ripcord which had not been pulled.

Marseille jumped from his aircraft, but for once luck had deserted him

Small numbers of 'Gustav-2s' were modified for the tactical reconnaissance role, with the cannon removed and a vertical camera mounted in the rear fuselage. The use of the Me 109 (and also the FW 190) for this purpose became necessary because the increasing enemy fighter opposition on each of the battle fronts meant that slower reconnaissance types incurred heavy losses. Modified versions of each of the new main variants of the Me 109 would be used for tactical reconnaissance for the remainder of the war.

The next major production version of the fighter, the 'Gustav-6', started to leave the assembly lines in the autumn of 1942. This differed from the G-2 in that it carried two 13mm heavy machine-guns on top of the engine cowling, in place of the earlier rifle-calibre weapons. To cover the larger breech mechanism of the 13mm guns, the fighter had two large bulges on the cowling in front of the windscreen.

■ 210mm ROCKETS ■

The Luftwaffe issued a range of field modification kits to allow units to 'customize' the new fighter for specific operational roles. The R-1 kit, for example, provided an under-fuselage rack to carry a single bomb weighing up to 550lb (249kg). The R-2 kit provided for a tubular launcher under each wing to carry a 210mm rocket, for use against enemy bomber formations or ground targets. The R-4 kit provided a blister mounting for a 30mm heavy cannon and ammunition, one to fit under either wing.

'WILD BOAR' MESSERSCHMITT 109s

Above: Me 109G-2s operating in the 'Wild Boar' single-engine night-fighter role to counter RAF bomber attacks, summer 1943.

From mid-1943, the Luftwaffe began to employ small numbers of single-engined fighters, including Me 109s, to engage RAF night bombers attacking cities in Germany. Over the target, the concentrations of searchlights, the fires on the ground and the Pathfinders' marker flares often combined to illuminate the bombers. The single-seaters patrolling high above the target could then make visual attacks on the raiders. To prevent conflict with the flak defences, it was agreed that the latter would engage bombers flying below a certain altitude, typically 18,000ft (5,500m). Above that altitude, the fighters would engage bombers. The single-engined night fighter tactics bore the apt title 'Wild Boar'. For the remainder of the war, these methods were an integral part of the German night air defence system.

WEAPONS INSTALLATION FITTED TO Me 109G-5 AND G-6

KEY:

a. MG 131 13mm heavy machine-guns

b. Electrical synchronization unit for firing MG 131s through the airscrew disc

c. Magazine for MG 131 ammunition

d. Empty case chute for port MG 131

e. Mountings for MG 131s

f. Ignition coil, to provide high voltage for electrically fired MG 131 ammunition

g. Mounting brackets for nose fairing

h. MG 151 20mm cannon firing through propeller spinner

i. Front mounting of MG 151

k. Magazine for MG 151 ammunition

l. Feed chute for MG 151 ammunition

m. Control column, with firing button for weapons

n. Revi 16B reflector sight

o. Arming switch for weapons

Also, the 'Gustav-6' had provision to carry one or two separate power-boosting systems, to inject a fluid into the supercharger of the DB 605 engine. To boost power at altitudes above 20,000ft (6,096m), the GM-1 system injected nitrous oxide (laughing gas) into the engine. The nitrous oxide was held in liquid form in a heavily lagged pressurized container in the rear fuselage, and the complete system weighed 670lb (304kg). To boost power

Above: Diagram from an official Luftwaffe handbook, showing the fuselage armament fitted as standard to Me 109 Gustav-5 and Gustav-6. These fighters had a 20mm Mauser cannon firing through the airscrew hub, and two 13mm Rheinmetall-Borsig heavy machine-guns above the engine cowling synchronized to fire through the airscrew. On some later aircraft, the engine-mounted cannon was replaced by a Rheinmetall-Borsig 30mm weapon.

Below: The 'Gustav' did not suffer fools gladly. If the pilot opened the throttle too quickly during take-off, the powerful engine torque was liable to lift the fighter off the ground before it attained flying speed. Often the fighter rolled upside down and smashed on the ground under full power, giving the pilot little chance of escape. (Schliephake)

orated. On each battle front in turn the Luftwaffe was thrown on the defensive. More and more fighters were required, and the 'Gustav', originally introduced as a stopgap type, was built in ever-greater numbers. During 1943, production of the Me 109 was twice that in the previous year, with more than 6,400 'Gustavs' delivered to the Luftwaffe.

One factor that led to demands for increasing numbers of air defence fighters was the daylight attacks by US heavy bombers on targets in Germany. What had started as infrequent raids by a few dozen bombers against fringe targets had grown into deep penetration attacks by several hundred bombers able to inflict severe devastation. To meet the new threat, several fighter Gruppen were withdrawn from the battle fronts to bolster the defences of the homeland.

In the summer of 1943, Unteroffizier Hans Seyringer was posted to IInd Gruppe of Fighter Geschwader 27, a day

The young pilot had only about 200 flying hours in his logbook

fighter unit based at Wiesbaden and equipped with the 'Gustav-6'. The young pilot had come straight from training and had only about 200 flying hours in his logbook. His recollections give a good impression of what it was like to serve with such a unit.

During bomber-interception missions the fighters usually carried a 66 gallon (300 litre) drop tank under the fuselage. The standard armament fitted to 'Gustavs' on Seyringer's unit was three 20mm cannon and two 13mm machine-guns. Some of the aircraft also carried two 210mm rocket launchers under the wings, though as an inexperienced pilot Seyringer never flew with these weapons.

When waiting on the ground at readiness, the aircraft were usually drawn up by Staffeln in line abreast. The four Staffeln, each with about a dozen 'Gustav-6s', were dispersed separately at 90-degree intervals around the perimeter of the grass airfield. Once the pilots had

Top: Me 109 'Gustav-2s' belonging to a tactical reconnaissance Gruppe. This version had the nose-mounted cannon removed, and a vertical camera fitted in the fuselage immediately behind the cockpit.
Above: Me 109 'Gustav-2' of Fighter Geschwader 11 at Jever during 1943, fitted with underwing launchers for two 210mm air-to-air rockets for use against US heavy bomber formations.

at altitudes below 20,000ft, the MW system injected a water/methanol mixture into the engine (the water cooled the charge and provided the extra power, and the methanol prevented the water from freezing at high altitude). The complete MW system weighed 300lb (136kg).

As the 'Gustav-6' entered service, Germany's war fortunes suddenly deteri-

Above: A close-up of the rocket installation on a 'Gustav'.

Left: Me 109 'Gustav' of the Finnish Air Force. The type entered that service in March 1943 and remained in use until 1954.

been brought to cockpit readiness, the order to scramble was given by firing a green flare from the control tower. From then on, it was important to get the Gruppe into the air and assembled into battle formation as rapidly as possible. To achieve this, two of the Staffeln on opposite sides of the airfield began simultaneous take-off runs, moving on parallel headings separated by a few hundred yards. As the first two Staffeln passed each other at the centre of the airfield, the other two Staffeln began their take-off runs also heading in opposite directions.

After take-off, the leader orbited once over the airfield so the individual Staffeln could start to move into position behind him. Then he turned on to his intercept heading and began a slow climb away. Once the formation was fully assembled, he increased his rate of climb.

These tactics provided the most rapid means of getting a Gruppe into the air and assembled into formation. There was little small margin for safety if anything went wrong, however. Seyringer recalled a nerve-racking incident when, due to incorrect fitting, a fighter taking off in

the opposite direction accidentally loosed off a couple of rockets. The missiles came scorching past Seyringer's Staffel just as the fighters were getting airborne. Their proximity caused considerable consternation but, fortunately for the pilots involed, no damage!

▪ TACTICS ▪

Once the ground controller had brought a fighter Gruppe within visual range of an enemy formation, the Gruppe leader decided on the type of attack to employ. Usually Seyringer's Gruppe attacked bombers from the rear, the fighters flying in four-aircraft units in line abreast or line astern. After their initial attack, the fighters split into pairs to make further firing runs. Sometimes Seyringer's Gruppe made head-on attacks, though he did not like this method. He felt that the time spent manoeuvring into position for such an attack was out of proportion to the very short firing pass that resulted.

Above: 'Gustav-6' carrying the white fuselage band and wing tips of a unit operating on the Mediterranean front.
Right: Unteroffizier Hans Seyringer of Fighter Geschwader 27, whose experiences are described in the text, pictured with his 'Gustav-6'. With a victory score of four enemy aircraft destroyed, he was shot down and wounded during an engagement with American escort fighters in February 1944. (Seyringer)

Until late in 1943, the American escort fighters lacked the range to penetrate deep into Germany. Serringer's unit had few encounters with them and he thought that was as well, for a heavily laden 'Gustav-6' was no match for a Thunderbolt.

To Hans Seyringer, the effect of the fighter's extensive development process on handling was all too evident. To put it simply, the 'Gustav' was too heavy and its engine too powerful for the fighter's small wing and tail surfaces. When carrying a full armament and drop tank, the aircraft required careful handling during take-off. If there was heavy-handedness of the controls, the fighter was liable to react viciously. If, for example, the pilot opened the throttle too quickly, the powerful engine torque was liable to lift the fighter off the ground before it attained flying speed. The 'Gustav' would drop its left wing, roll on its back and smash into the ground, giving the pilot little chance of escape. The 'Gustav' did not suffer fools gladly.

During 1943, the Luftwaffe tactics to counter the American heavy bomber raids were in a continual state of development. Home defence units used any type of weapon that came to hand. Fighter Geschwader 11 carried out experiments in air-to-air bombing, using

DISASTER FOR THE GERMAN DAY FIGHTER FORCE

In the spring of 1944, the American escort fighters were able to reach almost every part of Germany. The new Mustang was superior in performance to the Me 109, and it was usually present in greater numbers. As a result, the German day fighter units took increasingly heavy losses. At the end of April 1944, Generalmajor Adolf Galland reported: "Between January and April 1944 our day fighter arm lost more than 1,000 pilots. They included our best Staffel, Gruppe and Geschwader commanders. The time has come when our force is within sight of collapse." Now the German pilots had to fight for their very survival, and one by one even the best of them were being picked off. Gone were the days when the aces could 'play' enemy planes to allow their less experienced colleagues to get easy kills, as they did over Russia a couple of years earlier. One of those who died in action with the American fighters in April 1944 was Leutnant Otto Wessling, then credited with 83 victories, who had set up Walther Hagenah's first 'kill' described earlier.

time-fused 550lb (249kg) released from above the bomber formation. Initially, it seemed this tactic might have a good chance of success. Even if the bombs did not destroy the enemy planes, they might damage some of them sufficiently to force them to leave their formation. Other fighters could then finish off the wounded birds as easy prey. There were serious problems with this method, however. Carrying a bomb in place of a drop tank, the 'Gustav' had a short radius of action. Also, it proved difficult to vector the heavily laden fighter into position above a high-flying bomber formation. Moreover, since there was no effective proximity fuse then available, the problem of getting the bomb to

MESSERSCHMITT 109 G-2 VERSUS HAWKER TEMPEST

At the beginning of 1944, a captured Me 109 'Gustav-2' was flown in a comparative trial against the latest RAF fighter type, the Hawker Tempest Mark V. These extracts from the official report show that the German fighter was outclassed in almost every respect.

"**Maximum speed:** The Tempest possesses an advantage of 40–50mph [64–80km/hr] at heights below 20,000ft [5,850m] but at heights in excess of 20,000ft [6,096m] the advantage possessed by the Tempest rapidly diminishes. **Climb:** The climb of the Me 109 is superior to that of the Tempest at all heights but this advantage is not pronounced at heights below 5,000ft [1,520m]. When both the aircraft commence a dive at the same speed and are put into climbing attitude, the Tempest is slightly superior, but providing the Tempest possesses the initial advantage in speed, it has no difficulty in holding it providing the speed is kept in excess of 250mph [400km/hr]. **Dive:** Comparative dives between these aircraft show that the Tempest will pull away from the Me 109. This is not so marked in the early stages of the dive, but in a prolonged descent the Tempest is greatly superior. **Turning circle:** It was found that in this aspect of manoeuvrability the Tempest was slightly superior to the Me 109. **Rate of roll:** At speeds below 350 IAS [mph indicated, 564km/hr] there is practically nothing to choose between the two aircraft, but when this speed is exceeded the Tempest can out-manoeuvre the Me 109 by making a quick change of bank and direction. **Conclusions:** In the attack the Tempest can always follow the Me 109, except in a slow steep climb. In the combat area the Tempest should maintain a high speed, and in defence may do anything except attempt a climb at low speed."

Below: Comparative trials revealed that the Hawker Tempest Mark V, which entered service in the RAF early in 1944, was superior to the Me 109 'Gustav-2' in almost every respect.

detonate as it passed the target aircraft defied solution. Most of the bombs detonated well clear of their intended victims, and after a month or so the unit abandoned this form of attack.

During the spring of 1944, following the introduction of new and larger drop tanks, the American escort fighters were able to reach almost every part of Germany. The new Mustang fighters were superior in performance to the defending Me 109s, Me 110s, Me 410s and FW 190s. Moreover, the escort fighters operated in large numbers, and as a result the German fighter units took heavy losses.

■ HOME DEFENCE ■

By now the greater part of the Luftwaffe fighter force was committed in the defence of the homeland. And it was losing pilots faster than the German flying training schools could provide replacements. The Luftwaffe was being bled white. The only possibility of reversing this trend was with the large-scale deployment of the Messerschmitt 262 jet fighter. Yet this type was still not ready to enter mass production (see next section of this book).

Although the 'Gustav' was now well beyond its effective development life, new sub-types continued to appear. By optimizing it for a narrow range of combat roles, the fighter might survive in action. Thus, the 'Gustav-10', for example, was built specifically to engage in high-altitude fighter-versus-fighter combat. These aircraft carried the new Daimler-Benz 605D engine with an

enlarged supercharger and the GM-1 power boosting. Their armament was reduced to one 20mm cannon and two 13mm machine-guns. They were assigned to units whose task was to provide top cover for more heavily armed fighters delivering attacks on bomber formations. In addition, small numbers of 'Gustav-10s' were modified for the tactical reconnaissance role, with the two heavy machine-guns removed and a fixed vertical camera mounted in the rear fuselage.

■ A DESPERATE TIME ■

In the spring of 1944, the German aircraft industry underwent a major reorganization. The Luftwaffe,

Above: Damaged Me 109 'Gustav' trailing glycol smoke after being hit in the cooling system during an engagement with a US escort fighter. Soon after this picture was taken, the 'Gustav' was shot down. (USAF)
Below: Me 109G-6s of IIIrd Gruppe Fighter Geschwader 27 waiting at readiness at Wiesbaden-Erbenheim in 1944. The broad red band around the rear fuselage indicated that the aircraft belonged to a Reich air defence unit. (Schroer)

IN ACTION DURING THE FINAL MONTHS OF THE WAR

Leutnant Hans-Ulrich Flade flew the Me 109 'Gustav' and the 'Kurfurst' with IInd Gruppe of Fighter Geschwader 27 early in 1945. In previous months, the production of these fighters had reached an all-time high, and if an aircraft was damaged it was usually simpler to get a new fighter than repair the old one: "We simply went to the depot nearby, where they had hundreds of brand new 109s – G-10s, G-14s and even the very latest K models. There was no proper organization any more; the depot staff just said, 'There are the aircraft, take what you want and go away.'" But getting fuel, that was more difficult. Flade's Gruppe had a strength of about 20 pilots, but it was losing these at a rate of two or three each day. Morale on the unit was low. "Each morning we pilots had breakfast together, and the replacements would come in. The older pilots regarded the newcomers as though they had only days to live – and with reason, for the standard of fighter conversion training was now so low that most of the new pilots flew only two or three missions before they were shot down. I remember many conversations along these lines – not exactly a cheerful subject for a young man who had just joined his first operational unit!" The Gruppe operated in the top-cover role, to keep the American escort fighters off the backs of other German fighters making for the bombers. "We followed the old rules: dive as a pair or a four out of the sun, make a quick attack to break up their formation and make them drop their tanks, then climb out of danger and assess the situation. If conditions were favourable, we would go down for a second attack. Always the escorts were so numerous that it would have been foolish to get into a dogfight."

Left: The Me 109G-14 featured a larger rudder and a redesigned cockpit canopy to give better vision to the sides and the rear. This example belonged to IIIrd Gruppe of Fighter Geschwader 3, a unit that flew escort missions for more heavily armoured fighters delivering attacks on US heavy bomber formations. (Romm)

Below: Me 109 'Kurfurst', the final version of the fighter to go into production in Germany before the end of the war. As well as the revised tail surfaces and redesigned canopy fitted to the late production 'Gustavs', this variant featured a more powerful Daimler-Benz 605 engine and carried two 15mm cannons mounted on top of the engine.

by this time in a desperate situation, needed every modern fighter it could lay its hands on. Under the new Luftwaffe procurement plan, almost the entire capacity of the industry was turned over to the manufacture of fighter-type aircraft. At the same time, to render the industry less vulnerable to air attack, a large part of the aircraft construction and assembly work was dispersed into small factories and workshops dotted throughout the country.

Once the new system was in place, production of the Me 109 rose in leaps and bounds, despite the heavy and continual raids on German cities and industrial centres. For the Me 109, September 1944 was the peak month, with the Luftwaffe taking delivery of

Above and left: The unusual 'Mistel' weapon, an Me 109F mounted rigidly on top of a Junkers 88 bomber that had the cabin removed and a large warhead fitted in its place. The Me 109 pilot aligned the bomber on the target, then fired explosive bolts to separate his aircraft so that he could make his escape.

Below: The Avia S.199 was manufactured in Czechoslovakia after the war, using components for the Me 109 'Gustav' built in that country. The fighter was fitted with a Jumo 211 engine, which gave the unusual nose contours. (Hurt)

1,605 new aircraft. That year, 14,212 examples of this type of aircraft were delivered, more than twice as many as in the previous year, which had itself been a record. At this stage of the war, the units equipped with Me 109s always had plenty of aircraft, although there were worsening shortages of trained pilots and fuel as the tide turned inexorably against the German forces.

Despite the known poor handling qualities of the Me 109 'Gustav', work continued in attempts to squeeze yet more speed and combat capability out of the basic design. The final variant of the Me 109 to enter large-scale production was the 'Kurfurst', deliveries of which began at the end of September 1944.

PROLOGUE

"The Forts were dropping their bombs, but the sky was so black with flak that we could only occasionally see them as they flew through the solid wall of sooty explosions. Don was the first to see the Me 109.

"'Johnny, at six o'clock high there's a single bandit.'

"I looked back, and there he was, high above us. I gazed in disbelief as his nose dropped and he plummeted down on us.

"'Don, the crazy son of a bitch is bouncing us.'

"'I know. When I yell 'Break', you break right and I'll break left.'

"I watched as the 109 dropped closer and closer. 'Break, Johnny.'

"I pulled sharply to the right, and thought at first I had broken too late as the 109 pulled on to my tail. I tightened my turn and met Don halfway around as he tried to fire on the 109 in a head-on attack. I went around twice more with the Jerry on my tail before Don could reverse his turn and swing down for a rear attack. But this German pilot was a smart, capable flyer. As Don brought his guns to bear, he Split-S and dove to the ground. Don and I followed him, our motors roaring in pursuit. He pulled out of his dive and banked left, which brought him close to

me. I followed him and fired. He wasn't one to sit still, however, and changed his turn to swing into Don. I followed, firing intermittently. Don meanwhile had climbed for altitude, and I kept the Jerry busy in a tight turn. As I fired, I saw flashes on his wing, fuselage, and even his motor, but the pilot wouldn't bale out. Turning all the time and losing height, we were now just above the tree tops, and the 109's engine was spewing smoke. I had no fore-warning that my ammunition was running out, but as I prepared for the final burst, only silence came as I pressed the tit.

"'Finish him, Don, I'm out of ammunition.'

"Don, who had been manoeuvring above us waiting for the Jerry to break out of the turn, zoomed down in front of me and made one pass on the courageous German flyer. His shots hit home . . ."

■ COMBAT DUO ■

The two Mustang pilots in this successful combat were two of America's finest; Don Gentile (21 victories) and John T. Godfrey (18 victories). Members of the 336th Fighter Squadron, 4th Fighter Group in the spring of 1944, the deadly duo became legendary for their teamwork, even though they only flew as a pair on five occasions.

This combat was notable on several counts. The Me 109G opposing them was in many ways the equal of the Mustang, and it started the combat with the dual advantages of height and position. The German pilot showed great confidence in engaging after it became clear that the element of surprise had been lost, when the safe move would have been to disengage and climb away, using the excess speed generated in his attacking dive. As it was, he was evidently banking on disposing of Godfrey before

Left: Probably the greatest exponents of air combat teamwork in the USAAF were Captain Don Gentile, seen here in the cockpit of his P-51B *Shangri-La*, and Lieutenant John Godfrey, perched on the wing wearing flying helmet, goggles and Mae West (10 April 1944). On return to the USA, Gentile became an Air Force test pilot (KIFA 28 January 1951); Godfrey returned to action in August, was shot down by ground fire later that month, and became a prisoner of war (died 12 June 1958). (USAF)

GENTILE AND GODFREY VERSUS Me 109

(1) The two Mustangs break in opposite directions, and the Me 109 follows Godfrey's hard turn. (2) Gentile opens fire, misses, then turns away to reposition. Meanwhile, Godfrey flies tight circles to deny the Messerschmitt a shot. Gentile gets behind the German (3), who tries to disengage with a vertical dive (4) with Gentile in pursuit. Godfrey, now free, also dives to cut the 109 off (5). The German pilot pulls out of his dive (6) and turns towards Godfrey, but with Gentile still on his tail is forced to turn away. With Godfrey in an attacking position, Gentile pulls up and circles (7). Godfrey runs out of ammunition and calls Gentile, who dives and delivers a lethal burst (8).

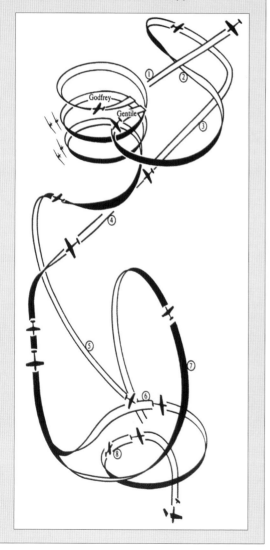

Gentile could intervene, then taking on the second Mustang in a one-versus-one combat.

That he failed was due to the excellence of the P-51B, which turned hard enough to deny him a valid shooting opportunity, and the skill of John Godfrey in holding him off until Gentile could take up an attacking position.

Having lost the initiative, and outnumbered two to one, he attempted to disengage with a near-vertical dive to ground level. The superb perform-ance of the two Mustangs allowed them to follow him down with relative ease, with Gentile in hot pursuit. Even then, he might still have escaped had it not been for the teamwork of the two Mustang pilots, one of whom held him in play while the other jockeyed for position, the leadership passing back and forth between them as opportunity offered. But against what was acknowledged to be the best fighting pair in the USAAF, flying aircraft fully the equal of his own, his bravery and flying skills availed him nothing.

■ PRECISION BOMBING RAIDS ■

When the United States of America entered the war, their policy in Europe was to carry out preci-sion bombing raids on selected targets. The main bomber type was the Boeing B-17 Flying Fortress, which not only had adequate range for the task, but carried very heavy defensive armament. In theory, this would allow the bombers, flying in close formation, to beat off massed attacks by German fighters. In practice, this did not work at all well. With shallow penetrations of enemy air-space, casualties were sustainable, as the time spent in the combat area was limited. However, with deep penetrations the German fighter arm was able to react in force over a considerable period, and US losses rose to unacceptable levels.

The only possible answer was to match fighters with fighters, but there were problems. Single-seat, single-engined fighters of the time were tradition-ally short-legged, while the longer-ranged twin-engined fighters were outclassed by agile enemy single-engined fighters. Germany had learned this lesson during the Battle of Britain, when the Me 110 took a series of heavy beatings from the nimble British Spitfires and Hurricanes. Somehow a single-seater, single-engined agile fighter with the required range had to be found.

The solution came in the unlikely shape of an American airframe initially developed for the RAF, married to the outstanding Rolls-Royce Merlin engine. The Mustang had almost double the fuel capacity of the Spitfire and a correspondingly greater radius of action. On late models, the addition of a large fuel tank in the fuselage and two drop tanks under the wings increased the range to the point where the American fighter could rove the length and breadth of the Third Reich. Wherever the bombers went, Mustangs could accompany them, to the dismay and discomfiture of the defending German fighters.

■ MERLIN ENGINE ■

The Merlin engine had been adopted to provide the high-altitude performance lacking in the original Allison-engined aircraft. That the airframe was good there was no doubt; the early model Mustang had proved itself to be an outstanding fighter at low and medium altitudes. The RAF used it in roles where high-altitude performance was not required, such as ground attack, army co-operation and low-level reconnaissance.

The USAAF was not slow to follow suit, with the attack version redesignated the A-36 Invader and the tactical reconnaissance aircraft the F-6. The fighter variant was at first known as the Apache in USAAF service; only later were both names abandoned in favour of Mustang, which, already used by the British, in the long run saved a lot of confusion.

While the Merlin-engined Mustang variants were by far the most important of the breed, and the type

Above: Wherever there was action, Mustangs were sure to be found. They ranged Europe from Norway in the north to Italy in the south, and from France in the west to Russia in the east. North African deserts, Burmese jungles, Chinese paddy fields, the vast wastes of the Pacific, even the skies over Japan – all heard the thunder of their engines. (Arvin Williams via JE)

gained undying fame in the skies of Western Europe, it was used in virtually every theatre of operations during the Second World War. A handful of Mustangs was supplied to the Soviet Union, although these were far too few to have any real impact. B-17 Fortresses on the so-called 'Shuttle' missions, which flew on to Russian bases after bombing Germany, were accompanied by Mustangs, which sometimes operated briefly on the Eastern Front. Mustangs were also based in southern Italy, from where they could range as far afield as Romania, Bavaria, or the south of France.

In the Far East, the Japanese were made well aware of the presence of the P-51, units of which were at various times based in India, Burma and China. Even in the vast Pacific Ocean, traditionally the domain of the US Navy carrier fleets, the Mustang's immense radius of action was put to good use. Based on Iwo Jima towards the end of the war, Mustangs escorted the huge B-29 Superfortresses during raids on the Japanese home islands.

Like all fighters of the era, the Mustang underwent a process of continuous development, and its performance started to approach the limits of what was possible with the internal combustion engine and not very efficient propeller. The other limit which had been pushed very hard indeed was pilot endurance. After a seven-hour mission over Germany, a pilot was completely exhausted. The answer had to be a second pilot to share the load.

Below: The combination of the British Rolls-Royce Merlin engine and the American P-51 Mustang airframe resulted in a superb fighter. With the addition of extra fuel tanks, it was able to escort the heavy bombers over previously unheard-of distances.

But how was this to be done without compromising performance?

The answer was the P-82 Twin Mustang. In essence, two Mustang fuselages and tails were coupled together with a central wing and tail section, with the outboard wings remaining unchanged. This gave two cockpits, while range and performance remained largely unimpaired; only manoeuvrability suffered, and that not to any great degree. Still later, an airborne interception radar was fitted, giving night and all-weather Twin Mustangs.

■ KOREA ■

The end of the Second World War coincided with the emergence of the new breed of jet fighters. Totally outperformed, the Mustang seemed as if its days as a front-line combat aircraft were numbered. It had, however, one remaining advantage. Early jet engines were incredibly thirsty, and their acceleration was sluggish. Consequently, endurance was almost non-existent by comparison with the Mustang, and they were unable to use short temporary airstrips from which the piston-engined fighter could operate with ease.

This endurance was to show to advantage in the war in Korea, which broke out in 1950. Japan-based jets could stay over the battle area for just a few minutes, whereas P-82s from the same base could loiter for much longer, and P-51s could be based 'in-country'. The final combat sortie of an American

P-51 took place from Korea in January 1953, but this was far from the final combat mission to be flown.

Above: Even in 1944, the German Me 262 jet gave the Mustang a hard time in combat. A far greater mismatch nearly occurred in 1963. If the confrontation between Malaysia and Indonesia had resulted in open war, Indonesian Mustangs would have had to face missile-armed Mach 2 Lightnings of the RAF. (BAe via author)

Israeli Mustangs flew in defence of the newly formed state from late 1948, and even in 1956 they took an important, if secondary, role in the Suez war before being phased out during the following year. In 1963, a confrontation took place between Malaysia and Indonesia. The main Indonesian fighter type was the Mustang. The air defence of Malaysia was largely in the hands of the Royal Air Force, equipped with the Mach 2-capable Lightning. In the event of overt hostilities, this would have been a tremendous mismatch; perhaps fortunately for the Indonesian fighter pilots, it did not occur. Finally, in what was perhaps the most ridiculous war ever, Salvadorean Mustangs fought with Honduran Corsairs and Thunderbolts. This was the combat swansong of the Mustang, which was soon after relegated to airshows and unlimited-class racing.

In what was to prove a final renaissance for the fighter, the Cavalier Aircraft Corporation PA-48 Enforcer made its maiden flight on 9 April 1983. A heavily modified Mustang, it was offered to the South American market as a light tactical aircraft. There were no takers, and the programme was finally terminated in 1986. The Mustang is long gone from the military scene, but its proud legend lives on. This part of the book is its story.

Below: 1945 saw the Mustang the dominant fighter in the USAAF, but it was outclassed and superseded by the new jet fighters, typically the Lockheed P-80 Shooting Star, shown here. (Author)

NORTH AMERICAN P-51B MUSTANG

1 Rudder trim tab (plastics) construction
2 Rudder frame (fabric-covered)
3 Rudder balance
4 Fin front spar
5 Fin structure
6 Access panel
7 Rudder trim tab actuating drum
8 Rudder trim tab control link
9 Rear navigation light
10 Rudder metal bottom section
11 Elevator plywood trim tab
12 Starboard elevator frame
13 Elevator balance weight
14 Starboard tailplane structure
15 Reinforced bracket (rear steering stresses)
16 Rudder operating horn forging
17 Elevator operating horns
18 Tab control turnbuckles
19 Fin front spar/ fuselage attachment
20 Port elevator tab
21 Fabric-covered elevator
22 Elevator balance weight
23 Port tailplane
24 Tab control drum
25 Fin root fairing
26 Elevator cables
27 Tab control access panels
28 Tailwheel steering mechanism
29 Tailwheel retraction mechanism
30 Tailwheel leg assembly
31 Forward-retracting steerable tailwheel
32 Tailwheel doors
33 Lifting tube
34 Fuselage aft bulkhead/ breakpoint
35 Fuselage break point
36 Control cable pulley brackets
37 Fuselage frames
38 Oxygen bottles
39 Cooling air exit flap actuating mechanism
40 Rudder cables
41 Ruselage lower longeron
42 Rear tunnel
43 Cooling air exit flap
44 Coolant radiator assembly
45 Radio and equipment shelf
46 Power supply pack
47 Fuselage upper longeron
48 Radio bay aft bulkhead (plywood)
49 Fuselage stringers
50 SCR-695 radio transmitter- receiver (on upper sliding shelf)
51 Whip aerial
52 Junction box

53 Cockpit aft glazing
54 Canopy track
55 SCR-522 radio transmitter-receiver
56 Battery installation
57 Radiator/supercharger coolant pipes
58 Radiator forward air duct
59 Coolant header tank/ radiator pipe
60 Coolant radiator – access cover
61 Oil cooler air inlet door
62 Oil radiator
63 Oil pipes
64 Flap control linkage
65 Wing rear spare fuselage attachment bracket
66 Crash pylon structure
67 Aileron control linkage
68 Hydraulic hand pump
69 Radio control boxes
70 Pilot's seat
71 Seat suspension frame
72 Pilot's head/back armour
73 Rearward-sliding clear-vision canopy
74 External rear-view mirror
75 Ring and bead gunsight
76 Bullet-proof windshield
77 Gyroscopic gunsight
78 Engine controls
79 Signal pistol discharge tube
80 Circuit-breaker panel
81 Oxygen regulator
82 Pilot's foot-rest and seat mounting bracket
83 Control linkage
84 Rudder pedal
85 Tailwheel lock control

86 Wing centre-section
87 Hydraulic reservoir
88 Port wing fuel tank filler point
89 Port .5in (12.7mm) machine-guns
90 Ammunition feed chutes
91 Gun bay access door (raised)
92 Ammunition box troughs
93 Aileron control cables

94 Flap lower skin (Alclad)
95 Aileron profile (internal aero- dynamic balance diaphragm)
96 Aileron control drum and mounting bracket
97 Aileron trim tab control drum
98 Aileron trim tab plastics (phenol fibre) construction
99 Port aileron assembly

125 Coolant pipes
126 Cowling forward frame
127 Coolant header tank
128 Armour plate
129 Propeller hub
130 Spinner
131 Four-blade Hamilton Standard
    Hydromatic propeller
132 Carburettor air intake,
    integral with 133
133 Engine mount front
    frame assembly
134 Intake trunking
135 Engine mount reinforcing tie
136 Hand crank starter
137 Carburettor/trunking vibration-
    absorbing connection
138 Wing centre-section front
    bulkhead
139 Wing centre-section end rib
140 Starboard mainwheel well
141 Wing front spar/fuselage
    attachment bracket
142 Ventral air intake (radiator
    and oil cooler assemblies)
143 Starboard wing fuel tank
144 Fuel filler point
145 Mainwheel leg mount/pivot
146 Mainwheel leg rib cut-outs
147 Main gear fairing doors
148 Auxiliary fuel tank (plastic/
    pressed paper composition);
    capacity 90 imp gal (409 litres)
149 Auxiliary fuel tank (metal)
    capacity 62 gal (284 litres)
150 27in (68.6cm) smooth-
    contour mainwheel
151 Axle fork
152 Towing lugs
153 Landing gear fairing
154 Main gear shock strut
155 Blast tubes
156 Wing front spar
157 Gun bay
158 Ammunition feed chutes
159 Ammunition boxes
160 Wing rear spar
161 Flap structure
162 Starboard aileron tab
163 Starboard aileron
164 Starboard aileron tab adjustment
    mechanism (ground setting)
165 Wing rib strengthening
166 Outboard section structure
167 Outer section single spar
168 Wingtip sub-assembly
169 Starboard navigation light
170 Detachable wingtip

100 Wing skinning
101 Outer section sub-assembly
102 Port navigation light
103 Port wingtip
104 Leading-edge skin
105 Landing lamp
106 Weapons/stores pylon
107 500lb (227kg) bomb
108 Gun ports

109 Machine-gun barrels
110 Detachable cowling panels
111 Firewall/integral armour
112 Oil tank
113 Oil pipes
114 Upper longeron/engine
    mount attachment
115 Oil tank metal retaining straps
116 Carburettor

117 Engine bearer assembly
118 Cowling panel frames
119 Engine altercooler
120 Engine leads
121 Packard (Rolls-Royce Merlin)
    V-1650 engine
122 Exhaust fairing panel
123 Stub exhausts
124 Magneto

BIRTH OF A FIGHTER

With war looming in the late 1930s, it became a matter of urgency for Britain and France to expand their air forces. With their home industries already heavily committed, it was only natural that they should turn to the United States.

The best of the American fighters of this period was the Curtiss P-40. The prototype of this had first flown in the autumn of 1938, more than two years after the Spitfire, but it was in fact little more than a re-engined Hawk 75 of rather earlier vintage. A large production order for the US Army Air Corps was placed in May 1939, and this meant that the manufacturers had little spare capacity to meet export orders for Britain and France in the immediate future. At this stage, the British Purchasing Commission, based in New York, sought a second-source manufacturer. Their choice lighted on North American Aviation, based at Inglewood, California.

At that time, North American was mainly noted for its NA-16 Harvard trainer, and its sole experience of fighter design consisted of a handful of NA-50s and NA-68s for Thailand. These were in essence Harvards with more powerful engines and armament. This notwithstanding, the idea of licence-production of the Curtiss fighter did not really appeal to North American. Studies for a new fighter had been underway since the previous summer, and these appeared to indicate that the company could design a fighter around the same Allison engine used by the P-40, but which would have far better performance than the Curtiss.

A proposal was made to the British in January 1940, which resulted in a contract for a prototype, designated

Left: Prior to the P-51, North American Aviation lacked experience in fighter design, its previous attempt in this field being a souped-up and armed version of the T-6 trainer, two of which are seen here with the Mustang prototype.
Below left: The NA-73X prototype. Sleek but angular, this was vaguely similar in appearance to the German Messerschmitt Me 109E, which gave rise to all sorts of unfounded rumours. From this angle, the wingtip shows the approximate configuration of the laminar flow section that was to play such a tremendous part in the Mustang's success. (AAHS via JE)
Opposite: The instrument panel of the early Mustangs was tidily laid out, as can be seen in this photograph taken during assembly, although it followed American rather than British practice. Another departure from British practice was the wrap-around perspex windshield, with an armoured glass screen behind it. If the windshield misted up, as frequently happened, the pilot was unable to reach past the armoured glass to wipe it. The answer was a revised windshield with an armoured glass panel incorporated; this was implemented on the second production batch. Also visible here are the reflector sight and the rearview mirror. (Roger Freeman)

NA-73X. Part of the mythology of the Mustang's origins was that the British insisted that the new fighter should be produced from scratch in just four months. In fact, this arose from a statement by NAA President Dutch Kindelberger, but it was never an element in the contract. Of course, the dice were loaded; design studies had, as we have seen, been underway for almost a year, and when the contract was signed on 23 May 1940, much of the detail design was already complete. It was, however, a remarkable achievement that the NA-73X was rolled out just 102 days later, even though it lacked an engine and the wheels had been borrowed from a Harvard!

The NA-73X was sleek but angular. For ease of production, curves were never used where a straight line would do. This gave the aircraft a superficial resemblance to the Me 109E, and thus started the canard that NAA designer Edgar Schmued was a German who had once worked on the Messerschmitt fighter. There was of course no truth in this, even though it was to appear in print many times.

One crucial decision was to use a laminar flow wing

Aerodynamic drag increases in direct proportion to the square of the speed; i.e. drag at 400mph is 16 times greater than the drag for the same aircraft at 100mph. The only way to obtain greatly improved performance over another fighter which uses the same engine is to substantially reduce drag, and NAA designers made every attempt to do this. At the same time, they made every effort to keep weight down by making many items serve more than one purpose.

One of the really critical decisions was to use a laminar flow wing. This had been researched by the National Advisory Committee for Aeronautics (NACA, the forerunner of the modern NASA). The normal aerofoil sections for

---

DESIGN CONSIDERATIONS

"Strictly for comparative purposes, we are including results of a study showing the difference in size and performance between the airplane offered and one which might be offered with a minimum of armament and without protective armor. This second design (P-509) incorporates only four machine-guns and is not fitted with protective armor, but is otherwise the same. It will be noted that the high-speed in this condition is 400mph with a wing area of 190sq ft. With a full complement of armament and armor plate protection front and rear, the weight is increased from 6,450lbs to 7,765lbs and the wing area is increased from 190sq ft to 230sq ft in order to maintain the same landing speed. The resulting performance is materially reduced and the high-speed is 384mph under the same conditions."

EXTRACT FROM LETTER FROM NORTH AMERICAN AVIATION, 1 MAY 1940

---

the period had their maximum thickness at roughly 20 per cent of the chord, the chord being the distance from front to back. They also had a distinct camber, with a convex upper surface and a concave lower surface. After the airflow passed the thickest point, it had a tendency to 'burble', or become turbulent. The thickest point on a laminar flow wing was more than halfway across the chord, and for all practical purposes it had no camber; both surfaces were convex in shape. In practice, this meant that the air tended to slip smoothly past both surfaces, giving a tremendous reduction in drag. There was of course a price to be paid for this; the lift generated was not as high as a more conventional aerofoil section, and for low speeds, large and powerful slotted flaps were needed.

■ ALLISON ENGINE ■

The NA-73X was of all-metal stressed skin construction. The wings, which had pronounced dihedral, contained a sheet-web main spar, and an almost equally strong rear spar, which carried the ailerons and flaps. The distance between spars was sufficient to fit the length of the .50in (12.7mm) Browning machine-gun, leaving only the barrel to project ahead of the main spar. The main gear legs were widely spaced, giving excellent ground handling, and retracted inwards towards the centreline. The main gear wheels were large, and to house them within the wing, the leading edge was kinked forward inboard to increase wing depth at this point. To minimize drag, the tail wheel was also retractable.

The only engine considered was the Allison V-1710, which was a liquid-cooled 12-cylinder inline producing 1,150hp. Contrary to popular legend, it had a geared supercharger, but power, and with it performance, fell away rapidly above 15,000ft (4,570m). At that time the USAAC had no requirement for high-altitude combat fighters, and all American fighters of the era were equally limited. Even as the NA-73X was being built, combat experience in Europe was proving otherwise, but while a turbo-supercharger was briefly considered, it was discounted at this stage. Traditional engine mountings of the day consisted of a frame of welded steel tubes. NAA differed in designing cantilevered beams, with the engine itself resting on rubber blocks to damp out vibration.

Location of the radiator beneath the fuselage

Another attempt to minimize drag involved the cooling system. Heat from the engine was led to a radiator which dissipated it into the passing air. Heat is of course a form of energy which, unless some means could be found to harness it, was wasted. Theoreticians on both sides of the Atlantic suggested that if the heated air was discharged rearwards at high pressure, it could actually provide a small increment of thrust, which in turn would partially offset the drag of the installation. It demanded great care in

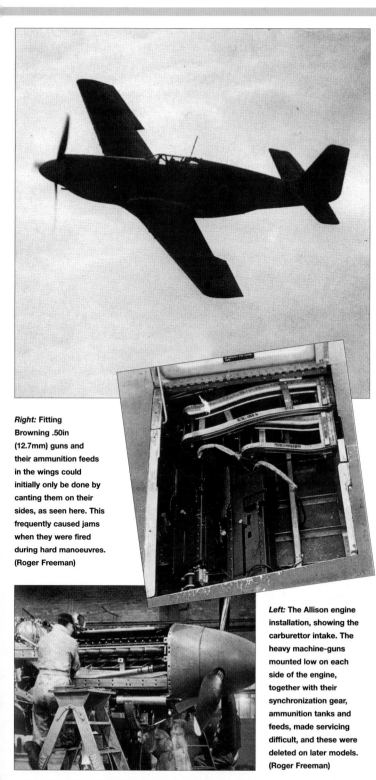

Right: Fitting Browning .50in (12.7mm) guns and their ammunition feeds in the wings could initially only be done by canting them on their sides, as seen here. This frequently caused jams when they were fired during hard manoeuvres. (Roger Freeman)

Left: The Allison engine installation, showing the carburettor intake. The heavy machine-guns mounted low on each side of the engine, together with their synchronization gear, ammunition tanks and feeds, made servicing difficult, and these were deleted on later models. (Roger Freeman)

designing the ducting for the intake and efflux, with moveable flaps to adjust the flow as necessary. While the principle was well known, early Mustang radiators did not produce thrust in this manner, and only later was this developed.

The optimum location for the radiator installation was found to be beneath the fuselage, just aft of the cockpit. A small penalty was paid in weight for the extra piping required, but in terms of performance it paid off. Not considered at that time was the danger of extra combat vulnerability, but even if this had been taken into account, it would probably have been deemed to be compensated for by increased performance.

■ 8MM SEAT ARMOUR ■

The controls were well harmonized, and instead of cables, which could slacken slightly, adversely affecting handling, the control runs were rods, again at a slight weight penalty. The control surfaces on the tail were fabric-covered, whereas the ailerons were aluminium.

The cockpit was roomy by British standards, with 8mm back armour to protect the pilot. To minimize drag, it was set low, and the roof line was faired into the fuselage. The view 'out of the window' was good, although, as with many contemporary fighters, rearward visibility could have been better. However, the canopy design drew adverse comments from some quarters. Whereas British fighters had sliding hoods, the canopy of the NA-73X was hinged. The panel on the left opened out and downwards, while the roof hinged open to the right. It could not be opened in flight, unlike the British-style canopies, although in an emergency it could be jettisoned. In this, it was not unlike the Me 109.

The NA-73X carried no armament, although dummy gun ports were painted on the leading edges of the wings. The proposed armament was heavy by any standards. Two .50in (12.7mm) Browning machine-guns were mounted

Above: Test pilot Paul Balfour came to grief on the fifth flight of NA-73X, when the engine cut. His forced landing in a cultivated field was a disaster, as can be seen here. Damage was extensive, and more than seven weeks passed before the aircraft could be flown again.

low on the nose, synchronized to fire through the propeller. These were staggered to allow their magazines to fit one behind the other. Two more .50in (12.7mm) Brownings were set outboard in the wings, with four .30in (7.62mm) Brownings further out. The magazines for the wing guns, holding two hundred .50in (12.7mm) rounds each or five hundred .30in (7.62mm) rounds each, were set well outboard, and fed by conveyor chutes.

The United States being a far larger country than Britain, Americans are perhaps more distance-conscious than their trans-Atlantic cousins. This showed in

the design fuel capacity of the NA-73X, which consisted of two 75 imperial gallon (90 US gallon/341 litre) tanks in the inboard wing sections. This was three-quarters as much again as the normal capacity of the Spitfire, and gave the new fighter the remarkable endurance of about four hours.

Fuel capacity – two 75 imperial gallon tanks in the wings

Although the airframe had been rolled out early in September 1940, Allison engines, also used in the P-38, P-39 and P-40, were in short supply. Not until early October did one become available. It was fitted quickly, and taxiing trials commenced. Then, on 26 October,

freelance test pilot Vance Breese lifted the new aircraft off the Mines Field runway for its first flight.

Three more successful test flights were made, which revealed only minor snags apart from a tendency of the engine to overheat. Modifications to the radiator inlet were needed, but before these could be put in hand, near-disaster struck.

On 20 November, company test pilot Paul Balfour took the NA-73X aloft on its fifth test flight. As he approached the runway he throttled back, and as speed bled off, the engine started to run roughly, then spluttered to a stop. With no power available, Balfour attempted a dead-stick landing in a cultivated field short of the runway. He selected gear down but, given the soft surface, this was an error. The wheels dug in and the aircraft nosed over on to its back. That there was no fire was fortunate on two counts. Balfour was trapped in the cockpit, the canopy of which was half-buried

Above: The first production aircraft, AG 345, in British markings. The short carburettor scoop has yet to be lengthened. The nose guns can be seen projecting, while some idea of the unorthodox layout of the wing guns is given by the vertically staggered ports, with the centre guns set lower than the others.

in the soft earth, and had to be dug free. Secondly, the precious prototype, although damaged, was repairable, and was returned to the flight test programme on 11 January 1941.

One of the more obvious modifications concerned the carburettor scoop. Due to the layout of the Allison engine, this was located on top of the engine cowling. Under certain flight conditions,

low airspeed, low revs and increased angle of attack, air ram recovery was insufficient. This had been responsible for the crash of the first prototype. The cure for it was to extend the intake forward to the very front of the cowling.

Ultimately the incident did not jeopardize the project. The urgency of the British requirement meant that the North American fighter had been purchased 'off the drawing board', an order for 320 having been placed in August 1940, following the original letter of intent of 11 April. Then, during December of that year, it was officially named Mustang by the British.

The first production aircraft was scheduled for delivery in January 1941, but, due to various problems, it did not take to the air

until 23 April. This machine was not delivered to the RAF; instead it was retained as a development aircraft by NAA, who flew it intensively in conjunction with the prototype.

■ FIRST MUSTANG ■ IN THE UK

The first Mustang to reach Britain arrived at Liverpool docks in a crate in October 1941, having survived the attentions of the U-boats en route. It was taken to Speke airport, where it was assembled, and made its first flight in its adoptive country on 24 October. From Speke it went to the Aeroplane and Armament Experimental Establishment at Boscombe Down, where all operational equipment, British gunsights, radios etc were installed, and evaluation began. Further evaluation of this aircraft and one other was made by the Air Fighting

Left: The first production Mustang flew on 23 April 1941. From this angle, the short carburettor scoop above the engine and the radiator housing beneath the fuselage can clearly be seen. The control surfaces on the tail were fabric-covered, which accounts for the different colour. (Paul Coggan via JE).

FLYING REPORT

"The aircraft is pleasant to fly, being extremely stable in all planes. The take-off is rather long, but with little tendency to swing, and as the engine is not fitted with an automatic boost control, care must be taken not to overboost. The landing is easy though the run is longer than taken by a Hurricane or Spitfire. The controls are well balanced and can be made light or heavy as required by adjustment of the servo-tabs fitted to ailerons and elevators. There is little tendency to heavy-up at high speeds. With the controls lightened by the tabs, the Mustang is as light as the Spitfire but far smoother in all manoeuvres. The aircraft handles extremely well in aerobatics and gives ample warning of the stall. In particular, it was found far more difficult to effect a high speed stall than in a Spitfire."

EXTRACT FROM AFDU REPORT, 5 MAY 1942

Development Unit at RAF Duxford from 28 January 1942. In fact, most of the first 20 Mustangs to arrive in Britain were initially used for evaluation and installation trials.

The AFDU at Duxford gave a very favourable report on the American fighter, praising its handling in particular. It noted that the cockpit, while generally spacious and comfortable, was a trifle cramped for a tall pilot. In addition, it was excessively hot, even in freezing conditions. Compared to the Spitfire VB, it was significantly faster at low and medium altitudes, but the speed advantage was lost at 25,000ft (7,600m). In rate of climb, the Mustang was significantly inferior to the British fighter, by which it was outmanoeuvred at all heights. It did, however, perform far better in the dive as a result of its aerodynamic cleanness.

■ A MAJOR FLAW ■

The fall-off in performance with increasing altitude was the one flaw in an otherwise superb fighting aeroplane. From the first days of air fighting, altitude had always been regarded as the most important tactical advantage. By 1942, most air combat took place at altitudes where the Mustang was less agile. This being the case, RAF Fighter Command could not risk it, and the majority of the first batch of Mustang Is went to Army Co-operation Command squadrons, where their sparkling low-level performance and outstanding range could be fully utilized in the low-level armed reconnaissance role. For this they were fitted with an F24 oblique camera mounted behind the pilot's head armour.

Even as prophets are traditionally without honour in their own land, so the Mustang was for a long time ignored by the USAAF. Reasons were not hard to find: existing fighters such as the P-38 and P-40 were undergoing further development, while several new and promising designs were coming along fast, among them Republic's enormous P-47 Thunderbolt. Consequently, there

Above: The seventh production Mustang I seen at the Air Fighting Development Unit, RAF Duxford, for which it had the yellow 'P' in a circle painted on the fuselage. The carburettor scoop on this machine has been lengthened, and the adjustable outlet at the rear of the radiator farm can be seen open.
Right: The fourth and tenth production Mustangs were retained by the USAAC for evaluation under the designation XP-51. This was a departure from standard practice, as the 'X' prefix was normally only given to true prototypes, which this was far from being. Seen here in RAF colours and apparently ready for delivery is AG 348, the fourth production machine, later renumbered as 41-038.

was little interest in what was primarily seen as a 'foreign' design. The USAAF did, however, acquire two examples of the type.

This had come about quite fortuitously. Before warplanes could be exported, the manufacturer needed a Foreign Release Agreement with the USAAC (as the USAAF then was). This agreement stated that the fourth and tenth production machines should be supplied for evaluation, with the designation XP-51. Although the first aircraft was flown on 20 May 1941, various delays ensured that it did not reach the test centre at Wright Field, Ohio (now Wright-Patterson AFB) until 24 August. The second XP-51 did not arrive until 16 December that year, by which time the official performance flight tests were all but complete.

The US government made credit available with Lend-Lease

The first batch of Mustangs for the RAF was a straight sale, but with the costs of all-out war escalating, British funds ran short. At this stage, the US government made credit available with Lend-Lease. Under this arrangement, the USAAF ordered aircraft as though for their own use, then passed them on. On 7 July 1941, the USAAF placed an order for 150 Mustangs on behalf of the RAF. These differed from the previous batch in that they were armed with four 20mm Hispano Suiza cannon in place of the previous eight machine-guns, a change arising from extensive combat experience. In RAF service these became Mustang IAs; to the Americans they were plain P-51s, with no suffix letter.

With flight testing at Wright Field in full swing early in December 1941, the treacherous attack on Pearl Harbor by the Japanese catapulted the United States into the war. While this was to have a lasting effect on the future of the Mustang, at first it served only to obscure matters as American fighter development

Top: 41-038 seen at the Wright Field, Ohio, test centre (now Wright-Patterson AFB) some time after 24 August 1942. With the exception of an anti-dazzle panel on the cowling and bright national markings, the aircraft is in bare metal. Surprisingly, the carburettor scoop has not been lengthened, while the gun ports have either been blanked over, or airbrushed out by the censor. (USAF via JE)

Middle: 41-038 survived the war, albeit in a sad and careworn state. Seen here at Freeman Field in Indiana in 1945 and scheduled for the scrap yard, it was rescued for the National Air and Space Museum. (Haney Collection via JE)
Bottom: Completely refurbished by the Experimental Aircraft Association after 30 years in storage, 41-038 flew again in 1980 as part of the Warbirds of America fleet.

XP-51 OFFICIAL PERFORMANCE SUMMARY

Level flight speed at design altitude of 13,000ft (3,950m) with a design gross weight of 7,934lb (3,600kg)

Maximum speed 382mph (615km/hr), 3,000rpm/1,100bhp
High speed 370mph (595km/hr), 3,000rpm/1,100bhp
Cruising speed 325.5mph (524km/hr), 2,280rpm/750bhp

Optimum range and endurance with 170 imperial gallons fuel
Cruising speed 780 miles (1,255km) 2.4 hours

Climb data with gross weight of 7,934lb (3,600kg)

Altitude	0/0	5,000/	10,000/	15,000/	20,000/	25,000/	30,800/
(ft/m)		1,524	3,0484	572	6,095	7,620	9,387
Climbing speed							
(mph/kh)	178/286	194/312	208/335	222/357	236/380	248/399	262/422
Engine (rpm)	3,000	3,000	3,000	2,600	2,600	2,600	2,600
Power (bhp)	1,050	1,095	1,140	820	680	550	-
Maximum climb							
ft/min	2,200	2,270	2,345	1,570	1,070	610	100
m/sec	11.18	11.53	11.91	7.98	5.44	3.10	0.51

and production was stepped up. The few Wright Field test pilots who had flown the Mustang were impressed, but they were lone voices crying in the wilderness. Only slowly were its sterling qualities recognized and accepted.

Of the 150 P-51s ordered for the RAF, only 93 were actually delivered to them. Of the remainder, 55 were retained by the USAAF, commencing in July 1942, by whom they were at first known as Apaches. Most of these were fitted with cameras to become F-6A tactical reconnaissance machines. The final two were earmarked for the XP-78 project, which involved a change of engine.

Massive expansion had caused budgetary problems for the USAAF, and by the time that it decided that it wanted the Mustang, the budget for fighters was exhausted. There was, however, still money in the kitty for an attack aircraft. Consultations between NAA and the Pentagon resulted in the A-36A Invader. In essence, this was a P-51 with the uprated -87 Allison engine, underwing racks to carry two 500lb (227kg) bombs, and dive brakes. Hydraulically actuated, these were of the perforated door type, set above and below the wings. The .30in (7.62mm) machine-guns in the wings were deleted.

■ DIVE-BOMBER PLOY ■

At this stage the USAAF had no requirement for a dive bomber, but modifying the P-51 in this way was a useful ploy for getting it into USAAF service. Be this as it may, this did not prevent the USAAF from evaluating the A-36A as a dive bomber. On 16 April 1942, a massive order for 500 A-36As was placed, long before this variant flew.

This was followed on 23 June (when the next year's budget became available) by another order for 310 P-51As. These used the latest model Allison V-1780-81 engine, which developed maximum power at 18,000ft (5,490m) and thus significantly improved high-altitude performance, although it still did not give the Mustang parity in this sphere with its European contemporaries. The other major change was in weaponry; the nose-mounted guns with their heavy and cumbersome synchronization gears, the latter necessary to prevent damage to the propeller, were deleted, as were the wing-mounted .30in (7.62mm) machine-guns. The number of wing-mounted .50in (12.7mm) Browning heavy machine-guns was increased to four.

This change in the armament offered several advantages. With the increasing

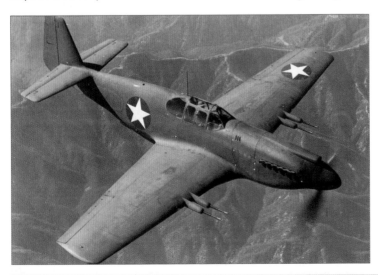

Left: The angular lines of the Mustang made it easily mistaken for the rather smaller Me 109E. Seen here is the most heavily armed Mustang of all, the P-51 (no suffix letter), which carried four 20mm cannon in the wings. (Roger Freeman)

Left: The A-36A Invader was the dive bomber variant, fitted with dive brakes above and below the wings. With an uprated Allison engine, it could carry one 500lb (227kg) bomb beneath each wing. The wing-mounted .30in (7.62mm) machine-guns were deleted, as seen here.

use of armour plate and self-sealing tanks by the enemy, light machine-guns had little to commend them, whereas the Browning .50s were adequate against all but heavy bombers, few of which were likely to be encountered. The projectile of the heavier gun had near-perfect ballistics (the world's first supersonic fighter, the Bell X-l, used the same shape for its fuselage) giving a long effective range. Weight saving was considerable. The complexity of the overlapping feeds for the wing guns was greatly reduced, while the logistical problems that arose from using two different sizes of ammunition were eliminated.

Right: P-51A of the USAAF. The wide spread of the main gear legs made it particularly suitable for operations from semi-prepared airstrips. (Roger Freeman)

USAAF reverted to the British name of Mustang

The A-36 made its maiden flight in the hands of test pilot Ben Chilton on 21 September 1942 – by which time the USAAF had reverted to using the British name of Mustang for all variants – and the same pilot also took the first P-51A into the air on 3 February 1943. With production by now in full swing, first deliveries of the latter took place

Above: Reconnaissance Mustang! The F-6B was a P-51A fitted with a twin K24 camera installation. This 9th Air Force example is from the 107th Squadron of the 67th Tactical Reconnaissance Group. It is fitted with the Malcolm hood, a field modification invented by the British to improve all-round view from the cockpit. (T. R. Bennett via JE)

FLYING REPORT

"The A-36 has excellent diving characteristics from the standpoint of a fighter, but it dives too fast for a dive bomber, the dive breaks slowing the airplane down approximately eighty-three (83) miles per hour. This is insufficient from the dive bomber standpoint, as the airplane will still dive with the dive breaks open to speed in excess of four-hundred-fifty miles per hour, necessitating bomb release at approximately four thousand (4,000) feet in order to pull out of the dive. The best diving angle is approximately seventy (70) degrees."

EXTRACT FROM FINAL REPORT ON TEST OF THE OPERATIONAL SUITABILITY OF THE A-36 TYPE AIRPLANE, 15 APRIL 1943

during the following month. Of the 310 P-51As, 35 were fitted with the twin K24 camera installation to become F-6Bs, while 50 were allocated to the RAF as Mustang IIs.

The Mustang was by now well and truly launched in both RAF and USAAF service. But the best this fighter could produce was still to come.

ALLISON MUSTANGS
IN SERVICE

The first Mustang delivery to an operational unit was made in late January 1942. The lucky recipient was No. 26 Squadron of Army Co-operation Command (ACC) RAF, based at Gatwick where the international airport now stands, but then just a grass field.

■ BRITISH MUSTANGS ■ (WESTERN EUROPE)

Experience in the Battle of France (albeit at the receiving end) had convinced the British that the key to success in land operations lay in close co-operation with the air. The RAF had long possessed dedicated army co-operations squadrons, but on the outbreak of

Left: Tactical reconnaissance Mustangs of No. 168 Squadron RAF overfly allied armour advancing across Normandy. They carry the invasion stripes adopted for instant recognition. (Roger Freeman)

war these were equipped with antiquated Hawker Hector biplanes and lumbering Westland Lysanders. Both types of aircraft were far too slow and vulnerable for modern warfare.

Army Co-operation Command (ACC) was formed in December 1940 as a Command in its own right, with the object of building an effective tactical reconnaissance and close air support force against

Above: Mustang I of No. 26 Squadron poses for the camera with a few degrees of flap. The vertically staggered gunports indicate some of the problems of getting three machine guns in the wings. (Roger Freeman)

Below: Same engine, different aircraft. A P-40 Tomahawk I in RAF service. The slightly ungainly appearance is due to its development from the radial engined P-36 (Crown Copyright via Bruce Robertson)

Above: The Mustang I supplanted the Westland Lysander in Army Co-operation Command. This is an aircraft of No. 225 Squadron. (via Bruce Robertson)

the day when the war could be carried to the Third Reich. Its first task was to re-equip with faster and more modern aircraft, but these were in short supply. ACC had to take what was available, which in this case was the Curtiss P-40 Tomahawk, rejected by RAF Fighter Command because of poor high altitude performance – although used effectively in North Africa with the Desert Air Force.

Re-equipment with the Tomahawk commenced in August 1941, but a high rate of unserviceability made this type unsatisfactory. The Mustang, also rejected by Fighter Command for shortcomings at high altitude, but with an outstanding performance at low level, came at the ideal time to replace it.

The army co-operation mission was still in the throes of development at this stage. For this reason, conversion on to type was a fairly leisurely affair, with both types operated during the conversion phase. This had the advantage of keeping all the squadrons operational rather than taking them out of the line to re-equip. By October of that year, no fewer than 14 squadrons had converted to the Mustang I or II.

Below: Mustangs of No. 400 Squadron RCAF, parked on a hardstanding at Dunsfold, Surrey, in 1943. These have flame dampers on the exhausts for Night Ranger missions. (Roger Freeman)

MUSTANG I AND II SQUADRONS IN ACC SERVICE, OCTOBER 1942

Sqn	Service	Prev A/C
2	RAF	Tomahawk
4	RAF	Lysander
16	RAF	Lysander
26	RAF	Tomahawk
63	RAF	Hurricane
169	RAF	Beaufighter
239	RAF	Tomahawk
241	RAF	Tomahawk
268	RAF	Tomahawk
309	Polish	Hurricane
400	RCAF	Tomahawk
414	RCAF	Tomahawk
430	RCAF	Tomahawk
613	R(Aux)AF	Tomahawk

No. 241 squadron never flew Mustangs operationally. In November 1942 it was sent to the Middle East to fly Hurricanes, and its aircraft were taken over by No. 168 Squadron.

In all, 24 British squadrons flew Allison-engined Mustangs during the war, although there were never more than 16 at any one time.

■ MUSTANG AND ■ 109 LOOKALIKE

A major cause for concern was the superficial resemblance between the Mustang and the Messerschmitt Me 109, particularly the 109E, which had squarecut wingtips. To make for easier identification, most Mustang Is in front-line squadrons carried painted yellow bands around the wings throughout 1942.

The combat debut of the Mustang came on 10 May, when a single aircraft of No. 26 Squadron flown by Flying Officer G. N. Dawson left Gatwick at first light for an armed reconnaissance. Crossing the coast south of Le Touquet, he shot up hangars in the corner of the airfield north of Berck

Plage, then attacked a goods train before returning safely. From such small beginnings, the Mustang legend grew!

The first major operation in which the Mustang was committed was the amphibious landing at Dieppe on 19 August. Virtually a dress rehearsal for the later invasion, it was a test of effectiveness of the army co-operation concept. Four ACC squadrons were involved; the already operational No. 26 and 239, with elements from the Canadian No. 400 and 414 Squadrons, whose operational debut this was.

Nine Mustangs were shot down by flak and fighters in the course of 72 sorties, while two more were damaged beyond repair.

Below: Practice run. Mustang Is of No. 63 Squadron hurtle low over Scotland in April 1943. The aircraft from which the picture was taken was obviously even lower than these two. (Roger Freeman)

Information on the tactical situation was available in England very quickly; and American pilot Hollis Hills, flying with No. 414 Squadron RCAF, claimed a Focke-Wulf FW 190 as the Mustang's first air combat victory. It was the first of many.

■ POPULAR OPS ■

The low-altitude armed photo-reconnaissance sorties which were the ACC Mustang's basic mission were codenamed Popular'. These sorties were normally flown by a section of two at 270mph (434km/hr) at very low altitude. The technique was to point the port wing at a target, then set the camera rolling. The task of the wingman was to protect his leader by keeping a sharp lookout for fighters. 'Populars' were only flown in conditions of seven-tenths cloud or more, With the cloud base at 1,500ft (460m) or less. This provided something in which to hide.

Below: German flying boats moored on a lake in the south of France burn under the guns of attacking Mustangs in 1944. (Roger Freeman)

LOW LEVEL TACTICS

Attacks should be alternated between the two members of the flight, one covering while the other makes the attack. Each pilot of the pair should be constantly searching for enemy aircraft so as to avoid a surprise attack by enemy pursuit (aircraft). Attacks should be made from one side of the railway, canal or roadway, to the other – never along. An attack should never be repeated even though the objective has been missed, because the protecting element of surprise is no longer present. At a speed of 270mph [434km/hr] and at zero altitude, the search area is comparatively limited and targets appear quickly. Experience and alertness are required to pick out those targets in time to make an attack . . . It has also been found that depressing the flaps 5° will have little effect on the speed, but it will change the attitude of the aircraft so that targets can more easily be seen over the nose.

BRITISH ARMY CO-OPERATION TACTICAL
EMPLOYMENT OF THE MUSTANG, 26 AUGUST 1943

After the Dieppe raid, 'Rhubarbs' became fashionable. These were low-level incursions aimed at specific ground targets, flown by two aircraft in weather conditions which would aid them in eluding the German defences. 'Rangers' were identical except that targets of opportunity were sought. Spitfires also flew these missions, but because the Mustang could penetrate twice as far into enemy territory it was far more useful in this role. In 18 months, a single Mustang squadron destroyed or damaged 200 railway engines, over 200 barges, and a number of enemy aircraft on the ground. Losses during this period were eight Mustangs: five to flak, two to unknown causes, and one to enemy fighters. Mustangs penetrated into Germany itself, to just outside Wilhelmshaven. Air combat was avoided if possible, but nearly 30 German fighters fell to the guns of Allison-engined RAF Mustangs. No. 400 Squadron RCAF claimed a dozen in the flrst year of operations, three alone falling to the guns of Flight Lieutenant Duncan Grant. From June 1943, this unit

also flew night intruder patrols, attacking German aircraft over their own bases. For these night missions, flame-damping exhausts were fitted.

ACC was disbanded in June 1943, and the Mustang squadrons, transferred to 2nd Tactical Air Force, set up specifically for the invasion of Europe. Production of Allison engined Mustangs had ceased at this time, and the attrition inherent in low-level operations caused a shortage of aircraft. Between June 1943 and January 1944, nine Mustang squadrons converted to other types.

By D-Day, 6 June 1944, only five British Allison-Mustang squadrons remained; Nos 2, 168, 268, 414 RCAF and 430 RCAF. By the end of the year only Nos 26 and 268 Squadrons still operated the type. No. 26 ceased to fly Mustangs late in 1943, but reconverted in October 1944 for the photo reconnaissance of V-2 rocket-launching sites in Holland. At the end of the war in Europe, only these two squadrons still flew Allison-Mustangs.

■ AMERICAN MUSTANGS ■ (WESTERN EUROPE)

With the invasion of Europe scheduled for mid-1944, the USAAF planned to have several squadrons of F-6As and F-6Bs in place in England for the event. However, the plan was foiled by the non-availability of Allison-engined Mustangs, and in fact only one unit was formed. This was the understrength 67th TRG, with a mere 24 F-6Bs, which took up residence at Membury in October 1943.

ALLISON-MUSTANG UNITS IN SERVICE IN ENGLAND, D-DAY, 6 JUNE 1944

No. 2	Squadron	RAF
No. 168	Squadron	RAF
No. 268	Squadron	RAF
No. 414	Squadron	RCAF
No. 430	Squadron	RCAF
67th	TRG	USAAF

■ AMERICAN MUSTANGS ■ (MEDITERRANEAN)

The first USAAF Mustangs in operation were the cannon-armed P-51s. In October they were followed by the A-36A Invader. Although the USAAF originally had no requirement for a dive bomber, training for this role began. The air brakes sometimes extended unevenly due to varying hydraulic pressures, and it was difficult to keep the aircraft aligned on its target. Structural failures sometimes occurred, causing the loss of both aircraft and pilot. The USAAF recommended that the type should be used for low attack only.

By March 1943, USAAF Mustangs were ready for action. Their combat debut came in North Africa, when the 68th Observation Group, based in Morocco, received 35 P-51s. They were really camera-equipped F-6As, but this designation was rarely used.

Above: American aircraft used by the RAF, seen at Speke in December 1941. In the foreground is Mustang I, later allocated to No. 430 (Canadian) Squadron; behind is a P-40D Kittyhawk, while left to right in the background are a Lockheed Hudson and two Douglas Boston light bombers. (Roger Freeman)

That same month, the A-36As of the 86th Bomb Group were also shipped to Africa, but for various reasons this unit was late getting into action. The combat debut of USAAF Mustangs took place on 10 April, on a photo-reconnaissance mission to Kairouan airfield in Tunisia.

By the end of May over 300 A-36As had arrived in North Africa. The American Mustang units in the Mediterranean theatre used yellow wing stripes for ease of identification.

It was the 27th BG that took the A-36A to war for the first time, when it dive-bombed the airfield on the Axis-held island

Opposite above: **Desert conditions played havoc with aircraft, not least their paint schemes, as shown by this camera equipped P-51 in North Africa. The Stars and Stripes on the tail was adopted for the benefit of local inhabitants who might have been unfamiliar with standard USAAF Insignia.**

Opposite below: **A-36A of 27th Fighter-Bomber Group in Sicily, 1943. The white bars on the nose carry the mission records. This aircraft, No 42-84067, is seen with a 500lb (227kg) bomb under each wing. (USAAF via Roger Freeman.)**

of Pantelleria on 6 June. Attacks on Sicilian targets followed; then, shortly after the successful invasion of that island, the 27th moved to Sicily, where it was joined by the 86th. Both Groups then took part in attacks on the Italian mainland.

The sequence of events for a dive-bombing attack was as follows. Target approach was between 8,000 and 10,000ft (2,400–3,000m). Air brakes out, then half-roll directly above the target and pull through into a vertical dive. The bombs were released as the speed built up through 300mph (483km/hr), which was usually at an altitude of between 2,000 to 4,000ft (600–1,200m), with recovery on the deck. Against heavy flak defences, bomb release and recovery were made much higher. Attacks were made by sections of four, who went down one after the other. This had the fault of putting all aircraft in the same chute; if the ground gunners missed the leader, they might easily get one of those following. Tail-end Charlie in a dive-bombing mission was not an enviable place to be!

■ DIVE-BOMBING ■

The difference between dive- and glide-bombing was purely the angle of dive on the attack run. Anything less than 72 degrees was regarded as glide-bombing. A true vertical dive gave greatest accuracy, but it was not easy to tell when this was achieved. There was only one foolproof way; an aileron roll would cause the aim to wander off if the dive angle was less than 90 degrees! One final canard should be disposed of; it has often been stated that the air brakes were wired shut. There was an early recommendation that they should not be used, due to handling problems caused by differential deployment. The wiring story, which is baseless, appears to have arisen from this. In fact, the problem was largely overcome by a simple modification.

While based on Sicily, the two A-36A groups several times provided escorts for B-17s and B-24s raiding targets in the Naples area. This was not a great success due to their lack of high-altitude capability but they were

Above: **An A-36A Mustang of the 27th FBG overflies the Vesuvius volcano south of Naples shortly before it erupted in 1944. (USAAF via Roger Freeman)**

the only fighters in the theatre with the range to get there and back. German fighter and flak defences were fierce, and several aircraft were lost on these missions.

The Salerno landing in September 1943 also saw the Mustang's long operational radius used to the full, although on this occasion they were not required to operate at high altitude.

HIGH SPEED

It became an excellent fighter-bomber, capable of delivering its load with extreme accuracy. Its high speed and good manoeuvrability make it an excellent aircraft for either dive or glide bombing, but it must be noted the accuracy obtained by glide bombing is much less than that obtained by using the dive brakes to secure vertical dives on the target.

NORTHWEST AFRICAN
AIR FORCE TACTICAL BULLETIN
No.23, 1 JULY 1943

DIVE-BOMBER

'Our most dangerous flights were down the straits between the toe of Italy and the island of Sicily, when we were assigned the task of bombing enemy barges, which were being used to get troops out of Sicily. The anti-aircraft fire was intense during these missions, which were successful but costly in terms of pilots and planes. We were very successful in hitting the barges during dive-bombing. I have no idea how many guns were mounted on the barges; we were too busy concentrating on our dive-bombing and strafing runs to count guns.'

WAYNE RUTHERFORD, 86TH FBG.

Then after a few days the 27th and 86th TRGs were moved to an airstrip on the beachhead itself. The missions were of short duration but very dangerous, as the Mustangs were under fire even during take-off and landing.

The mountainous terrain in Italy made dive-bombing necessary, even though losses in this form of attack were high. Where possible, low-level attacks were substituted. With no replacement aircraft forthcoming, the 27th and 86th, by now redesignated as Fighter-Bomber Groups, suffered a reduction in size from four squadrons to three. By March 1944, almost half the available A-36As had been lost or written off. Matters were made worse when a handful of A-36As were transferred to the 111th TRS of the 68th TRG, to supplement their F-6As. This situation could

not last. The 27th FBG re-equipped with P-40s that month, while in July the 86th FBG converted to P-47s. At much the same time, the 111th TRS handed in their remaining P-51 As and A-36As in exchange for Merlin-engined Mustangs. It was the end of an era.

■ AMERICAN MUSTANGS ■
(FAR EAST)

The 311th FBG arrived at Dinjan in north-east India in the late summer of 1943, having been shipped across the Pacific via Australia. Two squadrons were equipped with A-36As; the third

Below: P-51A Mustangs of the 1st Air Commando Group at an airfield outside Karachi before moving to Burma. The first operation of the 1st ACG was in support of the Chindits, the long-range penetration force led by Orde Wingate which operated behind Japanese lines. (USAF via JE)

Above: Conditions in the India/Burma theatre of operations were often primitive. This P-51A of the 1st ACG, seen being refuelled by hand pump from 40 gallon drums, was flown by Captain Robert L. Pettit. (USAF via JE)

flew P-51As. It was an all-can-do group, tasked not only with reconnaissance, attack and dive-bombing, but interception and bomber escort. In these last two it was rather less than succcssful.

The main Japanese fighter was the Nakajima Ki-43 Hayabusa 'Oscar'. This very lightly wing-loaded Japanese fighter outclimbed and out-turned the P-5IA at all altitudes and had a far higher ceiling. From low speeds it accelerated rapidly but it did have a relatively light armament of two 0.50in (12.7mm) machine guns, and general lack of protection for fuel tanks and pilot.

Tasked to provide protection for transports flying over the Himalaya, the A-36As were forced to fight at higher than optimum altitudes, and three went missing very quickly. The P-51A-equipped 530th FBS was detached to Kurmitola in Bengal to provide fighter escort for bombing raids on the Rangoon area, some 450 miles (725km) away. Fitted with two 60 imperial gallon (75 US gallon/284 litre) drop tanks, these were the first long-range escort missions to be undertaken by Mustangs.

While escorting Mitchells on a raid on Mingaladon airfield, the 530th was bounced by four Hayabusas. Out-manoeuvred in a low-level turning fight, two Mustangs were lost. At Insein, four Mustangs were lost for a single Hayabusa shot down and another badly damaged. After four escort missions, 530th FBS losses amounted to 50 per cent of strength.

P-51As were also used by two Air Commando units set up to support the Chindits on their deep penetrations behind Japanese lines. They operated from small strips carved from the jungle, carrying two 1,000lb (454kg) bombs, or triple Bazooka installations. A handful of P-51As also operated with USAAF units based in China.

THE ROLLS-ROYCE ENGINE

The margin between success and failure is always slim. As fighters sought ever greater altitudes, the British need for the Allison-engined Mustang diminished. As it was, the type was rejected for the pure fighter role due to its poor high-altitude performance. Had the RAF not had a requirement for low-level tactical reconnaissance, it might easily have been shunted off to some less important theatre of operations, there to languish largely unseen and unsung, until attrition removed it from the inventory.

On the other hand, the great wonder is that the Mustang was not designed with a more suitable engine from the start. Such an engine was available from the outset; the Rolls-Royce Merlin which powered the Spitfire and Hurricane, and a dozen other aircraft as well. As the Mustang was designed for the British, it is extremely surprising that such a power plant was not suggested at a very early stage. That the superb American airframe was eventually mated with the equally superb British engine appears to have been due to chance as much as anything. Be that as it may, it produced one of the truly great fighters of the Second World War, albeit rather belatedly.

■ SOMETHING BETTER ■

Late April 1942. The Mustang prototype had made its first flight almost exactly 18 months earlier, and AFDU was finalizing the test report on the production articles at Duxford. Meanwhile, a new German fighter, the Focke-Wulf FW 190A, had entered large-scale service on the Channel coast. It comfortably outclassed the standard British fighter of the day, the Spitfire V.

Almost overnight, the RAF had slipped from a slight technical advantage to a position of undoubted inferiority. Something better was needed, urgently. This was the state of play when Rolls-Royce test pilot Ronald Harker visited Duxford.

Part of Harker's brief was to evaluate the performance of aircraft powered by engines built by companies other than Rolls-Royce. This included not only British competitors, but American and captured German machines.

Opposite: **P-51B Mustangs of the 354th FG shepherd B-24 Liberators of the 458th Bomb Group over the sea. In proximity to the enemy, the American fighters would maintain a healthy distance from the guns of the bombers. (Roger Freeman)**
Below: **The Mustang X, a Rolls-Royce company conversion with a Merlin 65 engine. The intercooler radiator beneath the nose rather spoiled the sleek lines of the original aircraft. (Roger Freeman)**

Left: NAA converted two Mustangs to take Packard-Merlin V-1650 engines as XP-78s, later redesignated XP-51Bs. The first to fly, 41-37352, seen here, was originally built as a P-51 for the RAF, but was taken over by the USAAF when America entered the war. The 20mm cannon armament was retained. (USAF via JE)

Below: Drop tanks beneath the wings, a P-51B of 354th FG based at Boxted in Essex taxies out ready for take-off. This variant carried only four guns. (Associated Press via Roger Freeman)

On this particular day, 30 April, Wing Commander Ian Campbell-Orde, commanding AFDU, invited Harker to try out the Mustang. A 30-minute flight impressed him tremendously, although he noted the fall-off of power at altitude. At the same time, he realized that the new Merlin 61, with a two-stage supercharger, would make all the difference.

On his return to Rolls-Royce, he asked the chief engineer to calculate performance figures for such a machine. The results were startling. Maximum speed was 441mph (710km/hr). Not only was this 70mph (113km/hr) faster than the Allison Mustang, but it was achievable at 25,600ft (7,800m) – almost double the best altitude of the American fighter! If the calculations were correct, the combination was a potential world-beater. In some parameters it was better than the new Spitfire VIII powered by the same engine.

TEST FLYING

"Flying a new airplane I always put the power on easily at the start to get the feel of the airplane on the ground, then gradually gave it power. When I got airborne, a couple of hundred feet off the ground, I pulled up the gear and decided then I'd see how it would climb from scratch. I poured the coal to it and the aircraft snap-rolled! Rolls-Royce hadn't provided enough vertical fin area, and not enough offset."

LT COL. CAS HOUGH, USAAF

■ TWO-STAGE MERLIN ■

The advent of the Merlin 61 was almost as fortuitous. By mid-1941, the engine had neared its development limits, and the future was thought to lie with the larger Griffon. There was, however, a requirement for a turbo-charged Merlin to power a high-altitude bomber. But turbo-superchargers, as American engine manufacturers knew well, were heavy, bulky and complicated. As an alternative, Rolls-Royce hooked up two superchargers in series. The results were startling. Trial flights showed the full-throttle altitude was 29,750ft (9,070m); an amazing increase! Shortly after, the high-altitude bomber was cancelled and the new engine was developed for the Spitfire as the Merlin 61.

At first, interest in Harker's proposal was lukewarm, but as the new engine was expected to give the Spitfire little more than parity with the FW 190A, the prospect of a fighter which would clearly outperform the German machine was too tempting to resist. Five Mustang airframes were acquired for trials.

The Americans had meanwhile been keeping a close watch on developments. Arrangements had been made for Packard to licence-build the Merlin as the V-1650 as long ago as October 1940. By 1942, American production of the British engine was in full flood, and arrangements for production of the Merlin 61 were well in hand. North American were fully in the picture, and also started planning a Mustang with the new engine.

■ HIGHER AND FASTER ■

Fortunately not too many modifications were needed. The Merlin was dimensionally similar to the Allison, although it was some 300lb (136kg) heavier. The extra weight was more than offset by about 600hp extra, plus the high-altitude capability that was so desperately needed. Rolls-Royce chose to design a new engine mount. The intercooler for the supercharger installation led to a

Left: Fresh from the factory, this Block 1 P-51B shows off its beautifully clean lines, the low drag of which contributed materially to its superb performance.
Middle: Although seemingly a P-51B with USAAF insignia, this is actually a late-production Mustang III destined for the RAF (FX 883), and carries an RAF fin flash and RAF camouflage. The inboard kink of the wing leading edge is very apparent from this angle. (Paul Coggan via JE)
Bottom: A Texas-built P-51C. The only visible difference between this and a P-51B is in the radio mast at the rear of the cockpit. This is a late-production aircraft, completed at the time when bare aluminium was favoured over camouflage. While this was popularly supposed to increase maximum speed, differences between specific aircraft made it impossible to confirm. (Paul Coggan via JE)

small radiator under the nose, and this location also housed the carburettor intake, giving a rather bulged effect to the front of the aeroplane and spoiling its clean lines.

The first flight of the Mustang X, as it was designated, took place at Hucknall on 13 October 1942. While all went well, it was quickly evident that the formerly pleasant handling qualities had been adversely affected by the changes. Torque from the more powerful engine and the four-bladed propeller reduced directional stability, particularly in the dive. To overcome this, a small dorsal spine was added to the rear fuselage just in front of the fin, to give extra keel area. Despite the draggy nose contours, the first Mustang X attained a level speed of 433mph (697km/hr), and reached 20,000ft (6,100m) in 6.3 minutes; barely two-thirds of the time taken by the Allison Mustang. But the P-51X was purely experimental, with Rolls-Royce feeding information back to NAA in California.

■ TWO-SEATER ■

Meanwhile, NAA had also been moving fast. Authorization to convert two Mustangs to Merlins had been issued on 25 July. At first these were designated XP-78; only later did they become XP-51Bs. Whereas Rolls-Royce had spoiled the clean lines of the nose with

Above: A late-production P-51B, *Snoot's Sniper*, was given the Malcolm hood as a field modification. A sliding canopy, this could be opened in flight, unlike the previous 'lid and door' arrangement. This was an advantage on the landing approach in bad weather.

was easier said than done, and much redesign and intensive wind tunnel testing was needed to get it right.

Externally the P-51B differed little from the P-51A. The nose was slightly fatter, with the dorsal air scoop replaced by a less obvious ventral intake just behind the spinner. A Hamilton four-bladed propeller replaced the three-bladed one, and the radiator group under the mid-fuselage was slightly deeper. The structure had been beefed up internally, and hard points added beneath the wings to carry bombs. These were also plumbed for external drop tanks. Armament was standardized at four .50in (12.7mm) machine-guns in the wings.

The first flight of the XP-51B took place on 30 November 1942, almost seven weeks later than the Rolls-Royce conversion, and immediately superior performance was evident. NAA test pilot Ben Chilton achieved a level speed of 441mph (710km/hr) at 29,800ft

their conversions, with a consequent increase in drag and reduction in performance, NAA were extremely reluctant to do so. Urgent studies followed, which soon made it clear that the best location for the intercooler radiator was in with the group beneath the mid-fuselage. This

Above: With a 75-gallon drop tank beneath each wing, the range of the P-51B was extended sufficiently to allow it to act as a long-range escort fighter. Its success in this role completely changed the bombing offensive against Germany.
Above right: This Mustang had a chequered career. Still crated, it was dropped in the sea while being unloaded, and badly damaged. Condemned to be reduced for spares, it was rebuilt as a two-seater, in which configuration it is seen here. It was finally lost in the Irish Sea in 1944 due to engine problems. (George Gosney via JE)
Right: P-51B of Don Blakeslee's 4th FG, seen late in 1944 after the switch from camouflage to natural metal finish. (Roger Freeman)

(9,080m), while the rate of climb against that of the P-51A was almost doubled. An order for 400 P-51Bs had been placed even before the prototype flew, and more large orders followed. Mass production was initiated, with a shadow factory at Fort Worth, Texas. Fort Worth Mustangs were virtually identical to those from Inglewood, but were designated P-51Cs.

The first production P-51B flew on 5 May 1943, and the first P-51C on 5 August of the same year. Photo-reconnaissance was still a requirement, and 71 P-51Bs and 20 P-51Cs were converted to carry two K24 oblique cameras, or a K17 and K22. In this guise they became F-6Cs, most of which retained their armament.

■ ESCORT FIGHTER ■

By mid-1943 the USAAF 8th Air Force was carrying the fight to Germany, but it was becoming increasingly evident that the heavy bombers were unable to protect themselves sufficiently. A long-range escort fighter was needed. The P-47 Thunderbolt, although an excellent fighter in many ways, lacked range, while

Below: Winter 1943–44. An early shipment of P-51Bs lined up at Speke airport, awaiting allocation to front-line units. (Roger Freeman)

the twin-engined P-38 Lightning, though able to acquit itself well enough in theatres where the Allies held an overwhelming numerical advantage, was a turkey in the dogfight against the German single-engined single seaters.

The Fisher P-75A, an enormous, heavy and complicated beast

Several large and expensive fighters were under development for the long-range escort role. Fairly typical of these was the Fisher P-75A, an enormous, heavy and complicated beast, which first flew in November 1943. Early trials were unpromising, and a requirement was issued for an extra fuel tank to be fitted in the fuselage of a P-51B. With two external drop tanks, this increased the total fuel capacity of the Mustang to 348 imperial gallons (419 US gallons/1,586 litres). With this fuel load, the P-51B could do a round trip of over 1,200 miles (1,930km); rather more than the distance from England to Berlin and back.

Only the last few hundred P-51Bs and Cs were fitted with the fuselage tank as standard at the factory, although

P-51B/ MUSTANG III

Dimensions

Wingspan	37ft 0in (11.28m)
Length	32ft 3in (9.83m)
Height	13ft 8in (4.17m)
Wing area	233sq ft (21.65m²)

Weights

Empty	7,000lb (3,175kg)
Normal take-off	9,200lb (4,173kg)

Power

Packard V-1650-7 inline rated at 1,720hp war emergency

Performance

Maximum speed	422mph (711kph)
Climb	3,475fpm (18m/sec)
Range	950 miles (1,529km)
Ceiling	42,500ft (12,953km)

Armament

4 x .50in (12.7mm) machine-guns

some of the earlier production aircraft were retrofitted with it later. It did not feature on the Mustang III, as the P-51B was known in RAF and Commonwealth service.

There was, of course, a penalty to be paid. The extra weight so far back made directional stability rather marginal, and when half empty the petrol slopped about, affecting handling during what were quite mild manoeuvres. The drill was to take off, form up gently with the others, set course, then drone on steadily for the next hour or more, burning off fuel. Not until the fuselage tank was virtually empty could the pilot relax.

■ INTO SERVICE ■

Ordering a new aircraft type from the drawing board is unthinkable today, but during the war, things were different. A protracted development period, during which all the bugs were ironed out, simply meant that the in-service date might be delayed by a year, or even more. During this time, pilots would

Above: RAF Mustang IIIs in the Mediterranean theatre of operations retained the original canopy. This example is a P-51C of No. 260 Squadron, seen having a thorough overhaul in Termili, Italy. (Roger Freeman)

ROLL

"Upon returning from a mission with the right drop tank still attached, I flared out for landing with a 45 knot crosswind from 90° to the right. The airplane was trimmed heavily to the left, to hold up the right wing, due to the extra drag from the drop tank. As the airspeed decreased, just prior to touchdown, the tank dropped off. The right wing came up, and the wind started to roll the airplane to the left. I immediately applied full power. The torque, the wind, and the extreme left trim caused an immediate roll of 180°. I found myself inverted 50 feet off the ground and looking up through the canopy at pierced steel planking going by at 100 or so mph. I throttled back and sort of washed out in a half roll to the right.

LT WILLIAM G. COLONY USAAF,
5TH FS, 52ND FG, 15TH AF

have to make do with inferior or out-dated machines, and all too often pay with their lives for the privilege. An underdeveloped but superior-performing machine rushed into service could also be a cause of fatalities, but its performance gave its pilot a better chance in the hazard of battle. It was a question of which omelette required the fewest broken eggs, and in general this was the latter course of action.

The first Merlin-Mustang unit to see action reached England in October 1943. The 8th Air Force had been eagerly awaiting the arrival of the new long-range fighter, but an administrative error saw it assigned to 9th Air Force for ground attack. A compromise resulted in it being made available for bomber escort with the 8th until such time as further P-51B Groups arrived. Not until the following spring was the type operational in quantity.

Technical problems were rapidly encountered. Engines running rough, propeller seal leaks spilling oil on to the

Right: P-51Ds of three fighter groups in Italy. Left to right, 332nd FG; 52nd FG, to which William G. Coloney was assigned; and 31st FG. (Roger Freeman)

Below: Close-up of the Malcolm hood, which was fitted to all British-based Mustang IIIs, and not a few Mustang IIs. Not only did it give far better all-round visibility, but it could be opened in flight. (Roger Freeman)

windshield, overheating for whatever reason, faulty engine mounting bolts. All were gradually cured. Sometimes the underwing drop tanks failed to feed; the solution was to pressurize them.

Far more serious was the problem of gun jamming. To fit the Brownings in the wings, they had to be canted at an angle, with the ammunition belts feeding over and down into the breeches. In a turn of more than 2g, the forces exerted exceeded the limits of the mechanism, and they jammed. In the middle of a dogfight this could be very embarrassing. Booster motors were fitted, but these were a long time arriving.

The 68 imperial gallon (85 US gallon/ 322 litre) fuselage tank not only led to directional instability in flight, it also caused such severe tail-heaviness that even take-off was an activity fraught with peril. Before long, the load was restricted to 52 imperial gallons (65 US gallons/246 litres). A related problem was that a sudden pull on the stick caused a high-speed stall followed by a snap roll. This could, however, be put to good use by experienced pilots as an evasive manoeuvre that no enemy fighter was able to follow.

A procedure was initiated in which the fuel in the fuselage tank was used first, followed by that in the drop tanks. After a few instances in which Mustangs were

bounced by enemy fighters and forced to drop full wing tanks, this sequence was reversed.

Most serious of all was structural failure. Occasionally, the wings came off a Mustang in a high-speed dive. There were two main causes for this. At very high speeds, the large doors of the ammunition bays began to bulge outwards. This distorted the wing to the stage where the stresses imposed were too great, and it parted company with the fuselage. The second cause was a tendency for the undercarriage to extend

Above: **F-6C Mustang of the 111th Tactical Reconnaissance Squadron, 12th Air Force, seen in southern France, late 1944. The oblique camera port can be seen in the lower rear fuselage. (Roger Freeman)**

in flight, causing abnormal loads on the wing. These faults were eventually cured, but too late for some pilots.

The P-51B entered RAF service as the Mustang III. However, at this late stage, it was decided that the cockpit canopy was 'totally unsuited to European conditions', something that could have been determined way back in

Below: **One Mustang IV ready for delivery to the RAF. This is actually a Texas-built P-51K. In all, 875 Mustang IVs entered service, two thirds of which were P-51Ks. (AAHS via JE)**

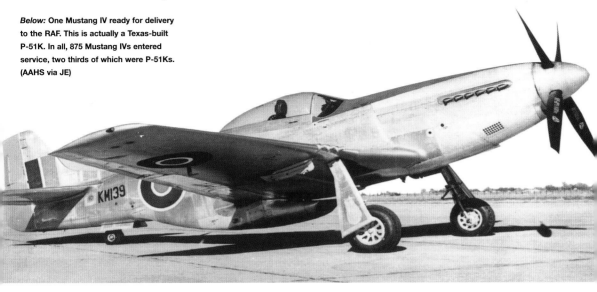

P-51K/ MUSTANG IV/IVA

Dimensions

Wingspan	37ft 0in (11.28m)
Length	32ft 3in (9.83m)
Height	13ft 8in (4.17m)
Wing area	235sq ft (21.83m²)

Weights

Empty	7,635lb (3,463kg)
Normal take-off	10,100lb (4,581kg)

Power

Packard V-1650-7 incline rated at 1,720hp war emergency

Performance

Maximum speed	437mph (703kph)
Climb	3,475fpm (18m/sec)
Range	1,710 miles (2,751km)
Ceiling	41,900ft (12,770m)

Armament

6 x .50in (12.7mm) machine-guns

1940, before the first Mustang ever flew. In a series of field modifications, the Mustang III was fitted with a bulged sliding canopy similar to that of the Spitfire. This was the 'Malcolm Hood', which vastly improved the all-round view, especially rearwards. A few Mustang IIs were also modified in this way.

As previously noted, the P-51B/C had several operational shortcomings, and NAA commenced work to rectify these. With ever-greater importance being placed on the all-round view from the cockpit, NAA modified a P-51B to take a one-piece tear-drop sliding canopy, which involved cutting down the rear fuselage to accommodate it. First flown on 17 November 1943, the new canopy gave a first class view through 360 degrees. With other modifications, it formed the basis of the definitive Mustang, the P-51D, or P-51K when built at Fort Worth.

The next improvement made was to the armament. Four .50 guns were

demonstrably inadequate, while the inability to fire in hard turns without them jamming was a serious handicap. Extensive redesign resulted in six .50s, all upright instead of canted, which virtually eliminated feed stoppages. The two inboard guns had 400 rounds each, while the other four each had 270 rounds.

The wing chord was increased at the root, making it slightly deeper and affecting the kink at the leading edge. The main gear was strengthened to take a much greater all-up weight, and the wheel bays were modified to suit.

> ### The P-51D was supplied to the RAF as the Mustang IV

Directional stability with fuel in the fuselage tank was always marginal, and cutting down the fuselage made matters worse. To offset this, a small dorsal fin was added. The P-51D was supplied to the RAF as the Mustang IV, and the P-51K, which differed only in having a slightly different propeller, became the Mustang IVA in British service.

As was the case with all other Mustang variants, some were converted for photo-reconnaissance. Two cameras, a K17 and a K22, were fitted in the rear fuselage just ahead of the tailwheel. Camera ship designations were F-6D and F-6K, and so far as is known, all retained their armament.

■ AUSTRALIAN ■ MUSTANGS

Only a handful of Mustangs were built outside the USA. The Commonwealth Aircraft Corporation of Australia obtained a licence to build the P-51D in 1944, starting with the assembly of knocked-down kits supplied by NAA. These resulted in 80 CA-17 Mustang XXs, the first of which flew in April 1945, while indigenous production provided 40 CA-18 Mustang 21s; 14 Mustang 22s fitted with an F24 camera; and 66 Mustang 23s, which differed in having British-built Merlins. However, no Australian-built Mustangs became operational until after the war.

Below: Many late P-51D/Ks had a small dorsal fin extension added to provide extra keel area and improve directional stability, which was always marginal with fuel in the fuselage tank. (Alvin Williams via JE)

Bremen, north-west Germany, 11 June 1943. "We did not know that the lead plane of the group ahead of us had two of its engines blasted by flak and had slowed to a crawl over that landscape from which came bomb bursts and legions of Focke-Wulfs and Messerschmitts.

"Mo (Colonel Preston) was trying to avoid over-running the bombers ahead of him. We were trying to avoid overrunning Mo, and so the group disintegrated . . . we had been taught that strict formation flying was as vital to us as the British square had once been to the infantry. Not for us the anarchic whooping attack en masse. To be uncovered from a formation's friendly fire was to be naked and next to dead.

"Seeing our ragged line zig-zagging on a bomb run, the enemy came at us like wolves after straggling sheep. We had moved in so close to Colonel Mo that our wing tip was almost within reach of his waist gunner. Bohn (the co-pilot) had never flown formation at high altitudes. Johnny (the pilot) was an experienced formation flyer, but he was sitting on an unexploded 20mm shell somewhere in his seat, and the thought paralysed him.

"Bohn's tactic was to follow Mo as a chick follows its mother. We were tucked in so tight that our spent shells bounced off the wings of a B-17 beneath us. We could see that in the low squadron there was not a single plane that did not have at least one feathered prop."

Above: The 379th BG, one of whose early exploits is described here, returns to base at Kimbolton after a raid on Germany.

◼ FLAK ◼

"When we came to a wide bay we saw the German smoke pots cloaking our target, Wilhelmshaven. Out of the smoke rose a storm of flak, rocking *Tondelayo*, sending fragments through her metal skin, biting into her delicate electric nerves.

"I called out the heading for the target, but Bob was already on top of his sight. We could not bomb as a Group, but only in train, following the plane ahead, hoping to hit the submarine pens we could not see. The explosions billowed up above the veil of smoke, but we could not be sure of whether we were plastering the shipping, the bay, the harbour or the bistros, whorehouses, shops, and homes of Wilhelmshaveners."

This was the first combat mission of Lieutenant Elmer Bendiner of the 527th Squadron of the 379th Bomb Group, based at Kimbolton, and a more frightening introduction to war could hardly be imagined. The cold at 25,000ft (7,600m) caused frost to form on the plexiglass windows of the bomber, obscuring the view and making enemy fighters hard to spot. Constant scraping was needed in order to keep them clear.

The Fortress's course had taken them over the German Bight, then a turn on to a southerly course towards Bremen, their primary target. Making landfall near Cuxhaven, they encountered accurate flak, its shrapnel rattling against their aircraft. Still heading south, German fighters had come thundering in from the east with guns blazing, and the B-17 gunners fired back, filling their machine with cordite fumes. A nearby bomber caught fire and spiralled down.

helmet, penetrated a bulkhead and then passed through one of the rudder pedals and the pilot's seat before finally lodging in his seat-type parachute.

As if this were not enough, Bremen was obscured by cloud and haze and the bombers turned west for Wilhelmshaven, their secondary target, where, as related, the bombing proved fairly haphazard. On return, Bendiner's B-17 was found to have sustained multiple hits but, with the exception of damage to the hydraulic braking system, most were superficial.

From an Air Force point of view, the raid was moderately satisfactory. Of the 168 bombers that set out that morning, only eight failed to return. But as so often happened, the brunt of the losses had been borne by a single unit. Bendiner's 379th Bomb Group lost six aircraft on this one mission, and of that six, four were from the 527th Squadron.

Narrow escapes were the order of the day, not only for Bendiner and his pilot. Another B-17F from Kimbolton was hit in the cockpit and both pilot and co-pilot were seriously wounded. The aircraft was flown back and successfully landed by one of the gunners under instruction from the pilot. The standard tour of duty was 25 operational missions, but to the survivors of the 527th Squadron, it seemed that they would not have to go this far.

Above: The 379th BG lost 141 aircraft missing in action, but despite extensive flak damage to the nose, this Fortress was not one of them. (USAF via Alfred Price)

■ ALTERNATE TARGET ■

Almost simultaneously, *Tondelayo* was hit by a 20mm cannon shell from an FW190. It made a jagged hole beneath Bendiner's window, grazed his

Above: The right tailplane of this 91st BG was knocked off by a 'friendly' bomb over Bremen in June 1943. (USAF via Alfred Price)

Above: Bombs go down on the Focke-Wulf aircraft factory near Bremen. Attacks on German aircraft production were given priority at an early stage of the American daylight bombing campaign. (USAF via Alfred Price)

■ TACTICS ■

American bombers flew in close formation for mutual protection against fighters, thereby unfortunately providing a massed target for flak as well as sometimes engendering problems on the bombing run. When the lead aircraft of the leading Group lost two engines on the same side, it threw the following 379th Group into total disarray. As luck would have it, the German fighters arrived on the scene just when the formation was at its most vulnerable, and this, more than anything else, accounts for the heavy losses sustained by this unit. Throughout the war, formations and tactics were continually modified to find the best solutions to these problems.

As the war progressed, Fortresses ranged the length and breadth of Europe, the Mediterranean and North Africa, not to mention the Pacific theatre. Their first operational bombing sorties were made by the Royal Air Force even before the USA entered the war, and the type served with the British throughout, mainly with Coastal Command on anti-U-boat patrols over the Atlantic. Others flew over Germany at night in the electronic warfare role.

■ PACIFIC/FAR EAST ■

In American service they were present on Hawaii and the Philippines when Japan attacked Pearl Harbor, and were later seen in the skies of India, Java, New Guinea and Australia. Fortresses played a

Above: A German fighter pounces on a straggler from the 100th BG. (USAF via Alfred Price)

Above: **While nose art was frequently of the 'girlie' type, it depended more on the predilections of the aircraft captain. The pilot of *Hard Seventeen* appears to have been a gamblin' man! (Ralph Trout)**

peripheral role in the decisive naval Battle of Midway in June 1942, but were largely supplanted by B-24 Liberators in the Pacific Theatre of Operations from September 1943. But it is the strategic bombing of Germany for which they are best remembered, penetrating to the farthest corners of the Third Reich. Even when casualties were at their highest, the Fortress raids never turned back. The operational swan song of the Fortress came long after the war, when Israel used it against Egypt.

The practice of naming individual aircraft was almost universal in the United States Army Air Force, and was usually illustrated by graphic nose art. For example, *Tondelayo* was a character portrayed by Hedy Lamarr in a Hollywood film called *White Cargo*, depicted on the aircraft in a state of semi-undress. But not all the inspiration came from the cinema. Some aircraft bore warlike names, while others were references to crewmen or home towns. The most famous of all was of course *Memphis Belle*, the first B-17 to complete a full tour of 25 operational missions before returning to the USA in triumph to help sell war bonds.

Naming endowed a machine with a personality and carried with it the tacit belief that she – never it, always she – would bring her crew safely through. The aeroplane thus became a lucky charm, an amulet belonging to the entire crew, within which they were protected. When the aircraft's luck ran out, as it so often did, the crew went with it. But if, as happened from time to time, a Fortress brought its crew back but was so badly damaged that it had to be scrapped, it was sometimes the case that the replacement aircraft was given the same name with the suffix II added, thus transferring the luck from the old to the new.

1   Rudder construction
2   rudder tab
3   Rudder tab actuation
4   Tail gunner's station
5   Gunsight
6   Twin .50in (12.7mm)
     machine-guns
7   Tail cone
8   Tail gunner's seat
9   Ammunition troughs
10   Elevator trim tab
11   Starboard elevator
12   Tailplane structure
13   Tailplane front spar
14   Tailplane/fuselage attachment
15   Control cables
16   Elevator control mechanism
17   Rudder control linkage
18   Rudder post
19   Rudder centre hinge
20   Fin structure
21   Rudder upper hinge
22   Fin skinning
23   Aerial attachment
24   Aerials
25   Fin leading-edge de-icing boot
26   Port elevator
27   Port tailplane
28   Tailplane leading-edge
     de-icing boot
29   Dorsal fin structure
30   Fuselage frame
31   Tailwheel actuation
32   Toilet
33   Tailwheel (retracted) fairing
34   Fully-swivelling retractable
     tailwheel
35   Crew entry door
36   Control cables
37   Starboard waist hatch
38   Starboard waist .50in
     (12.7mm) machine-gun
39   Gun support frame
40   Ammunition box
41   Ventral aerial
42   Waist gunners' positions
43   Port waist .50in (12.7mm)
     machine-gun
44   Ceiling control cable runs
45   Dorsal aerial mast
46   Ball turret stanchion support
47   Ball turret stanchion
48   Ball turret actuation
     mechanism
49   Support frame
50   Ball turret roof
51   Twin .50in (12.7mm)
     machine-guns
52   Ventral ball turret
53   Wingroot fillet
54   Bulkhead
55   Radio operator's compartment
56   Camera access hatch
57   Radio compartment windows
     (port and starboard)
58   Ammunition boxes

59   Single .30in (7.62mm)
     dorsal machine-gun
60   Radio compartment roof glazing
61   Radio compartment/bomb bay
     bulkhead
62   Fire extinguisher
63   Radio operator's station
     (port side)
64   Handrail links
65   Bulkhead step
66   Wing rear spar/fuselage
     attachment

67   Wingroot profile
68   Bomb-bay central catwalk
69   Vertical bomb stowage racks
     (starboard installation shown)
70   Horizontal bomb stowage
     (port side shown)
71   Dinghy stowage
72   Twin .50in (12.7mm)
     machine-guns
73   Dorsal turret
74   Port wing flaps
75   Cooling air slots

76   Aileron tab (port only)
77   Port aileron
78   Port navigation light
79   Wing skinning
80   Wing leading edge
     de-icing boot
81   Port landing light
82   Wing corrugated inner skin
83   Port out wing fuel tank
     (nine inter-rib cells)
84   No. 1 engine nacelle
85   Cooling gills

BOEING B-17 FLYING FORTRESS

115 Flight deck underfloor control linkage
116 Wingroot/fuselage fairing
117 Wing front spar/fuselage attachment
118 Battery access panels (wingroot leading-edge)
119 No. 3 engine nacelle spar bulkhead
120 Intercooler pressure duct
121 Mainwheel well
122 Oil tank (nacelle inboard wall)
123 Nacelle structure
124 Exhaust
125 Retracted mainwheel (semi-recessed)
126 Firewall
127 Cooling gills
128 Exhaust collector ring assembly
129 Three-blade propellers
130 Undercarriage retraction struts
131 Starboard mainwheel
132 Axle
133 Mainwheel oleo leg
134 Propeller reduction gear casing
135 1,000hp Wright R-1829-65 radial engine
136 Exhaust collector ring
137 Engine upper bearers
138 Firewall
139 Engine lower bearers
140 Intercooler assembly
141 Oil tank (nacelle outboard wall)
142 Supercharger
143 Intake
144 Supercharger waste-gate
145 Starboard landing light
146 Supercharger intake
147 Intercooler intake
148 Ducting
149 No. 4 engine nacelle spar bulkhead
150 Oil radiator intake
151 Main spar web structure
152 Mid-wing fuel tank rib cut-outs
153 Auxiliary mid spar
154 Rear spar
155 Landing flap profile
156 Cooling air slots
157 Starboard outer wing fuel tank (nine inter-rib cells)
158 Flap structure
159 Starboard aileron
160 Outboard wing ribs
161 Spar assembly
162 Wing leading-edge de-icing boot
163 Aileron control linkage
164 Wing corrugated inner skin
165 Wingtip structure
166 Starboard navigation light

86 Three-blade propellers
87 No. 2 engine nacelle
88 Wing leading-edge de-icing boot
89 Port mid-wing (self-sealing) fuel tanks
90 Flight deck upper glazing
91 Flight deck/bomb-bay bulkhead
92 Oxygen cylinders
93 Co-pilot's seat
94 Co-pilot's control column
95 Headrest/armour
96 Compass installation
97 Pilot's seat
98 Windscreen
99 Central control console pedestal
100 Side windows
101 Navigation equipment
102 Navigator's compartment upper window (subsequently replaced by ceiling astrodome)
103 Navigator's table
104 Side gun mounting
105 Enlarged cheek windows (flush)
106 Ammunition box
107 Bombardier's panel
108 Norden bombsight installation
109 Plexiglass frameless nose-cone
110 Single .50in (12.7mm) machine-gun
111 Optically-flat bomb-aiming panel
112 Pitot head fairing (port and starboard)
113 D/F loop bullet fairing
114 Port mainwheel

The Boeing Airplane Company was versatile, surviving the lean years after the First World War, and the world recession, by building a wide variety of aircraft: fighters, seaplanes, mail planes, transports, and even, a twin-engined bomber, the B-9A. The vast experience gained on these projects stood it in good stead when, in May 1934, the USAAC mooted the idea of a really big bomber.

The standard USAAC bomber at that time was the Martin B-10 and only just entering service. The B-10 was state of the art, an all-metal cantilever construction monoplane with retractable main gears, enclosed crew positions, including a gun turret in the nose, and an internal bomb bay. Its two 775hp Wright Cyclone radial engines were fitted with variable pitch propellers, itself a considerable innovation, and gave it a maximum speed of 213mph (343km/hr); fast enough to make interception by the fighters of that era extremely problematical. At cruising speed it could haul a bomb load of just over one ton out to a target 300 miles (480km) away.

At that time, the United States had retreated into near-isolationism, and was only concerned with its own defensive needs. Neither of the adjoining countries, Canada and Mexico, was regarded as potentially hostile and the Atlantic and Pacific Oceans appeared to rule out the possibility of air attack across them. The perceived threat was of

Left: Nose gun position, showing the ring and bead sight. The semi-kneeling position allows the gunner to move more freely.

enemy fleets approaching the coast; not only of the continental USA, but of Alaska and Hawaii also. The proposed counter to this was a very long-range bomber.

■ THE BIG BOMBER ■

The operational requirements specified exceeded all other attempts. They called for a wingspan of 150ft (46m); a maximum weight of 60,000lb (27,200kg); a still air range of 5,000 miles (8,050km) and a bomb load of 2,000lb (900kg). The project was called XBLR-1 (Experimental Bomber, Long Range, No.1), later abbreviated to project A. Basically it was a technology demonstrator to determine precisely what was possible. Both Boeing and the Glenn Martin company were invited to submit proposals by 15 June, just one month later.

On 28 June, Boeing received a contract for the design and construction of a single aircraft. This brought problems in its train, caused by the sheer size

of the machine. Special jigs had to be made, and it was built in sections in two different plants. By the time it was complete, more than two-thirds of a million man-hours had been expended on the Boeing Model 294, while the USAAC had redesignated it the XB-15.

XB-15, BOEING MODEL 294

DIMENSIONS
Wingspan: 149ft 0in (45.41m)
Length: 87ft 7in (26.69m)
Height: 18ft 1in (5.51m)
Wing area: 2,780sq ft (258.27m²)

WEIGHTS
Empty: 43,000lb (19,505kg)
Max. loaded: 70,706lb (32,072kg)
Bomb load: 8,000lb (3,629kg)

ENGINES
4 × P & W R-1830-11 Twin Wasp radials rated at 850hp each.

PERFORMANCE
Max. speed: 200mph (322km/hr)
Cruise speed: 152mph (245km/hr)
Service ceiling: 18,900ft (5,760m)
Max. range: 5,130 miles (8,254km)
Endurance: 24 hours

XB-15

With nothing to give it scale, the sleek lines of the Boeing Model 294, military designation XB-15, belie its enormous size. Compared to the standard bomber in services with the USAAC at that time, it was double the size and nearly four times heavier, and was expected to carry a similar bomb load seven times further. The huge wings were so deep that crawlways in them enabled mechanics to make adjustments to the engines in flight. With round-the-clock endurance, it needed extra crew and sleeping and cooking accommodation. Its influence on the design of the smaller B-17 is obvious. (Bruce Robertson)

Above: 'Grandpappy', as the XB-15 was known, had a larger wingspan than the B-29 Superfortress. Over an 18-month period it carried more than 100,000lb (45,000kg) of cargo and 5,350 passengers without incident.

The XB-15 suffered from galloping weight, and maximum weight increased by nearly one-fifth, leaving it underpowered. It was to have been powered by four Allison in-line engines each rated at 1,150hp, but it finally emerged with four Pratt & Whitney Twin Wasp radials of a mere 850hp each.

The wings contained crawlways for crewmen to reach the engines in flight to make minor adjustments. Two crews were necessary, and bunk space and a small galley with cooking facilities was provided. Two petrol-driven generators were installed, providing power for all the electrical systems. There was also an automatic pilot, de-icing and fire protection system, plus large flaps to reduce take-off and landing speeds. Defence against air attack consisted of four .30 and two .50 calibre machine guns, in nose, dorsal, ventral and two side blister positions. First flight took place at Boeing Field, Seattle, on 15 October 1937. It was clearly evident that the power of the four Pratt & Whitney Twin Wasp radial was insufficient to provide the required level of

performance. But, the XB-15, quickly dubbed 'Grandpappy', handled well enough by the standard of the era. Accepted by the USAAC in March 1938, it served through most of Second World War as the XC-105 troop and cargo-carrier, and was extensively used as flying test bed.

Mass-producing an aircraft such as the XB-15 would be a tremendous drain on resources, both technical and financial. If it could be shown to be a resounding success, then it might be worth the effort. But flight trials were still three years in the future, and it was not practicable to wait so long. The USAAC hedged its bets and thought smaller.

■ RETHINKING ■

Less than eight weeks after the contract for the XB-15 was placed, a new requirement was issued in the form of Circular 35-26. What was

wanted was a 'multi-engined', which in those days usually meant twin-engined, bomber.

The specification was issued with firm requirement that had to be met, combined with a 'wish list' of 'nice to have' parameters. The proposed new aircraft would carry a bomb load of 2,000lb (900kg) and have a maximum range of at least 1,020 miles (1,640km) and possibly 2,200 miles (3.540km). Maximum speed was to be at least 200mph (322km/hr) but preferably 250mph (402km/hr), and a cruising speed of 170mph (274km/hr) or 220mph (354km/hr). Finally, the service ceiling fluctuated from a low of 20,000ft (6,100m) to a high of 25,000ft (7,600m).

A flying prototype had to be ready in just 12 months, but in August 1935 no develpment funding was available. A feature was that the maker of the aircraft selected would receive a contract to build no fewer than 220 bombers. later cut back to 185. This was quite a substantial order for the

Below: Minus engine cowlings and with nose shrouded, Model 299 is prepared for its press debut on 16 July 1935. The Seattle Daily Times report of the event called it a '15-ton flying fortress', which was later adopted by Boeing. (G.S.Williams)

time, which made Boeing very keen to compete.

While it was expecting the contenders to be twin-engined, the USAAC had objection to four. This world normally have been suprising but the service knew what it was about. The order placed would be for either 185 twin-engined bombers, or 65 four-engined types.

While the lesser number may have appeared less attractive Boeing's decision to use four engines was made to enhance flight perfomance. Work on the Boeing Model 299, as it became, was conducted under conditions of semi-flight perfomance, thereby greatly increasing thier chance of success. Prior to this time four engines were traditionally used to improve take-off.

Work on the Boeing Model 299, as it became, was conducted under condition of semi-secrecy. Technology was taken from the XB-15, and the earlier Model 247. The former provided the wing design, scaled down and given tubular truss spars, while the latter influenced the shape of the fuselage. The tail surfaces of all three showed a strong family resemblance.

The urgency of getting the Model 299 ready in time caused it to race ahead of the XB-15 and it was rolled out and shown to the public on 16 July, only 11 months after the go-ahead had been given.

■ 15-TON ■ FLYING FORTRESS

The *Seattle Daily Times* carried a feature the next day together with a photograph bearing the caption '15-ton Flying Fortress'. This caught the imagination of Boeing's management, and they duly registered the name. It was very suitable for an aircraft which, like the XB-15, was intended for maritime reconnaissance and anti-shipping roles.

On the ground, the Model 299 was impressive. In polished aluminium and with colourful

BOEING MODEL 299	
DIMENSIONS	
Wingspan: 103ft 9in (31.62m)	
Length: 68ft 9in (20.95m)	
Height: 18ft 4in (5.59m)	
Wing area: 1,420sq ft (131.96m²)	
WEIGHTS	
Maximum: 32,432lb (14,711kg)	
Bomb load: 4,800lb (2,175kg)	
ENGINES	
4 × Praft & Whitney R-1690-E Hornet radials, each rated at 750hp	
PERFORMANCE	
Max. speed: 236mph (380km/hr)	
Cruise speed: 140mph (225mph)	
Service ceiling: 24,620ft (7,500m)	
Max. range: 3,010 miles (4,840km)	

USAAC Wing and tail markings, the sleek, cigar-shaped fuselage looked exactly right. The four radial engines spoke of power, while four stream-lined blisters, concealed machine guns.

The maiden flight of the Model 299 took place on the morning of 28 July. All went smoothly. Serveral more flights followed before the prototype was delivered to the USAAC at Wright Field, Ohio, for official evaluation. The non-stop journey of 2,100 miles (3,380km) took just over nine hours, giving an average speed of 233mph (375km/hr), which in 1935 was quite exceptional.

The two other contenders for the contract were Glenn Martin's B-12 and Douglas' DB-1, Which was based on the DC-2 airliner, forerunner of the immortal DC-3 Dakota. Against these the Model 299 demonstrated a clear performance advantage, which made it appear certain that it would be the winner. But on the morning of 30 October,

Y1B-17

One of the major differences between the prototype and the Y1B-17 was a redesigned single strut main gear leg. This had several effects. It saved weight and complexity, and made changing a wheel or a tyre a far simpler operation. Many other changes had been made, but many were still to come. Also clearly visible from this angle is the turbo-supercharger exhaust above the engine nacelle, the efflux from which interfered with the slipstream and caused buffeting. This aircraft is the sole Y1B-17A. (Roger Besecker)

the Model 299 stalled and crashed just off the end of Wright Field runway. It was totally destroyed, and with it died Leslie Tower, and USAAC test pilot Major Ployer Hill. The cause was human error. Control locks, fitted to prevent the moving surfaces from being flapped around by wind while on the ground, had not been released prior to take-off. Once in the air, Model 299 had become uncontrollable.

At the time that the disaster occured, the final stage of testing, consisting of evalution flight by service crewmen, had still to take place. With the Model 299 out of the competitions, the DB-1 was declared the winner. It entered service as the B-18 Bolo, and after just a few years was to vanish quietly.

The short while that Boeing Model 299 had been evaluated at Wright Field had been long enough to convince many people of its worth. On 12 January 1936 a contract was issued for 14 aircraft, one of which was a static test bed. A new designation was issued, YB-17, the Y prefix denoting pre-production machines, which included modification that had been found to be desirable during the trials of the prototype .

The main modification was the use of the Wright R-1820-39 Cyclone engine, rated at 850hp. Fabric-covered flaps replaced the original metal items, and the main areas were given single legs in lieu of the original doubles. This made wheel changing a much simpler process. Other changes affected the fuel system, instrument layout, de-icing and oxygen systems. In November of that year, the designation changed once more to become Y1B-17, but this reflected funding arrangements rather than hardware changes. The first Y1B-17 flew on 2 December 1936. Problems were encountered on only its third flight. Engine overheating caused the flight to be cut short; then on touch-down the aircraft tipped on to its nose, fortunately without any injury to the crew.

The brakes had overheated on take-off, then on being retracted while still too hot had seized up solid. A feature of this model was that the panelled transparent nose was able to rotate through a complete circle, allowing the machine gun installed a wide field of fire.

■ INTO SERVICE ■

The first delivery to an active service unit was made on 1 March 1937, at Langley Field, Virginia. A further 11 followed, making the 2nd Bombardment Group the first four-engined bomber outfit in the USAAC. The thirteenth Y1B-17 remained at Wright Field for development work.

It was planned to have two B-17 Groups, one on the east coast, the other on the west. A further 50 B-17s were ordered for 1938, plus 11 more for development work. Meanwhile the 2nd Bombardment Group was to develop operational techniques for the new bomber. During this work, several records were broken, while the high spot was a goodwill visit to Buenos Aires in February 1938 by a formation of

Above: Y1B-17 of the 2nd BG, which was charged with the operational evaluation of the type.

Below: Part of the 2nd BG over New York City on its way to Buenos Aires in February 1938.

Above: The 38th Reconnaissance Squadron was unusual in that it operated Y1B-17s in other than the strategic bombing role.

Above: The Fortress was tough; All American of the 97th BG returned to base despite being nearly cut in half in a collision with a German fighter. (Boeing)

six aircraft. The 5,000 mile (8,050km) flight from Miami was made in just two stages, the big bombers calling at Lima, the capital of Peru, en route.

It was during this period that interservice rivalry reared its ugly head. The US Navy had always regarded itself as the defender of the American coastline, and now observed the activities of the 2nd Bombardment Group with suspicion. Their chance came in May 1938, when three Fortresses of the 2nd Bombardment Group carried out a practice interception of the Italian liner *Rex*.

What really upset the Navy was that the liner was more than 700 miles (1,100km) out in the Atlantic at the time, and the exploit received a lot of publicity. They reacted by accusing the USAAC of poaching on their patch; successfully, it would seem, because from then on, the 2nd Bombardment Group was restricted to within a limit of 100 miles (160km) of the coast! This was followed by a directive from the Secretary of State for War that in 1940 the USAAC was to procure only tactical bombers.

This was reversed by the Munich crisis in September, when it was planned to make a significant increase in air striking power. Meanwhile, the 2nd Bombardment Group had flown a total of 9,293 hours without a single serious accident, and had developed suitable navigation methods and tactics.

The development machines provided valuable data, none more so than one that flew into a thunderstorm, where it was exposed to structural stresses far greater than those planned for the ground test article. The Y1B-17 ended in a spin, from which it recovered, remarkably

for such a large aircraft. The evidence of structural integrity made the stastic test machine redundant, and it was assigned to flight trials with turbo-superchargers fitted as the Y1B-17A.

First flight was made on 20 November. The exhaust from the turbo-superchargers was initially expelled above the engine nacelles, but this caused buffeting. A redesign brought the exhaust below the wing, which cured the problem.

■ TRIALS COMPLETED ■

The increase in performance was dramatic. Maximum speed increased to 311mph (500km/hr), while service ceiling went to 38,000ft (11,600m). These figures were of course for a lightly loaded aircraft; a full load of fuel and bombs reduced these figures significantly. The Y1B-17A set a record by carrying 11,000lb (5,000kg) over a distance of 620 miles (1,000km) at an average speed of 238mph (383km/hr). A typical operational capability was 2,400lb (1,100kg) of bombs for 1,500 miles (2,400km).

Below: Nose cupola 'more appropriately located in an amusement park than in a war aeroplane' was the comment of Air Commodore Arthur Harris RAF on inspecting the Y1B-17.

B-17B

Only 39 B-17Bs were built. They were very similar in external appearance to the Y1B-17, the main changes being turbo-supercharged Wright Cyclone engines as standard, giving a significant performance increment, a large, redesigned rudder for greater lateral stability at high altitudes, and a revised transparent nose with an optically flat panel in front of the bombsight. Many other changes took place under the skin. It was a step in the right direction.

With operational trials completed, Y1B-17s became B-17s, while the single Y1B-17A became the B-17A. The initial production batch of Fortresses was ordered. These started life as Boeing Model 299Es, but the performance demonstrated by the B-17A resulted in the adoption of turbo-supercharged engines, among other things. They then became 299Ms or, in USAAC service, B-17Bs.

The maiden flight of a B-17B came on 27 June 1939. Externally it looked very similar to its predecessor. Engines apart, the main differences were a larger and reshaped rudder and a new nose tranparency with an optically flat panel for bomb aiming replacing the previous ventral window.

Internally, crew positions were revised as a result of 2nd Bombardment Group experience; the pneumatic brakes were supplanted by a hydraulic system, and the top-secret Norden bombsight was fitted. This last

was to become notorious, less for its alleged accuracy than for the tight security measures that surrounded it. It was installed, still under wraps, in the aircraft shortly before take-off, and removed again right after landing, always with an armed guard in attendance.

Y1B-17

The waist gun blisters of the Y1B-17 were innovative but not very practical. They were an attempt to provide the greater field of fire of a turret while minimizing aerodynamic drag. In service it was found that while they gave a reasonable arc of fire, elevation and depression were very limited, while drag was considerable, and disturbance of the slip-stream adversely affected the tailplane and elevators. As protection against attacks from astern they were ineffective, as even at maximum traverse they left a considerable arc uncovered, while the tailplane shielded a significant area.

All 39 B-17Bs were delivered between 29 July 1939 and 30 March 1940, and this variant became the first to equip an operational Air Corps outfit. But even before the first arrived, work was in hand on an improved variant, of which 38 were ordered in 1939. This was the Model 299H, or B-17C.

This new aircraft featured several modifications, many of them influenced by the twin demands of greater survivability and improved performance. Externally, the greatest changes made were to the defensive gun positions. The lateral blisters had been found to provide an inadequate field of fire, and in any case caused unnecessary drag. They were consequently replaced by teardrop-shaped transparencies flush with the cylindrical fuselage, with pintle-mounted machine guns which gave a wider field of fire. The ventral blister gun was supplanted by a

B-17C

The B-17 was the first Flying Fortress to see action. Among other changes it did away with the stylish but aerodynamically and defensively unsound gun blisters. The waist positions were flush, although the original teardrop-shaped opening was retained so as to minimize structural changes. The ventral position was replaced by a much more solid bathtub, while the dorsal blister was omitted altogether and replaced by a sliding transparent fairing. The revised and enlarged rudder first introduced on the B-17B is seen to advantage here on this B-17C, in RAF service as the Fortress I.

B-17C DATA

DIMENSIONS
Wingspan: 103ft 9in (31.62m)
Length: 67ft 11in (20.10m)
Height: 15ft 5in (4.70m)
Wing area: 1,420sq ft (131.96m²)

WEIGHTS
Empty: 31,150lb (14,130kg)
Max. loaded: 49,650lb (22,520kg)
Bomb load: 4,800lb (2,180kg)

ENGINES
4 × Wright Cyclone R-1820-65 turbo-supercharged radials each rated at 1,200hp.

PERFORMANCE
Max. speed: 320mph (515km/hr)
Cruise speed: 232mph (373km/hr)
Service ceiling: 36,000ft (11,000m)
Normal range: 2,100 miles (3,380km)
Climb rate: 1,300ft/min (6.60m/sec)

Other changes included armour protection for the crew and self-sealing fuel tanks. All-up weight increased to 49,650lb (22,500kg), and the engines were Wright Cyclone R-1820-65 radials each rated at 1,200hp, driving constant speed, fully-feathering three-bladed propellers

■ THE B-17C ■

The first flight of a B-17C took place on 21 July 1940, by which time the Second World War had been running for ten months.

While the ground war in Western Europe remained static until May 1940, British, French and German bombers had all been active. Much early combat experience, particularly that of the Royal Air Force, which set great store by heavily armed strategic bombers, had filtered back across the Atlantic, influencing American thinking.

This resulted in the B-17D, of which 42 were ordered. The USAAC recognized the need for greater defensive fire power and for increased survivability. The dorsal and ventral gun position were modified to accept twin .50 calibre machine guns, while more armour was added. Cowl flaps were introduced on the engine nacelles, the bomb racks were redesigned, with a new release mechanism, and 24 volt electrics replaced the original 12 volt system. Deliveries of the B-17D began in February 1941, and the order was completed by the end of April. B-17Cs in USAAC service were also modified to D standard. But at the end of the day, the Dog was still an interim type.

Below: The B-17E featured a complete redesign of the entire rear fuselage and tail unit to make room for a tail turret. (Frank F. Smith)

longer and more solid 'bathtub'. The dorsal blister was removed, and replaced by a sliding transparency faired to the contours of the fuselage. Finally, the central nose gun was replaced by two gun mountings in side windows.

By an irony of fate, the Flying Fortress did not make its combat debut in either its designed role of coastal defence, or even in the service of its country of origin. Instead, it went to war as a high-altitude bomber with the Royal Air Force.

Even with the British, the Fortress got off to an unpromising start. With war looming, a British Purchasing Commission visited the United States in 1938 to investigate the possibility of acquiring American aircraft. With it was a certain Air Commodore Arthur Harris, later to become famous as Commander-in-Chief of RAF Bomber Command between 1942 and 1945. Among other types, he inspected a Y1B-17 of the 2nd Bombardment Group at Langley Field. Never a man for mincing words, Harris was scathing on the subject of its gun armament, and

concluded that it was far too vulnerable against any modern fighter. His comment on the nose cupola was that it was "more appropriately located in an amusement park than in a war aeroplane".

At the time, this was of course fair comment. But as we saw in the preceding section, Boeing and the USAAC were aware of these and other shortcomings, and were making every effort to correct them. By the end of 1940, the single most glaring deficiency was the lack of a power-operated gun turret.

Above: Boeing got the serial letters wrong on the batch of Fortress Is for the RAF; they should be AN, not AM. On the left is Air Chief Marshal Sir Hugh Dowding, the former head of RAF Fighter Command during the Battle of Britain. (Bruce Robertson)

By this time, the RAF had discovered through hard and bloody experience that daylight raids on targets in the Third Reich, where strong fighter opposition might be encountered, were likely to incur unacceptable losses. There did, however, seem to be one possible solution to this.

Left: As the Japanese swept across the Pacific, the Panama Canal took on a new importance. B-17s spent many weary hours patrolling the area. This is a B-17E with the early ventral turret. (USAF)

Below: A Messerschmitt Me 109 can just be seen in front of B-17F *Virgin's Delight* of the 91st BG, performing the Split-S breakaway manoeuvre. (USAF)

Me 109E

The Messerschmitt Me 109E was the standard German interceptor during 1940 and most of 1941, and thus was the fighter that the Fortress I had to defeat. Powered by a Daimler-Benz 601 liquid-cooled engine, it could achieve a maximum speed of 354mph (570km/hr) at 12,500ft (3,800m). While its service ceiling was marginally better than that of the Fortress I, speed, rate of climb and manoeuvrability were all greatly reduced at extreme altitudes.

Above: **Belly landing! A B-17 of the 379th BG touches down tail-first at Kimbolton. The ball turret has been jettisoned and all looks good. This group flew more sorties and dropped a greater weight of bombs than any other. (Bill Smith)**

The standard German day fighter of the period was the Messerschmitt Me 109E. Leaving aside the brochure figures quoted for rate of climb and time to altitude of this aircraft, and instead allowing for a standing start scramble, time to join up, and a formation battle climb, which was always slower than could be accomplished by a single machine, it would take something over 30 minutes for the fighters to reach 30,000ft (9,150m). And once they did get there, both their maximum speed and their manoeuvrability would be greatly reduced.

■ WAS HEIGHT ■ THE KEY?

In the space of 30 minutes, a bomber cruising at 180mph (290km/hr) would cover a distance of 90 miles (145km). At that time there was little information about the German early warning system, but unless this could provide significantly more than half an hour's notice of impending attack, the chances were that the bombers would be able to do their work and be long gone before the fighters arrived. And even if adequate early warning was available, ground control would need to be very precise in order to position the fighters correctly for an interception.

Flying at such extreme altitudes appeared to offer bombers relative immunity from fighter interception, and almost total immunity from flak. A trio of British four-engined heavy bombers was entering service at about this time, but they were unable to reach such a high perch. Only the Flying Fortress had sufficient altitude capability, and of course this was coupled with the much-vaunted accuracy of the the top-secret Norden bombsight.

■ TRIALS AND ■ TRIBULATIONS

Initial British approaches for the Fortress were made in the summer of 1940, but not until the end of the year was the request approved, when 20 B-17Cs were released. Unfortunately, these were not fitted with self-sealing fuel tanks, and had to be returned to Boeing for these to be installed. The delay thus caused was considerable, and not until April 1941 were the first four aircraft ready for delivery.

The first B-17C, known in RAF service as the Fortress I, arrived at Watton in Norfolk on 14 April. Others followed, and by the end of the third week in May, 14 had been delivered. Certain modifications were needed: standard British radio and signals equipment, identification lights etc, and all guns except the one in the nose were replaced by .50 Brownings. Most important of all

FORTRESS I

Fortress I of No. 90 Squadron, RAF Bomber Command, the specially formed unit which pioneered very high-altitude bombing, and with which the Flying Fortress made its combat debut. This aircraft, AN 530, *F for Freddie*, had an eventful career. It arrived in England on 10 July 1941; just too late to take part in the initial raid on Wilhelmshaven but, as one of the more reliable aircraft, it was selected for the abortive Berlin raid on 23 July. On 2 August it fought off attacks by three Me 109Fs of 3/JG 52, shooting down Feldwebel Wilhelm Summerer and damaging the other two. It was later transferred to No. 220 Squadron of Coastal Command and struck off charge in September 1943. (Bruce Robertson)

was the bombsight. The Norden was still top secret and had not been released; however RAF Fortresses were to have the Sperry Mk 0-1, similarly precise but rather more complex. This was duly installed, together with a Sperry auto-pilot system which, coupled to the sight, allowed the bomb aimer to make flat turns while lining up on target.

The recipient of the Fortress I was No. 90 Squadron, which was faced with the initial task of selecting men physically capable of standing up to the extremely demanding high-altitude operational environment. This was far from easy; nearly two-thirds of applicants failed for medical reasons. This made progress in forming the squadron slow.

As soon as sufficient personnel had been accepted and crewmen had been converted on to type (with the aid of a few selected American flyers and ground crew), high-altitude training was initiated. This revealed a number of problems.

The USAAC considered the optimum bombing altitude to be 20,000ft (6,100m), whereas the RAF proposed operating the Fortress I at least 50 per cent higher, and probably even more, in temperatures of -40° Celsius or even lower.

■ PROBLEMS ■

Two related factors caused unexpected problems; the first was the extremely low temperature and atmospheric pressure encountered at 30,000ft (9,150m) and above; the second was the delta temperature and atmospheric pressure; the difference between ground level and high altitude. These played havoc with the engines and other systems.

The former caused many Cyclones (but not all) to throw oil from the crankcase breather pipes. The turbo-superchargers became unduly sensitive to hamfisted control movements, surging at the least provocation, with the turbine blower breaking up in consequence. Heated window panels were needed to keep them clear of frost, while the auto-pilot/bombsight coupling caused violent yaws if the gyros had not been synchronized beforehand. The extreme changes in temperature and pressure during the course of a standard mission caused engine exhaust flanges to fracture, and

Above: The 305th BG which, under the command of Curtis LeMay, did so much to get the tactics right. Station-keeping in the formation ahead appears to leave much to be desired. (USAF via Alfred Price)

was responsible for hydraulic leaks which allowed air to infiltrate the system; a circumstance that was hardly con-ducive to effective braking.

Watton was a grass field not really suitable for such heavy machines, and pending the completion of a new air-field at Polebrook, with hard runways and taxiways, No. 90 Squadron moved to Great Massingham. It was during a flight from here, shortly before the projected move to Polebrook, that the first serious accident occurred.

The first USAAF casualty on active service occurs

It was June, the month in which the US Army Air Corps became the US Army Air Force. A Fortress I on a train-ing flight over Yorkshire failed to climb above a thunderhead, and instead entered it. Once inside, the giant bomber was pounded by huge hailstones, while a thick layer of ice built up on the wings. This destroyed the lift, forcing the huge bomber into a death-dive. As it tumbled from the sky, the forces exerted on the unlucky machine wrenched off a wing, then tore the fuselage in half. The only

survivor was Flight Lieutenant Steward, a medical officer from the Royal Aircraft Establishment at Farnborough, who managed to parachute to safety. Among the dead was Lieutenant Bradley, an experienced American B-17 pilot. He was the first airman of the newly consti-tuted USAAF to die on active service.

■ FIRST ACTION ■

The essentials for a very high-altitude bombing mission were two-fold: clear weather and near-perfect visibility. However good the aircraft and its crew, and however accurate the bombsight may be, if the target area cannot be identified from many miles away, and what is more, the actual target cannot be clearly seen from nearly 6 miles (9km) up, there is little point in even starting out. These conditions were met on 8 July, and three Fortresses were duly despatched from Polebrook. The crews, led by the squadron commander, Wing Commander MacDougall, were perhaps not as well trained as they might have been, but political pressure was exerted

Above: Damaged over Bremen, this 100th BG Fortress made a spectacular crash-landing when a propeller came off after touch-down. Over 800 holes were counted from the radio room aft. (John Kidd)

by those eager to see how the big bird would acquit itself in action.

The target was Wilhelmshaven. The three Fortress Is were to fly there in loose formation, closing up only if fighters were encountered. They would bomb the naval base individually from 30,000ft (9,150m) with four American-type 1,100lb (500kg) bombs, then, divested of their loads and homeward bound, climb away from the target area to make the task of interception even more difficult.

As Robbie Burns once observed, "The best laid plans of mice and men gang oft agley!" He might have added aviators. On the climb-out from base, all four engines of one Fortress started throwing oil, which streamed back and froze on the tail surfaces. This set up intense vibration, forcing its pilot to abandon the main mission and seek a target of opportunity.

The other two pressed on. They reached Wilhelmshaven and attacked with no intervention from the defences, but two bombs on the leading aircraft failed to release due to a frozen solenoid. This was the first of many failures caused by a combination of extreme cold and high humidity. On trials, the Americans had not gone so high, nor was there

much humidity over the bombing ranges in Nevada or Utah. Humidity in particular bedevilled Fortress operations for the next two years. But even the bombs that did drop missed their targets. It was later concluded that the physical problems encountered at high altitude in unpressurized aircraft were greater than had been thought, and made bombing accuracy very hard to achieve. All in all, it was hardly to be regarded an auspicious combat debut.

After the Fortresses left the target area, two black specks were sighted climbing towards them by Tom Danby, a beam gunner in the squadron commander's aircraft. Fighters! The Fortresses lifted their noses and climbed labori-

ously, but to no avail. The Messerschmitt Me 109s easily drew level with Danby's aircraft, passed across the nose as if taking the measure of this enormous stranger, then one started to turn in astern. Danby lined up his sight and took first pressure on the trigger. As he did so, his pilot commenced a gentle turn towards the direction of attack. This forced the German pilot to tighten his turn, but as he did so, his wings lost their grip on the rarified air and he literally fell out of the sky! No shooting was done by either side, which was probably just as well, because there was more than a fair chance that the guns of the Fortress were frozen up.

The next raid was a complete fiasco. On 23 July, three Fortresses set out to attack Berlin in daylight. Over Denmark they started leaving long white contrails, pointers in the sky that led the fighters straight to them. Far below, the crewmen could see menacing black specks, frantically grabbing for height but as yet nowhere near them. Over Denmark, the three Fortresses turned southwards towards Berlin, only to be faced with a solid wall of cloud. With no chance of locating their targets through it, they turned back, frozen and frustrated.

Below: Pillars of dark smoke denote hits on an oil refinery by the preceding wave, as more bombers bore in to attack. (USAF via Alfred Price)

Above: **Fortress I, formerly of No. 90 Squadron, seen here in the colours of No. 220 Squadron Coastal Command, escorting a convoy across the Atlantic. (Alfred Price)**

Other raids followed. On 24 July Brest was attacked, and hits were claimed on the battle cruisers *Scharnhorst* and *Gneisenau*. Emden was raided two days later. So far the German fighters had failed to intercept, but this situation did not last. On 2 August a Fortress was attacked north of Texel at only 22,000ft (6,700m) by three Me 109Fs, which made seven passes at the bomber, hitting it, but fortunately not seriously. Remarkably, one German fighter was shot down into the sea, a second was damaged and force-landed, while the third suffered some minor damage from the Fortress's return fire.

The first high-altitude fighter engagement that took place was a much more

Below: **Nineteen B-17Fs served with RAF Coastal Command as the Fortress II. This aircraft was written off in the Azores in 1944 after a taxiing accident. (Bruce Robertson)**

deadly affair. The same crew was caught at 32,000ft (9,750m) over Brest by seven Messerschmitts on 16 August and subjected to 26 attacks in quick succession.

Even at high altitude the B-17 proved vulnerable to fighters

The pilot put the big bomber into a shallow dive for maximum speed, taking evasive action against each attack. Eventually he escaped into cloud, but not before two crewmen had been killed and another two wounded. The Fortress crashed on landing and burned. Then a four-aircraft attack against the German pocket battleship *Admiral Scheer* at Oslo on 8 September also encountered fighters. One bomber was shot down, another went missing without trace. The third returned too badly damaged to be repairable. The writing was on the wall.

Even at high altitude, the Fortress I was proving too vulnerable in daylight, the bomb load was too small and the bombing too inaccurate.

The final Fortress operational mission from Polebrook was flown on 25 September, bringing the total to 48 sorties, 26 of which were aborted for various reasons, the most frequent of which was cloud obscuring the target. At this point, four aircraft were detached to Egypt, from where they carried out maritime reconnaisance missions over the Mediterranean, and night attacks on Tobruk and other North African targets. It was, however, found that the heat and dust of the desert reduced performance and serviceability quite spectacularly, and the two survivors of this period were sent to India, where they were eventually handed over to the USAAF.

Back at Polebrook, experimental high-altitude flights continued for a while. By this time the oil throwing and freezing-up of the guns had largely been cured, and the main purpose was to investigate the physiological problems more fully. This finally came to an end, and the remaining Fortress Is were transferred to No. 220 Squadron of Coastal Command, with whom they ranged far out over the Atlantic on anti-submarine patrols.

■ PACIFIC CRUCIBLE ■

By December 1941, the USAAF was in possession of about 150 Flying Fortresses. Mainly these were based in the continental USA, but some flew anti-submarine patrols from Newfoundland. These were reconnaissance missions only, because America was still officially neutral. Yet other Flying Fortresses were deployed in the Pacific.

Above: Action replay of the Pearl Harbor attack, as a 'Japanese Zero' swoops down on a landing Fortress at the annual air show at Oshkosh. The B-17 has been specially modified to put one main gear and the tail wheel down to simulate battle damage. (Eric Lundahl)

Below: Conditions in the Pacific could be primitive. This aircraft made a wheels-down forced landing on a Papua New Guinea beach. After repair, the locals were enlisted to help lay a steel matting runway to allow it to take off. (Both Frank F. Smith)

The 19th Bombardment Group was based at Hickam Field, right next door to Pearl Harbor on Oahu in the Hawaiian Islands. In the Philippines, at that time an American Protectorate, were 35 B-17Cs and Ds of the 7th Bombardment Group, based at Clark Field. Both Groups were about to be reinforced, and a dozen aircraft were in transit to them. This was the situation when Japanese carrier aircraft made a surprise strike against the American fleet at Pearl Harbor on the 7th of the month, an attack which finally brought America into the war.

At Hickam Field, the 19th Bombardment Group was caught on the ground by the Japanese attack, and all 12 aircraft were destroyed. Worse was to follow. The reinforcements for the 7th and 19th Bombardment Groups arrived at the height of the raid; low on fuel and un-armed, they were unable to defend themselves. Four were destroyed and all the others damaged, some by Japanese fighters, others by 'friendly' ground fire.

Just hours later, the Japanese turned their attention to the Philippines, destroying 14 B-17s of the 19th Bombardment Group on the ground at Clark Field. It was fortunate that a single squadron from this group had been deployed to Del Monte on Mindanao, 200 miles (320km) further south, so some of the group escaped this attack unscathed.

The surviving Fortresses of the 19th were employed against the Japanese invasion force, with little success, for ships at sea proved elusive targets. Hits were often claimed, but in fact little damage was done.

Fighter opposition at this time was provided by the redoubtable Mitsubishi A6M2 Zero, and two notable encounters with Fortresses took place in the first few days of fighting. On 10 December, a Japanese landing force consisting of one light cruiser, six destroyers and four transports was off-loading at Vigan on Luzon. At an altitude of 18,000ft (5,500m) above them flew 27 covering Zeros, one of them piloted by Saburo Sakai, later to become the top surviving Japanese fighter ace (62 kills).

ZERO ATTACK

"This was our first experience with the B-17, and the airplane's unusual size caused us to misjudge our firing distance. In addition, the bomber's extraordinary speed, for which we had made no allowance, threw our rangefinders off. All through the attack the Fortress kept up a steady stream of fire at us from its gun positions. Fortunately the accuracy of the enemy gunners was no better than our own."

SABURO SAKAI, ZERO PILOT

Six B-17Ds of the 14th Bombardment Squadron were sent against the invaders. They bombed from 25,000ft (7,600m), and succeeded in doing little damage. One of their number, piloted by Lieutenant Colin Kelly Jr, was spotted after the attack, and seven avenging Zeros set off in hot pursuit.

The Zeros were slower than their European counterparts, and in any case had additional height to gain. Not until 100 miles (160km) further on did they catch the speeding bomber. Even before they could gain a firing position, three other Zeros appeared ahead and attacked from above, but with absolutely no effect.

At last the pursuers caught up, and joined with the other three in line astern, making pass after pass, again with no apparent effect. The chase lasted a further 50 miles (80km), taking them over the US base at Clark Field. Sakai then took a hand. With two other fighters in attendance he closed right in, braving

ZERO FIGHTER

The Mitsubishi Zero was optimized for dogfighting rather than bomber interception. Japanese engines of the time lacked power, and to maximize manoeuvrability and performance by reducing weight, the Zero had no armour plating, no self-sealing fuel tanks, and often no radio. It was therefore very vulnerable to return fire.

Above: Some had it easier than others. General MacArthur's personal transport, Bataan, had reclining seats and hot and cold running water installed. (USAF)

Below: Declared 'war-weary' on the arrival of the B-17F, this E-model became a personal transport for General George Kenney. (USAF)

the defensive fire. Fuel streamed back from the ruptured tanks of the bomber, its gunners ceased firing, and fire broke out in the fuselage. It was the end. His crew baled out, but Kelly himself did not manage to escape. It was the first Flying Fortress to fall to Japanese fighters in the Pacific.

Four days later, a battle against even heavier odds ended differently. On 14 December, a B-17D of the 19th Bombardment Group piloted by Lieutenant Hewitt Wheless became separated from its formation. When he was just about to bomb a Japanese freighter from low altitude, he found himself bounced by 18 Zeros.

The Japanese fighters made attack after attack on the lone bomber, knocking out the left outboard motor, the radio and the oxygen system, shooting off the tail wheel, riddling the fuselage, holing the fuel tanks, damaging the control runs and killing one crewman. The Fortress gunners fought back desperately, claiming three fighters shot down, but their guns either jammed or ran out of ammunition. It looked like the end of the road, but fortunately the remaining Japanese fighters had also run out of ammunition.

This was perhaps less surprising than it may seem. Zeros carried a mere five seconds' worth of ammunition for their 20mm cannon, while their rifle-calibre machine-guns were virtually useless against a Fortress, which was an extremely tough aircraft indeed. Wheless'

B-17D sustained over 1,000 hits and still kept flying, although it was eventually wrecked in the ensuing forced landing on Mindanao.

■ THE B-17 ■ ENTERS SERVICE

The Japanese overran the Philippines by the end of December, and the handful of Fortresses were pulled back to Darwin in Northern Australia. From here it was about 1,500 miles (2,400km) to targets in the southern Philippines, which meant that even with auxiliary fuel tanks in the bomb bay, the bomb load that could be carried was exceedingly small – less than 2 tons in many cases. Shortly after, the B-17s were sent to Java. There were so few of them, but they were the only aircraft available with the necessary range to reach Japanese bridgeheads in Borneo and elsewhere, and even then they needed to stage through those Allied airfields which had not yet fallen.

By now, the improved B-17E was entering service, and more than 50 of these were sent to reinforce the theatre, although due to Japanese successes they were forced to come the long way round, via Africa and India. Attrition was heavy; nearly two-thirds of the available Fortresses were lost in the first three months of the Pacific War, to accidents as well as enemy action. During this period, Fortresses claimed to have sunk three warships, including the battleship *Haruna*, and eight transports, in the course of some 350 sorties. One bombardier actually claimed hits on ships when bombing from 35,000ft (10,700m), which says as much for his optimism as his eyesight. In fact, Japanese records showed that only two transports probably succumbed to air attack by Fortresses.

After two months operating out of airfields on Java, the Allies had to evacuate in the face of Japanese advances, and once more the surviving Fortresses found themselves back in Australia. But by this time, very few of the original B-17Cs and Ds were left, and their replacement, the B-17E, was a very different bird indeed.

When in December 1941 the USA entered the war, both the RAF and the USAAF were agreed on one thing: for the immediate future, the Third Reich could only be effectively attacked from the air. The primary disagreement was as to how. As a result of hard and bloody experience, the RAF had, with a few notable exceptions, abandoned daylight raids in favour of the cover of darkness, and argued strongly that the Americans should join them in this.

The USAAF, however, was not convinced. The British night effort at this time was fairly agricultural, with many crews unable to land their bombs within 5 miles (8km) of their targets. It consisted of little more than exporting bombs to 'somewhere in Germany'. Area bombing, which was to devastate German cities in the next three years, had not yet matured. The truth was that while night attacks tied down valuable

Left: Fortresses of the 381st BG leave contrails emblazoned across the sky, while two fighters hurtle across them high above. (USAF)
Below: Typical European weather made navigation, target finding and accurate bombing far more difficult than the USAAF expected. This is B-17F *Meat Hound* of the 306th BG in cloudy skies. (USAF)

Above: 8th AF commander General Jimmy Doolittle talks to a weather reconnaissance crew on their return. Second from left is Flying Officer Eldridge, an RAF weather observer. (USAF)

German resources in the shape of flak and night fighters, they were at that time doing little real damage.

The USAAF view was that precision attacks on industrial targets would be far more effective, and these could only be carried out in daylight. Daylight made accurate navigation much easier, and also the precise identification of industrial complexes. The American Norden

German fighters. The new and better protected B-17E and F were coming on stream, and the vulnerability against attack from astern had been reduced. The British prophesied disaster, but the Americans were confident in adopting the 'wagon train' approach of their forebears.

But before operations could start, there was much to be done. RAF Bomber Command was expanding fast, and new airfields sprang up like mushrooms across England. Even more airfields were needed for their American allies, and providing these took time.

■ THE FIRST ■ BOMB GROUP

Nor was the USAAF ready initially. The basic unit was the Bombardment Group (BG), which consisted of a headquarters and three squadrons, quickly increased to four, each of which had an establishment of 8–10 aircraft. The demand for personnel, training and aircraft initially outstripped supply. Matters were not helped when many production Fortresses were sent to units in the Pacific. It was months before the first USAAF Bombardment Group (Heavy) was able to take off and point its Fortresses eastwards, across the cold grey Atlantic.

Above: Airfields for the USAAF bombers were hastily prepared. This photograph shows an open-air bomb dump at Framlingham, with tented accommodation. (USAF)
Left: "Fill 'er up and check the oil, please!" For a raid on Germany, 2,000 gallons of fuel per aircraft was not exceptional. (USAF)

The ultra-high-altitude bombing pioneered by the RAF in late 1941 was not repeated. Instead, the American heavy bombers attacked in close formation from rather lower levels, relying on the massed firepower of their defensive armament to beat off the

tachometric bomb sight was inherently far more accurate than the British Mk XIV vector sight. On the bombing range in peacetime in clear visibility, releasing from an altitude of 10,000ft (3,050m), circular error probability (the radius within which the best 50 per cent of bombs fall) was about 300ft (90m) for the Norden and 775ft (235m) for the Mk XIV.

In combat, things were less simple. Heavy and accurate flak forced the bombers to much greater altitudes. Not only did circular error probability increase significantly with height, but shrapnel rattling against the wings and fuselage was a considerable distraction to the bombardier. European weather conditions bore no similarity to those of California, and frequently the target was obscured or semi-obscured by cloud. All these factors conspired against the highly accurate Norden bombsight. But all else being equal, there was no substitute for practical experience, and the USAAF decided to press ahead and see for itself.

B-17 UNITS THAT BECAME OPERATIONAL IN ENGLAND 1942

Group No.	Squadrons	Base	First mission	Notes
97	340, 341, 342, 414	Polebrook	17 Aug 42	To North Africa, Nov 42
32	301, 352, 353, 419	Chelveston	5 Sep 42	To North Africa, Nov 42
92	325, 326, 327, 407	Alconbury	Sep 42	Training unit after four missions, returned to ops May 43 with YB-40
306	367, 368, 369, 423	Thurleigh	9 Oct 42	Last mission 19 Apr 45
91	322, 323, 324, 401	Bassingbourn	7 Nov 42	Last mission 25 Apr 45
303	358, 359, 369, 427	Molesworth	17 Nov 42	Last mission 25 Apr 45
305	364, 365, 366, 422	Grafton Underwood	17 Nov 42	Last mission 25 Apr 45

Above: The Yanks are coming! Fortresses on Iceland, 21 July 1942.

The first unit to arrive in England was the 97th BG, equipped with B-17Es; it was followed by other units with the newer B-17F. The recently formed US 8th Air Force had received its first weapons. Intensive training followed, and a period of acclimatization to European weather conditions.

The first mission was flown by the 97th BG, which was based at Polebrook, on 17 August 1942. Twelve B-17Es raided the Sotteville marshalling yards at Rouen, strongly escorted by four RAF Spitfire squadrons. Visibility was good, and about half the bombs landed in the target area. Two bombers were slightly damaged by flak. It was a promising

Below: Early loss. A Fortress breaks up and goes down over northern France after being hit on the way to the target. (USAF)

Above: They're here! Two B-17F Fortresses of the 91st BG arrive in England late in 1942. In the foreground are a Hurricane (left) and a Fairchild Argus (right) of the RAF. (Merle Olmsted)

debut, and all seemed set fair for the 8th AF, with the 301st BG in pre-combat training and the 92nd BG arriving. Due shortly were the 306th, 91st, 303rd and 305th BGs.

The 97th was given no time to rest on its laurels. Two dozen B-17Es bombed Abbeville airfield on 19 August during the Dieppe Raid, and the next day 12 aircraft attacked the Amiens marshalling yards, again with a Spitfire escort. All the bombers returned unscathed on both occasions, having seen little of German fighters.

Shallow penetrations over enemy territory continued for the rest of the month; sometimes the bombing was accurate, at others it was less so. In September, the 301st and 92nd BGs became operational, and joined the fray. Then on 6 September, the Luftwaffe reacted strongly, penetrated the escort-ing fighters and shot down two of the 20 B-17s. The loss of 10 per cent of the raiding force came as a nasty shock.

In November, just as the B-17 force was getting into its stride, the 97th and 301st BGs were transferred to the 12th Air Force in North Africa, while

the 92nd BG became a B-17 'finishing school', and did not return to action until September of the following year. This left only the 306th BG in the front line, although it was joined dur-ing the month by the 91st, 303rd and 305th BGs. The latter two units flew their first mission on 17 November.

It was not an auspicious start. The target was the U-boat base at St Nazaire, but it was obscured by heavy cloud. Those that managed to bomb were met with fierce flak, though they all returned. The 303rd had no such luck. They completely failed to find the tar-get, and brought their bombs home. On the following day, the 303rd managed to bomb St Nazaire. The problem was over 100 miles (160km) away! This was

the very thing that daylight raiding was supposed to avoid. Then, four days later, only 11 out of 76 bombers despatched were able to find Lorient.

The final months of 1942 were very much a proving period for the B-17 units. Methods and tactics were in a continual state of flux. Formations were changed in an attempt to use the heavy defensive armament to its best advan-tage, while allowing concentrated bombing. The leader in this field was Colonel Curtis LeMay, commanding the 305th BG at Chelveston. One of the problems to be overcome was that of bomb aiming. It was impossible to keep a tight formation yet still have every air-craft aim individually, without risking multiple mid-air collisions. Having sort-ed out his optimum formation, LeMay solved the aiming problem by having everyone drop when they saw the leader's bombs go down. Sophisticated it was not, but against all but pinpoint targets it was good enough, and at least it ensured concentration. As 1942 drew to a close, the 8th had neither raided Germany nor attempted a deep penetra-tion so far. But this was not far off.

■ 1943 ■
THE TEMPO INCREASES

The Casablanca Directive, signed on 21 January 1943, listed target types in order of priority. They were: U-boat

Below: The 91st BG returns to base at Bassingbourn after a sortie. (USAF)

REVISED 18-AIRCRAFT GROUP DEC 1942

The revised 18-aircraft Bomb Group formation, introduced in December 1942. The requirements were threefold: a concentrated bomb pattern which called for a narrow frontage; concentration of defensive firepower, which called for close formation; and freedom from masking the defensive guns, which demanded vertical staggering of aircraft. Formations changed throughout the course of the war, culminating in 1945 with a 36-aircraft BG occupying a frontage of 1,170ft (356m), with four nine-aircraft squadrons staggered through 1,150ft (350m) vertically.

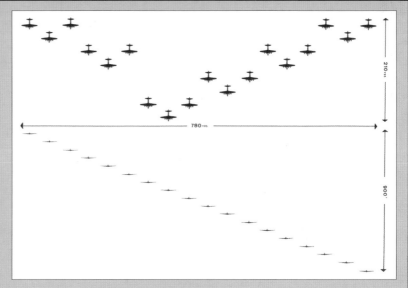

construction; aircraft construction; transport; fuel; and other industries. Six days later, the 8th AF put this into practice as 67 B-17s set off to raid the U-boat construction yards at Vegesack, the first German target scheduled.

As was so often the case, the primary target was socked in by cloud, and the

The 8th AF begins its assault on Germany

secondary, which was Wilhelmshaven, was attacked instead, although with unimpressive results. Fortunately the flak was ineffective, and the FW 190 pilots of JG. 1, lacking experience in estimating range against anything as large as a B-17, failed to press home their attacks. Three

bombers were shot down for 22 German fighters claimed, which seemed a good rate of exchange.

Appalling weather foiled planned raids on Germany over the next few months, while the Luftwaffe fighters polished their tactics and became ever more effective. Although much of the early bombing effort was directed against the U-boats, it quickly became apparent that measures against the fighters were badly needed. In the largest raid so far, 115 B-17s took off on 17 April, their target the Focke-Wulf factory at Bremen.

Fighters arrived in force as the bombing run commenced, and wave after wave of them attacked from head-on. The leading wing, consisting of the 91st and 306th BGs, suffered the worst of the onslaught. In the former, the entire low squadron went down, while the latter lost 10 out of 16 aircraft. Total losses for the mission were 16; one to flak, the rest to fighters. This amounted to 14 per cent of the entire force, while another 48 bombers returned with varying

Right: A tight 'ladder' of bombs goes down from a B-17F of the 96th BG. In the background are other groups in rather ragged formations, while flak bursts stain the sky. (Boeing via Alfred Price)

54-AIRCRAFT COMBAT WING FORMATION INTRODUCED MARCH 1943

The 54-aircraft Combat Wing, consisting of three Bomb Groups each of 18 aircraft, was introduced in March 1943. Its aims were basically those of the Bomb Group formation: bombing concentration and defensive security. At first, it occupied a box of sky some 1⅓ miles (2km) wide, 1,800ft (550m) from front to rear, and 2,900ft (880m) vertically. This proved unwieldy, and it was condensed into just over ½ mile (900m) wide, 1,275ft (390m) front to rear, and 2,700ft (820m) vertically.

the RAF and USAAF mounted diversionary operations. This worked in part, but one of the diversionary forces suffered heavily. The main force landed just under 25 per cent of their bombs on target, which was a good result for the time. The plant was out of action for a month and production reduced for five months thereafter. Sixteen Fortresses of the main force failed to return, a more acceptable 6.8 per cent, one of them a YB-40 hit by flak, but no fewer than 170 were damaged.

The weather improved in late July, and a series of heavy raids was made by forces of 250–300 bombers. The deeper penetrations were often combined with raids on targets in occupied Europe by medium bombers, splitting the defender's strength. Then on 28 July, bombers returning from Oschersleben beset by German fighters were met at the Dutch border by more than 100 P-47s equipped

degrees of damage. This rate of attrition could not be sustained. The one apparent bright spot was the claim for 63 German fighters destroyed, but this turned out to be misleading.

■ GUNNER CLAIMS ■

Overclaiming has always been a feature of air warfare, and arises from confusion caused by the rapidity of events. This was inevitable. Several dozen gunners blazed away at one fighter; if it went down they all claimed it in good faith. Even the most expert debriefer could not sort out the tangle with any degree of accuracy. Figures for the period allowed 450 claims for fighters destroyed to be upheld, but the true figure was in all probability fewer than 50. Total bomber losses for the same period amounted to 103. The false picture thus presented gave rise to unfounded optimism in the USAAF.

Escort fighters were desperately needed. The British Spitfire was too short-legged for the task; the Republic P-47 Thunderbolt was better, but not by

much, while the twin-engined Lockheed P-38 Lightning was no match for the agile Focke-Wulfs and Messerschmitts in a dogfight. It was at this point that the 92nd BG returned to operations, bringing with them the YB-40 gunship, of which so much was hoped. As related previously, these were a failure and were withdrawn from service in September of that year.

On 22 June came the deepest penetration yet, when 235 Fortresses raided the synthetic rubber plant at Huls, in the Ruhr. To minimize fighter opposition, a feint course was flown to deceive the German fighter controllers, while both

Right: **Not all losses were attributable to enemy action. A B-17F of the 91st BG sheds its load without realizing that another aircraft has strayed almost directly beneath it. The first bomb strikes the tailplane without detonating, bending it down. In the final picture, the unfortunate Fortress goes down out of control; the victim of poor look-out and less than perfect station-keeping. (Boeing via Alfred Price)**

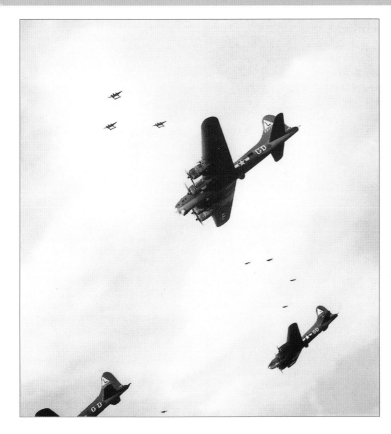

celebrated with the most ambitious deep penetration yet. Early that morning, 147 Fortresses took off to attack the Messerschmitt works at Regensburg, escorted by Thunderbolts as far as the German border. Shortly after, another 230 B-17s would take off, bound for the ball-bearing factories at Schweinfurt. These had no escort, as the German fighters would be on the ground refuelling and rearming. At least, that was how it was planned. In the event, the second wave was delayed by fog, and got away hours later.

The German fighters waited for the Thunderbolts to turn back before launching their attack on the first wave. Then dozens of single and twin-engined fighters pounced. For the next 90 minutes they tore into the bombers, concentrating on the rearmost bombardment wing, which lost 13 Fortresses. Four more went down from the two leading wings. Only as the target hove in sight did the attacks cease. Visibility was excellent, and the bombing, led by Curtis LeMay, was accurate. The force then veered to the southwest, crossed Italy and landed in North Africa, the first of the so-called 'shuttle' missions. On arrival, 24 B-17s were missing; one had crash-landed in Italy; two more, badly damaged, had sought sanctuary in Switzerland, while four had ditched in the Mediterranean out of fuel. Refuelled and rearmed, the German fighters waited in vain for the return flight.

They were, however, rewarded by the arrival of the second wave, now three

The 8th AF lose 60 bombers against Regensburg and Schweinfurt

Top: **Lockheed P-38 Lightnings escorting Fortresses of the 381st BG late in 1943. (USAF)**

Above: **Flames streaming from the starboard wing and separated from its formation, a Fortress is remorselessly hunted down by a FW 190 after raiding the aircraft plant at Oschersleben. (USAF)**

with new drop tanks to extend their radius of action. These shot down nine of their assailants in short order. It was the shape of things to come.

■ SCHWEINFURT ■

It was 17 August 1943, the anniversary of the raid on Rouen, and the event was

hours behind schedule. This time they concentrated on the leading bombardment wing. Twenty-one bombers were shot down by fighters on the way to Schweinfurt and one more was lost to flak over the target. The second wave did not head for North Africa; instead it returned to England, losing 14 more en

Above: Aircraft of the 381st BG lined up on the runway at Ridgewell prior to a mission. (USAF)

route. Schweinfurt was heavily hit, although accuracy was less than had been achieved at Regensburg.

Losses on this two-pronged raid were 60 Fortresses lost on the day, or 16 per cent. But worse was to come. When the remnants of the first wave returned from Tunisia, it was without 55 bombers too badly damaged to make the return flight. In all, the raid cost 118 aircraft, an unacceptable attrition rate of 31 per cent. American gunners claimed an incredible 288 fighters destroyed, later reduced to 148. Actual German fighter losses were just 25. Nor was the damage on the ground particularly rewarding. Production resumed a few days later, and was normal after a few weeks.

■ BOMBING THROUGH ■
THE WEATHER

The weeks following the Schweinfurt raid were quiet, with shallow penetrations only, as losses were made good. The B-17G started arriving in England at about this time, ready for its combat debut. The 8th did not sally forth in force again until 6 September, when 338 Fortresses set out for Stuttgart. This time, the main enemy was the weather. Heavy cloud covered much of Western Europe,

Right: A Messerschmitt 110 curves away after attacking Fortresses of the 91st BG. (USAF)

Stuttgart was socked in, and few so much as saw it; formation cohesion was lost. German fighters attacked in force over the target area, and again near Paris on the return flight. The result was a disaster. Eleven B-17s were lost to fighters; a round dozen came down in the Channel out of fuel; at least two more crashed on landing, while five lost or damaged machines set down in Switzerland. All this with hardly a bomb anywhere near the target.

The weather was kind to Germany over the following weeks, and the remainder of the month passed with raids on French and Belgian objectives. On 15 September, two 1,000lb (450kg) bombs were carried on racks externally for the first time, one of the rare occasions on which this was done. Meanwhile, measures to overcome the worst effects of cloud were in hand.

In August 1943, the 482nd Bomb Group was formed at Alconbury, as the 8th Air Force's sole Pathfinder unit. It was made up of two B-17 and one B-24 squadrons equipped with British gadgets. The first was Gee, a comparatively short-ranged navigational device. The second was Oboe, which, using signals from English ground stations, allowed fairly accurate blind bombing. The third was H2S, a primitive (by modern standards) ground mapping radar, later slightly improved to become H2X. The former was carried in a bathtub under the chin, the latter initially in a retractable dome in the same position, although production aircraft had this fitted in place of the ball turret. All Pathfinder aircraft carried smoke markers. Dropped above a solid undercast on radar indications alone, these left a distinctive trail above the clouds, obscuring the target, providing a point at which successive waves of bombers could aim.

Pathfinding with H2S was pioneered on 27 September, with an attack on

SCHWEINFURT

"I watched two fighters explode not far beneath, disappearing in sheets of orange flame, B-17s dropping out in every state of distress, from engines on fire to control surfaces shot away, friendly and enemy parachutes floating down and, on the green carpet far beneath us, numerous funeral pyres of smoke from fallen aircraft, marking our trail."

COL. BEIRNE LAY

Above: A direct hit by heavy flak has torn the front fuselage and port inner engine clean away from this B-17, which goes down blazing furiously. (USAF)

Emden. The leading Wing dropped with the Pathfinder aircraft; the second Wing dropped on the smoke markers, while the third was able to find a gap in the cloud and bombed visually. Post-strike reconnaissance showed that only the Pathfinder-led units had hit Emden; the visual bombers were miles adrift. It was a promising start. A blind bombing leader was to become a standard part of most 8th AAF raids. But first the technique had to be refined, and sufficient crews trained.

In 1943, the life expectancy of a Fortress was a mere 11 missions; a tour of duty was 25 missions. When a crewman completed his tour – and a surprising number did – he was statistically dead twice over! However, progress was being made. Carpet, a gunlaying radar jammer, gradually entered service, and this equipment decreased the effectiveness of the flak. While flak destroyed only a small proportion of the bombers, it was

responsible for most of those which returned damaged, while forcing them to bomb from ever higher altitudes, with a corresponding decrease in accuracy. Carpet was a British invention that saved many American lives.

The following month saw a return to Schweinfurt on the 14th by 291 Fortresses. As was by now standard procedure, the defending fighters held back until the bombers passed Aachen, when their escorts turned back. They then struck, in a way described by American official historians as "unprecedented in its magnitude, in the cleverness with which it was planned, and in the severity with which it was executed".

■ SCHWEINFURT ■ AGAIN!

By the time that Schweinfurt was reached, 28 bombers had gone down and many others were badly damaged. Despite this, the bombing was heavy and

accurate, and only one aircraft was lost to flak in the target area. But now they had to run the fighter gauntlet once more on the homeward leg. Again they were assailed from all sides, and by the time that they reached the relative safety of the escorts, formations were breaking up, all cohesion lost.

Three ball-bearing factories had been hard hit, but once again the price was high. Sixty Fortresses were lost; five more crashed on reaching England, and 12 were written off with battle damage; over 26 per cent of the total. A further 121 were damaged but repairable. Barely one in every three returned unscathed, and these figures might have been still worse had it not been that the RAF sent fighters with long-range tanks to the aid of the hard-pressed American Thunderbolt and Lightning escorts.

The defenders had taken the measure of the Fortresses. They used 21cm rockets to break up the closely packed bomber formations, then attacked en masse from head-on. The B-17 was a tough bird, able to sustain severe damage and keep flying, and it normally took several attacks on one machine to bring it down. The essential thing, from the German point of view, was to isolate it so that it could be picked off at leisure.

The second Schweinfurt raid underlined what many had said all along – that unescorted bombers, no matter how well armed, could not fly daylight missions against determined fighter opposition without incurring unacceptable losses. The price was too high; long-range escort fighters were needed more desperately than ever.

Using drop tanks, P-47s were able to penetrate a little way into Germany; P-38s a bit further. Then in December came the answer to the problem. The P-51 Mustang was a happy marriage of an American airframe and a British engine. Using drop tanks, it could range deep into Germany and go all the way to most targets.

■ BIG WEEK ■ AND BERLIN

Operations continued following the Schweinfurt raid, but increasingly poor weather meant that many of them were radar bombing missions led by Pathfinders. Few visual attacks could be made, and in January 1944 the 8th concentrated mainly on V-1 launch sites in the Pas-de-Calais. Not until late February did the bombers really get into their stride again, as the clouds parted, giving clear skies over Germany.

Big Week, the period from 20–25 February, saw a concerted attempt by the Allies to cripple the German aircraft industry. At last with escort fighters able to accompany them, the bombers raided Focke-Wulf plants at Tuetow and Oschersleben; Messerschmitt factories at Augsburg, Regensburg, Gotha, Brunswick, Furth and Erla/Leipzig; the Junkers works at Bernberg, Aschersleben and Halberstadt; and Heinkel's facility at Rostock. Immediate German production losses were estimated at 1,000 aircraft, and many more over the next few months. Total bomber losses, B-17s and B-24s, amounted to 226; just under 6 per cent of the 3,800 sorties flown. Fighter escort losses during Big Week amounted to 28, but the low figure of bomber loss underlined their worth.

B-17 UNITS THAT BECAME OPERATIONAL IN ENGLAND 1943

Group No.	Squadrons	Base	First mission	Notes
94	331, 332, 333, 410	Bassingbourn	13 May 43	Last mission 21 Apr 45
95	334, 335, 336, 412	Alconbury	13 May 43	Last mission 20 Apr 45
96	337, 338, 339, 413	Grafton Underwood	14 May 43	Last mission 21 Apr 45
351	508, 509, 510, 511	Polebrook	14 May 43	Last mission 25 Apr 45; film star Clark Gable flew with this group
379	524, 525, 526, 527	Kimbolton	29 May 43	Last mission 25 Apr 45; flew most sorties, dropped greatest bomb tonnage
381	532, 533, 534, 535	Ridgewell	22 Jun 43	Last mission 25 Apr 45
384	544, 545, 546, 547	Grafton Underwood	22 Jun 43	Last mission 25 Apr 45; dropped last 8th AF bombs of war
100	349, 350, 351, 418	Podington	25 Jun 43	Last mission 20 Apr 45
385	548, 549, 550, 551	Great Ashfield	17 Jul 43	Last mission 20 Apr 45
388	560, 561, 562, 563	Knettishall	17 Jul 43	Last mission April 45; flew 19 Aphrodite missions
389	568, 569, 570, 571	Framlingham	27 Sep 43	Last mission 20 Apr 45
482	812, 813, third sqn flew B-24s	Alconbury	27 Sep 43	Last mission 22 Mar 44; pioneer Pathfinder unit also operational research
410	612, 613, 614, 615	Deenethorpe	26 Nov 43	Last mission Apr 45
447	708, 709, 710, 711	Rattlesden	24 Dec 43	Last mission 21 Apr 45

Note: The 422 BS commenced operations as part of 305 BG in Nov 42; then pioneered night bombing for 8th AF in Sep/Oct 43. Night leaflet sqn from 7/8 Oct 43. Based at Chelveston, redesignated 858 BS in June 44, re-equipped with B-24s the following month.

marker. They were intercepted on the homeward leg, but the Mustang escorts fought heroically to protect them, losing 23 of their number. Five Fortresses failed to return, a surprisingly small loss under the circumstances.

Two days later, the 8th tried again. The force consisted of 561 Fortresses, tasked against a ball-bearing factory in the Erkner suburb and against the Bosch factory at Klein Machnow, plus 249 Liberators which were to attack the Daimler-Benz engine works. Fighter cover was provided by 691 Thunderbolts, Lightnings and Mustangs, some of the latter RAF, working in relays. The distance to Berlin ensured that no deceptive course changes could be used; the German fighters would have plenty of time to deploy.

Such a force could not be hidden. The time-consuming process of assembling such a massive armada in its correct order meant that it was under radar observation long before it left the English coast. In the occupied countries and in Germany, fighter units were brought to readiness; on this day they were to meet numbers with numbers.

The bomber stream was 94 miles (150km) long, thundering eastwards at 180mph (290km/hr), but some four hours after the first bomber had taken

Top: H2X ground mapping radar, fitted in a retractable dome in the nose compartment, allowed blind bombing through cloud. This was an experimental installation. *Above:* Radar-equipped pathfinder of the 401st BG, showing the retractable radome fitted in place of the ball turret. (Ralph Trout) *Right:* A heavily armed Messerschmitt Me 410 commences its firing pass on a B-17F of the 390th BG.

On 4 March, the bombers set off to Berlin, the only major German target not yet attacked in daylight. Once again, the weather turned sour and the recall signal was issued, but one combat wing of 29 Fortresses failed to receive it and carried on. Realizing this, headquarters allowed part of the escort to continue also. Fighters were encountered as the bombers neared the target, but they pressed on, releasing their loads on a Pathfinder's

Above: Long-range escort fighters wheel protectively above B-17F Fortresses of the 390th BG. They tipped the balance against the defenders decisively. (USAF via Alfred Price)

Right: Flying Fortresses over the German capital. The low squadron is barely in the contrail belt. (USAF)

off, it had become disorganized. The head of the stream, well protected by Thunderbolts, had inadvertently veered southwards. The 13th Combat Wing was running behind schedule, and had lost visual contact with the aircraft in front. Not realizing this, it continued on the correct course, thus forming an offset in the formation.

The first German fighters attacked over Haselunne, just east of the Dutch border, to meet the 13th CW head-on. Only eight Thunderbolts were on hand to greet 107 Me 109s and FW 190s, and this was not enough to hold them off. The German fighters flashed between the bombers, guns blazing, and narrowly avoided collisions with

them. Damaged Fortresses dropped out of formation in all directions; easy meat for the waiting fighters as they swung round to re-engage. Black smoke from burning aircraft stained the clear sky; white parachutes blossomed below.

Calls for help brought more P-47s from all directions; these took some of the pressure off, but there were simply not enough of them. The unengaged German fighters regrouped for another head-on attack. In all the battle lasted 45 minutes.

Above: Target Berlin! Tempelhof airfield can be seen near the right wingtip of this 452nd BG Fortress as it lines up on its primary target. (USAF)

one fell to unknown causes. This was the largest bomber loss ever suffered in one raid by the 8th Air Force. However, it was not enough to stop the 8th. Over the next three days, two raids of similar strength were visited upon the German capital, and a third on 22 March.

With the invasion of Europe looming, priorities switched. Attacks against communications centres intensified, while tremendous efforts were made to reduce

The 8th prepare for invasion; oil and transport the targets

Meanwhile, the front of the bomber stream was faring almost as badly. Attempting to get back on course, it crossed several flak zones before meeting up with another huge German fighter formation. The escorting Mustangs were in the right place, but failed to avert the blow completely. More bombers went down, although the German interceptors paid a heavy price for their success.

At last, the bombers reached Berlin, only to run into the most vicious flak

that most of them had ever seen. Partial cloud foiled the bomb runs on two of the primary three targets, but widespread damage was caused in the city. The return flight was marked by skirmishes with small numbers of German fighters, which were generally held at bay by the escorts. There was, however, one exception. Forty-four German fighters managed to assemble near the Dutch border; they cost the 388th BG six Fortresses.

Losses on the Berlin raid amounted to 73, of which 56 were Fortresses. Of these, three reached Sweden in a damaged state, while four were struck off charge in England. Fighters accounted for 45, fighters and flak for four, flak alone for six, while

the German oil industry. On 12 May, 935 heavy bombers raided oil plants at Bruex, Bohlen, Leuna, Lutzendorf and Zwickau. Meanwhile, 15th Air Force was raiding the Romanian oil fields at Ploesti. Raid followed raid, and aviation fuel production slumped from 175,000 tons in April to 52,000 tons in June, 35,000 tons in July, and a mere 7,000 tons in September. This caused a tremendous reduction of German fighter effectiveness.

Below: A large hole through her fin making control difficult, *Boche Buster* of the 401st BG breaks formation to seek safety in neutral Sweden, 7 October 1944. (Bert Hocking)

FORTRESSES THROUGH THE BERLIN FLAK

"A dark puffy veil that hung like a pall of death covered the capital city. It was the heaviest flak I had ever seen. It almost seemed to swallow up the bomber formations as they entered it. One ship blew up and three others dropped away from their formations. . . It didn't seem that anything could fly through that. But there they were, Flying Fortresses sailing proudly away from the scene of devastation."

Lt LOWELL WATTS, 388TH BG

By October 1944, the bombing campaign against the Third Reich had sapped the strength of the German day fighter arm. Lack of aircraft was not the cause; widely dispersed plants scattered throughout Germany maintained production at record levels, and the depots were full of replacements.

The critical shortage was of trained pilots. Under the constant battering of the massive American raids, which were increasingly covered by long-range escorts, the German fighter units had suffered swingeing losses. Experienced men were irreplaceable; novices rarely lasted long. Then, as the fuel shortage bit ever harder, training was curtailed, and the quality of replacement pilots dropped still more. To make matters worse, even the ever-shrinking band of old stagers sometimes found themselves grounded for lack of fuel. From this time on, only on rare occasions were they able to put up serious opposition to the American armadas. Fortress operations over Germany gradually became safer, so much so that in the closing months of the war it was possible to fly a full tour and never encounter a German fighter in the air! On the other hand, the flak defences were strengthened, and losses to this cause began to exceed those of the fighters, although without reaching anywhere near the same proportions. This reduction in risk was acknowledged by the USAAF, who increased the number of sorties in a tour of operations from 25 to 30, and eventually to 35.

While in the early months the loss rate of Fortresses was horrendous, a few – and they were very few indeed – survived to complete more than 100 missions. Yet others had taken such a beating that they were no longer sufficiently reliable for operations, although still flyable. One

Left: The 91st BG unloads over Berlin on smoke markers dropped by lead aircraft in February 1945. The nearest aircraft is a late model B-17G, with the taller dorsal turret. (USAF)

use for some of these was as assembly ships. Shuffling a formation of many hundreds of bombers into the correct order before sallying forth was far from easy. One solution was to paint war-weary aircraft in brilliant colours and strange patterns. These unmistakeable psychedelic monsters were then launched and took up their assigned place in the assembly area, where their assigned formations took station on them. When all was in order, they returned to base.

■ APHRODITE ■

Another use for war-weary B-17s was as radio-controlled flying bombs. Stripped of all unnecessary equipment, these were packed with 20,000lb (9,000kg) of Torpex high explosive. For Project Aphrodite, as it was known, these were flown off by a two-man crew, who parachuted to safety near the English coast. Control was then handed over to a specially equipped 'mother' aircraft, which remotely guided the flying bomb to its target. The hazardous Aphrodite

Above: Mustangs escort B-17G *Patches* on a 15th AF shuttle mission to Russia. The long reach of the American fighter transformed American deep penetration missions. (USAF)

missions were flown by the 388th BG from Fersfield, an isolated airfield in the wilds of Norfolk, but the difficulties of accurately guiding them on to their targets, plus a couple of unfortunate accidents, ensured that only a handful of missions were flown.

Other experiments carried out from Fersfield involved Batty, a system using a television-guided bomb. Rather ahead

B-17 UNITS THAT BECAME OPERATIONAL IN ENGLAND 1944

Group No.	Squadrons	Base	First mission	Notes
	803	Oulton	5 Jun 44	Countermeasures Squadron, 8 B-17Fs and 2 B-17Gs; largely replaced by B-24s from August 44
486	832, 833, 834, 835	Sudbury	1 Aug 44	Last mission 21 Apr 45 (prev B-24s)
487	836, 837, 938, 839	Lavenham	1 Aug 44	Last mission 21 Apr 45 (prev B-24s)
490	848, 849, 850, 851	Eye	27 Aug 44	Last mission 21 Apr 45 (prev B-24s)
493	860, 861, 862, 863	Debach	8 Sep 44	(prev B-24s) Last mission 20 Apr 45; last BG to become operational in 8th AF
25 (R)	652 Sqn only with B-17, others with B-24	Watton	Nov 44	Composite unit, weather reconnaissance
34	4, 7, 18, 391	Mendlesham	17 Sep 44	(prev B-24s) No losses to fighters over enemy territory

low – less than one-third of a per cent. One B-17 was lost to a Me 262 jet fighter, while four more went down to flak, which damaged a further 85 aircraft. Just to show it was no fluke, 1,193 heavies went out on the following day, losing only two of their number. The pattern continued.

Whereas the British Lancaster routinely carried bombs of up to 12,000lb (5,400kg), Fortress (and Liberator) bays could not accommodate a bomb larger than 2,000lb (900kg). This was of little use against hardened targets, and the Disney bomb was introduced to correct this shortcoming. Weighing 4,500lb (2,000kg), it used rocket propulsion to pierce 20ft (6m) of reinforced concrete.

Nine B-17s of the 92 BG each carried four Disney bombs on underwing racks to the U-boat pens at Ijmuiden on 14 March 1945. Only one hit was

scored, and a further raid was mounted, but soon the Allied advance overran the area, making further attacks unnecessary.

Just four days later, the 8th mounted its final major attack on Berlin with 1,327 heavy bombers. They were met by an estimated 40–50 Me 262 jet fighters, which accounted for a mere eight Fortresses. The remaining 16 bombers which failed to return, plus a further 16 which force-landed in Russian-held territory, all fell to flak. The loss rate of 3 per cent, while heavy for 1945, was a far cry from the first Berlin raid just over a year earlier.

Final rounds in Europe; operations continue in the Pacific

By now, worthwhile targets were becoming few and far between, and on 16 April, General Spaatz stated that the strategic air war was over; from then on only tactical targets remained. The final 8th AF bombs of the war were dropped on the Skoda Armament Works at Pilsen on 25 April 1945, by a B-17 of the 384th BG.

of its time, Batty was beset with technical difficulties, and achieved little.

To return to the bombing of Germany, some idea of the reduction of defensive effectiveness was given on 22 February 1945, when 1,411 heavy bombers attacked communication centres all over the Third Reich from the unprecedentedly low altitude of 10,000ft (3,050m), chosen to achieve bombing accuracy against small targets. Losses were remarkably

B-17 OPERATIONAL STATISTICS 8TH AF

BG No.	Missions	Sorties	Bombs (tons)	Aircraft missing	Sorties/ missing
303	364	10,721	24,918	165	64.98
306	342	9,614	22,575	171	56.22
91	340	9,591	22,142	197	48.68
305	337	9,231	22,363	154	59.94
379	330	10,492	26,460	141	74.41
94	324	8,884	18,925	153	58.06
95	320	8,903	19,769	157	56.70
96	320	8,924	19,277	189	47.21
384	314	9,348	22,415	159	58.79
351	311	8,600	20,357	124	69.35
92	308	8,663	20,829	154	56.25
100	306	8,630	19,257	177	48.78
388	306	8,051	18,162	142	56.70
390	300	8,725	19,059	144	60.59
381	296	9,035	22,160	131	68.97
385	296	8,264	18,494	129	64.06
447	257	7,605	17,103	97	78.40
410	255	7,430	17,778	95	78.21
452	250	7,279	16,467	110	66.17
457	237	7,068	16,916	83	85.16
398	195	6,419	15,781	58	110.67
97	14	247	395	4	61.75
301	8	104	186	1	104.00
TOTALS	**6,034**	**181,828**	**422,788**	**2,935**	**av. 61.95**

1) At least four BGs converted from the B-24 to the B-17 in the summer of 1944, but their records include data for both aircraft, and have not been included here.

2) Missing aircraft are just that; no allowance has been made for those that reached base but crashed on landing, or were struck off charge. A rough approximation based on available sources gives about one-third as many again.

3) At one point early in the war, the life expectancy of a B-17 was just 11 sorties. The sorties/missing aircraft ratio shows how much safer things had become in the later stages. This is particularly noticeable with BGs formed late in 1944. Three factors were decisive: sufficient numbers of long-range escort fighters; from spring 1944 many missions were flown over occupied France; and in the final months of the war, the Luftwaffe was a spent force.

As by far the majority of Fortress operations in the Second World War were flown by the US 8th Army Air Force based in England, it was only to be expected that the narrative would mainly concern itself with these. But the B-17 served well and faithfully with other air forces and in other theatres.

We have already touched on the early years of the Pacific War. While those Fortresses there at the start gave sterling service, ably backed by such reinforcements as could be got through, this period was essentially tactical. There was little scope for strategic bombing until the Japanese advance had been halted, which did not happen until mid-1942. While the Fortresses helped to hold the ring, there was little more they could do. Vulnerable to fighters at medium and low altitudes, they yet lacked the precision to hit either small fixed targets or moving ships from high altitude.

This was all too clearly demonstrated at the decisive Battle of Midway in June 1942, when 19 B-17s were based on the island. During the four days of battle, they flew over 80 sorties in the course of seven missions. They first attacked the invasion force; the main Japanese carrier force twice; two cruisers; a solitary destroyer; and finally an American submarine under the impression that it was a Japanese cruiser. They claimed hits on two battleships or heavy cruisers; two transports; three aircraft carriers, and finally 'sank' the 'cruiser'. During this flurry of activity, two B-17s were lost. In actual fact, there was not even a

Left: The Boeing B-29 Superfortress commenced operations in the Far East in June 1944, as B-17 production was being run down. (Author)

293845

Above: Tail gunners rarely carried cameras, which makes this view of B-17Gs of 15th AF setting out from their Italian base the more interesting.

near-miss. The sunk 'cruiser' had of course crash-dived to safety.

This is not to denigrate the efforts of the Army fliers, but it does provide an illustration of the difficulties; first of hitting moving targets from a level bomber, secondly of distinguishing bomb hits from other signs of battle, and thirdly of ship recognition by aviators, all from 3 miles (5km) up!

When at last the situation stabilizes and the Japanese were forced on to the defensive, high-altitude bombing came once more into its own. However, the distances in the Pacific were so vast that the longer-ranged Liberator was preferred to the Fortress, which from mid 1943 had vanished from the scene. A few aircraft went to India, but the same factors applied.

In any case, the days of the Flying Fortress were numbered; a specification for an ultra long-range bomber was issued in 1942. The B-29 Superfortress was far larger than its predecessor, better armed, longer ranged, and could carry a much bigger bomb load as well as bigger bombs. B-29 bases in the Marianas Islands become operational from October 1944, and from then on, Japanese targets were under constant attack, culminating in the nuclear raids on Hiroshima and Nagasaki which

brought the war in the Pacific to an abrupt close. B-17 production peaked in March 1944, but was thereafter run down in favour of the B-29 Superfortress.

■ MEDITERRANEAN ■ THEATRE

Two B-17 groups were detached from the 8th AF in November 1942 and transferred to the newly formed 12th AF, commencing operations from Maison Blanche in Algeria on the 16th of that month. They were joined in the spring of 1943 by the 2nd and 99th BGs, and carried out raids on targets in the western Mediterranean area.

Once German resistance in North Africa had ceased, they moved forward to raid Sicily, softening it up for invasion.

Distances in Europe were generally shorter; fighter escort, often from bases on Malta, was usually available; and the German and Italian flak and fighter defences far weaker. The weather was better, and usually the primary target was bombed from high altitude. The Fortresses then flew in very low over the sea, under the enemy radar coverage, before pulling up to a moderate altitude to bomb.

When bases on the Italian mainland became available, a new command, 15th AF, was formed. While a considerable portion of heavy bomber strength in Italy consisted of Liberators, the Fortress strength was increased with the arrival of more B-17 BGs, although Fortress numbers never exceeded one fifth of the B-17 strength of the 8th AF. As the Axis forces were driven back in 1944, so 15th AF joined in the campaign against oil targets with raids on Ploesti in Romania.

Shuttle mission were not an 8th AF prerogative. On 2 June 1944, 130 B-17s of 15th AF bombed communications targets in Hungary

before continuing to Russian airfields near Kiev. Two days later they attacked targets in Romania from the Kiev area, before once more raiding Romania while returning to Italy.

■ ROYAL AIR FORCE ■

Reference has already been made to Fortresses in RAF Coastal and Bomber Command service. In the former they were mainly used on anti-submarine patrols, operating from stations as diverse as Chivenor in Devon, Benbecula in the Hebrides, and the Azores, from where they helped to close the infamous mid-Atlantic Gap. The Azores, some 900 miles (1,450km) east of Lisbon, are part of Portugal, and Portugal was neutral during the Second World War. Permission to use Lajes airfield on the island of Terceira was granted when Britain invoked a Treaty of Alliance dating back to 1386!

European weather comes mainly from the southwest, and other Coastal units were Meteorological Reconnaissance squadrons, whose aircraft also ranged far out into the Atlantic, recording weather conditions which would allow the accurate forecasting so necessary for planning bombing raids.

Finally two squadrons equipped with Fortress IIIs (B-17Gs) flew with

Below: Coastal Command Fortress IIs and IIa's of No. 220 Squadron at Lajes in the Azores, December 1943, from where they played a sterling role in containing the U-boat menace. (Bruce Robertson)

the No. 100 group of Bomber Command from Tempsford and Oulton, packed with black boxes on electronic countermeasures sorties.

■ BLACK CROSSED ■ BOEINGS

There was however a third major combatant which operated the B-17. The Luftwaffe was naturally very interested in this new opponent, which was frequently encountered in the autumn skies of 1942. What were its strengths and weaknesses? Shot-down Fortresses were eagerly examined and deductions made. Then, with Christmas approaching, the Germans received a present when a fairly intact B-17F made a wheels-down landing in northern France. It was taken to the flight test centre at Rechlin where all its secrets were laid bare, after which it was used for fighter affiliation trials. Nine months after its capture, it was sent to I/KG.200, a unit engaged in clandestine operations. Over the next 15 months it was joined by two more B-17s, and they were given the fictitious designation Dornier Do 200.

The black-crossed Fortresses task was the dropping of agents behind Allied lines. The area covered by these operations was vast, from Ireland in the west to Trans-Jordan in the east and Algeria in the south. Just one of these aircraft survived the war, and was recaptured at Altenburg in April 1945.

■ ODDBALLS ■

During and shortly after the war, many Fortresses were converted for uses other than bombing. Transport was an obvious choice, although the circular fuselage cross-section did not particularly lend itself to this.

Four Fortresses were evaluated as transports. One, fitted with side windows and 38 seats, became the XC-108; this was later used in the Pacific by General MacArthur as a personal transport. The second was fitted with a large side-loading cargo door to become the XC-108A. The third was fitted out as an executive transport as the YC-108, while the fourth was converted to a fuel tanker as the XC-108B. None entered production. More numerous was the CB-17, a conversion of war-weary bombers to the transport role.

Yet another wartime conversion was the F-9. This was a long-range reconnaissance machine based on the B–17F, which carried both vertical and oblique cameras. Depending on the equipment carried, these became F-9As, Bs and Cs.

At the end of the war, the USAAF converted B-17Gs to the search and rescue role as the B-17H. This was fitted with a sea search radar under the chin, and a para-droppable lifeboat under the belly. The US Navy also had its own uses for the type; fitted with an APS-20 search radar it became a pioneer airborne early

Above: Dornier Do 200. A captured B-17 wearing Luftwaffe markings at Orly Airport, Paris, in December 1942. (Roger F. Besecker)

warning aircraft, with the designation PB-1W.

The PB-1W also carried out maritime reconnaissance and anti-submarine missions. Yet another user was the US Coast Guard with the PB-1G, a long-range air-sea rescue machine, which was occasionally used for iceberg reconnaissance sorties. But despite these conversions, there were far too many Fortresses. The vast majority were scrapped.

POST-WAR B-17 DESIGNATIONS

Transports	CB-17G
	VB-17G
Reconnaissance	FB-17F
	FB17G
	RB-17F
	RB-17G
AEW/Maritime Reconnaissance	1PB-1W
Air/Sea Rescue	PB-1G
	SB-17G
Target Drone	MB-17G
	QB-17G
	QB-17L
	QB-17N
	QB-17P
Drone Remote Controller	CQ-4
	DB-17G
	DB-17P
Engine Test Bed	EB-17G
	XPB-1W
Pilot Trainer	TB-17G

RAF SQUADRONS OPERATING FORTRESSES

BOMBER COMMAND
No. 90, high-altitude bombers, Fortress I Nos 214 & 223, electronic countermeasures, No. 100 Group, Fortress III

COASTAL COMMAND
Nos 206 & 220, anti-submarine, Fortress I, II, IIa and III, Nos 59 & 86, anti-submarine, Fortress III Nos 251, 517, 519 & 521 meteorological, Fortress III

Above: Waist gun positions in a B-17F, June 1943,
showing the gun mounting and ammunition feeds.